ELEMENTARY SOCIAL STUDIES

ELEMENTARY SOCIAL STUDIES

Challenges for Tomorrow's World

Dorothy J. Skeel

Harcourt Brace College Publishers
Fort Worth Philadelphia San Diego New York Orlando Austin San Antonio
Toronto Montreal London Sydney Tokyo

Publisher	Ted Buchholz
Acquisitions Editor	Jo-Anne Weaver
Developmental Editor	Tracy Napper
Project Editor	John Haakenson
Production Manager	Thomas Urquhart IV
Senior Art Director	Don Fujimoto

Cover Image courtesy of Harcourt Brace School Department

Copyright © 1995 by Harcourt Brace & Company

All rights reserved. No part of this publication may be reproduced or transmitted in any form or by any means, electronic or mechanical, including photocopy, recording or any information storage and retrieval system, without permission in writing from the publisher.

Requests for permission to make copies of any part of the work should be mailed to: Permissions Department, Harcourt Brace & Company, 6277 Sea Harbor Drive, Orlando, Florida 32887-6777.

Address for Editorial Correspondence: Harcourt Brace College Publishers, 301 Commerce Street, Suite 3700, Fort Worth, TX 76102.

Address for Orders: Harcourt Brace & Company : 6277 Sea Harbor Drive, Orlando, FL 32887-6777. 1-800-782-4479, or 1-800-433-0001 (in Florida).

(Copyright Acknowledgments begin on page 279, which constitutes a continuation of this copyright page.)

Printed in the United States of America

ISBN: 0-15-501100-6

Library of Congress Catalog Card Number: 94-76298

4 5 6 7 8 9 0 1 2 3 039 9 8 7 6 5 4 3 2 1

To Darby Amanda—
and all the children of the world
may they make tomorrow's world
a better place to live

**In memory of my parents and a dear
friend, Arlene Gallagher**

PREFACE

Teaching social studies in the elementary school presents challenges to any teacher, new or experienced. These challenges result from the problems facing our society and the world—most especially what information and skills will our children need? Challenges also come from the unique content of the social studies and its contribution to children's understanding of their world. The content of the social studies is derived from the social sciences, which investigate the actions of human beings. Through social studies, teachers attempt to help children understand themselves, develop an awareness of the multicultural composition of society and its global nature, and foster an atmosphere for acceptance of varying opinions and beliefs. In addition, teachers must help them develop problem-solving and decision-making skills and foster an active citizen participant role in society.

These challenges would be sufficient without the added concern of selecting appropriate content, teaching methods, and materials to successfully achieve the goals of social studies in the elementary school. The wide divergence in current social studies curricula, the many suggested methods of teaching, and an overabundance of available materials confounds the teacher's task. This textbook is designed to aid social studies teachers by presenting current thinking in all these areas.

Elementary Social Studies: Challenges for Tomorrow's World begins by introducing the reader to the great variety of children, teachers, classrooms, and schools. It then introduces teachers who hold various conceptions of social studies and how it should be taught in the classroom. These teachers discuss how their new textbook series will fit with their view of social studies. The textbook goes on to delineate the contributions of the social sciences and how social scientists would study and attempt to solve the problem of pollution from each one's perspective.

A section on teacher decision making in curriculum development includes planning for instruction through the development of a unit and the discussion of selected content, current issues, global, law-related, and economic education. The diversity the teacher will find within the classroom and ways of celebrating that diversity are discussed. Teaching strategies for concepts, inquiry, valuing, and map and globe skills follow. Evaluation strategies are included with the unit planning and teaching strategies. A final chapter discusses the effective use of the textbook and other instructional materials.

Many people have contributed to the development of this book: James P. Levy, who has always had faith in my writing; Ellen Kronowitz, who pushed me to write this book, reviewed it and gave support; and Ronald E. Sterling, a long-time colleague, who reviewed the manuscript and gave excellent suggestions.

My editors, Jo-Anne Weaver and Tracy Napper, provided continual guidance. John Haakenson was my able project editor, assisted by Charles Naylor, copy editor. No one could ask for better typists than Alice Kinnard, Carole

Terrill, and, most of all, Pat Bryan. Special thanks go to my nieces, Jill Richards who developed the graphics, and Shelly Richards who provided support.

Others who reviewed sections of the manuscript were John Anfin, Winthrop University; Kenneth Craycraft, Sam Houston University; Ann Lockledge, University of North Carolina, Wilmington; Lynn Nielsen, University of Northern Iowa; Ron Pahl, California State University, Fullerton; Carrie Sorensen, Saginaw Valley State University; and Elizabeth Stimson, Bowling Green State University.

ABOUT THE AUTHOR

Dr. Skeel has long-standing involvement in professional activities related to social studies. She is editor of the elementary section of *Social Education;* chaired the NCSS Task Force on Social Studies for Early Childhood/Elementary School Children—Preparing for the 21st Century; chaired and served as a committee member of the NCSS Early Childhood/Elementary Committee; board member of the College and University Assembly of NCSS; fellow of the Longview Foundation for Education in World Affairs and International Understanding; state coordinator for the "We the People—The Citizen and the Constitution" program; member of the Teacher Education Board of the Special Youth Committee on Citizenship Education of the American Bar Association; director of the Peabody Center on Economic and Social Studies Education; recipient of the Excellence in Education Award presented by the College of Education of The Pennsylvania State University; and author of elementary social studies textbooks, method texts, curriculum books and numerous articles and chapters on social studies topics.

CONTENTS

PREFACE   vii

PART I   INTRODUCTION   1

1. WHAT IS SOCIAL STUDIES?   3
   Who Are the Children?   3
   Who Are the Teachers?   5
   What Are the Classrooms Like?   7
   What About Schools?   8
   What About Social Studies?   9
       Defining the Social Studies   11
       Developing Objectives/Outcomes   13
   Summary   13
   Selected References   14
   Learning Activity   15

2. THE SOCIAL SCIENCES   29
   What Are the Social Sciences?   29
       History   31
       Geography   32
       Political Science   33
       Economics   35
       Sociology   36
       Anthropology   37
   Social Scientists Meet to Discuss Pollution Problems   38
       Summary   47
       Selected References   47
       Learning Activity   47

PART II   PROGRAM PLANNING AND CONTENT SELECTION   49

3. CURRICULUM DEVELOPMENT   51
   Teacher Decision Making   51
       Assessment of the Children   52
       Community Influences   54
       Historical Perspective of the Social Studies
           Curriculum   54
   Local School Guidelines and Textbook   58

A Sample Program   58
State Requirements and Guidelines   62
   California Framework   63
   Tennessee Framework   63
National Agencies and Projects   64
   Project Social Studies   64
   National Commission on Social Studies   65
     Grades K–3   65
     Grades 4–6   66
   Bradley Commission on History in the Schools   67
   Joint Committee on Geographic Education   67
   National Council on Economic Education   68
   Law-Related Education (LRE)   68
Summary   69
Selected References   69
Learning Activity   70

4. PLANNING FOR INSTRUCTION   71
Organizing for Instruction   71
   Developing Objectives   72
     Knowledge and Understanding   73
     Attitudes and Values   74
     Skills   75
   Unit Planning   76
   Developing the Unit   78
     What Will You Teach? How Do You Decide?   78
     Components of a Unit   79
     Objectives for the Unit   79
     Content   80
     Bibliography   91
     Evaluation   91
Summary   97
Selected References   98
Learning Activity   98
An Alternative Learning Activity   98

5. MULTICULTURAL EDUCATION   100
Cultural, Racial, Ethnic, and Religious Groups   103
   Learning Experiences   105
   Curriculum Development   106
   Teaching Strategies   107
Physically and Mentally Disabled Groups   108
Gender Stereotyping   109
Living in Poverty and Homelessness   110

        Role of the Child in the Classroom   112
        Classroom Conditions   113
        Role of the Teacher   113
        Selection of Content   114
        Special Instructional Considerations   116
            Organizational Patterns   117
            Teaching Methods   117
            Activities   120
    Summary   120
    Selected References   121
    Learning Activity   122

6.   SELECTED CONTENT FOR EMPHASIS: CURRENT ISSUES, GLOBAL, LAW-RELATED, AND ECONOMIC EDUCATION   123
    Current Issues   124
        Goals/Anticipated Outcomes   125
        When to Start   126
        Learning Experiences   127
        Controversial Issues: Social, Economic, Political, and Environmental   130
            Social Issues   131
            Economic Issues   132
            Political Issues   133
            Environmental Issues   133
        Resources   135
    Global Education   136
        Goals/Anticipated Outcomes   136
        Learning Experiences   138
        Atmosphere of the Classroom   141
        Resources   142
    Law Related Education   143
        Goals/Anticipated Outcomes   143
        Learning Experiences   144
            Classroom Rules and Constitutions   144
            Why We Have Laws   145
            Mock Trials   146
            Published Materials   146
        Classroom and School Environment   147
        Resources   148
    Economic Education   148
        Goals/Anticipated Outcomes   149
        Learning Experiences   150
            Scarcity   150
            Needs and Wants   150

Consumers and Producers 152
Barter and Money 153
Division of Labor and Specialization 153
Summary 154
Resources 154
Summary 154
Learning Activity 155

PART III TEACHING STRATEGIES 157

7. TEACHING CONCEPTS 159
   Introducing and Extending Concepts 161
   Introduction of Concepts 161
   Taba's Model 161
   Parker Model 163
   Gagne Model 165
   Extending Concepts 166
   Brainstorming 166
   Series of Pictures 166
   Storybooks 167
   Summary 167
   Selected References 168
   Learning Activity 168

8. PROBLEM SOLVING THROUGH INQUIRY 169
   Developing Thinking Skills 169
   Advantages and Disadvantages of Problem Solving
     Through Inquiry 171
   Questioning Skills 172
   Classroom Conditions 176
   Role of the Teacher 177
   Responsibility of the Child in an Inquiry-Centered
     Classroom 179
   Goals/Outcomes 179
   Problem Selection 180
   Initiation 181
   Incident 181
   Problem-Solving and Inquiry Activities 182
   Presentation of Facts 182
   Wastebasket Technique 184
   Discrepant Data 184
   Role Playing 185
   Tape Presentations 186

Continuing Activities   190
Evaluation/Assessment of Problem
Solving/Inquiry/Critical Thinking   190
Summary   192
Selected References   193
Learning Activity   194

9. SKILLS OF VALUING/MORAL REASONING:
   A BASIS FOR MORAL EDUCATION   195
   Cognitive-Developmental Approach   196
   Character Development   199
   Values Clarification Approach   200
   Values Analysis Approach   204
   Summary   207
   Selected References   208
   Learning Activity   209

10. MAP AND GLOBE SKILLS   210
    Learning Experiences for the Themes   211
    Theme One: Location   211
    Skills by Grade Levels   213
    Kindergarten   213
    First Grade   213
    Second Grade   213
    Third Grade   214
    Fourth Grade   214
    Fifth Grade   214
    Sixth Grade   214
    Theme Two: Place   215
    Kindergarten   215
    First Grade   215
    Second Grade   215
    Third Grade   216
    Fourth Grade   216
    Fifth Grade   216
    Sixth Grade   216
    Theme Three: Relationships Within Places   216
    Kindergarten   217
    First Grade   217
    Second Grade   217
    Third Grade   217
    Fourth Grade   218
    Fifth Grade   218
    Sixth Grade   218
    Theme Four: Movement   218

Kindergarten 218
First Grade 218
Second Grade 219
Third Grade 219
Fourth Grade 219
Fifth Grade 219
Sixth Grade 219
Theme Five: Regions 220
Kindergarten 220
First Grade 220
Second Grade 220
Third Grade 220
Fourth Grade 221
Fifth Grade 221
Sixth Grade 221
Problems to Determine the Extent of Children's Skills 221
Using Interest Centers to Increase Skill 224
Urban Map Skills 224
Maps and Globes 225
Summary 226
Selected References 226
Learning Activity 227

PART IV USING THE TEXTBOOK AND OTHER MATERIALS 229

11. USING THE TEXTBOOK AND OTHER MATERIALS 231
Introduction 231
Teaching Strategies with the Textbook 232
Concept Development and the Textbook 233
Group Reading 238
Vocabulary Developmen 239
Flashcards 239
Illustrated Concepts or Vocabulary Dictionary 240
Language Experience Chart 240
Journal Writing 240
Using the Textbook with Valuing Strategies 240
Children's Trade Books 247
Simulations and Games 249
Without Computers 249
Simulations with Computers 250
Cartoons 251

             Without Computers   249
             Simulations with Computers   250
        Cartoons   251
        Graphs and Charts   252
        Pictures   256
        Multimedia/Many Media Kits   258
             Multimedia Kits   258
        Videos and Filmstrips   259
             Videos   259
             Filmstrips   260
        Summary   260
        Selected References   261
        Learning Activity   262
        Criteria For Evaluating Textbook Materials   264
        Evaluation of Teaching Aids   267
Subject Index   269
Name Index   274
Credits   279

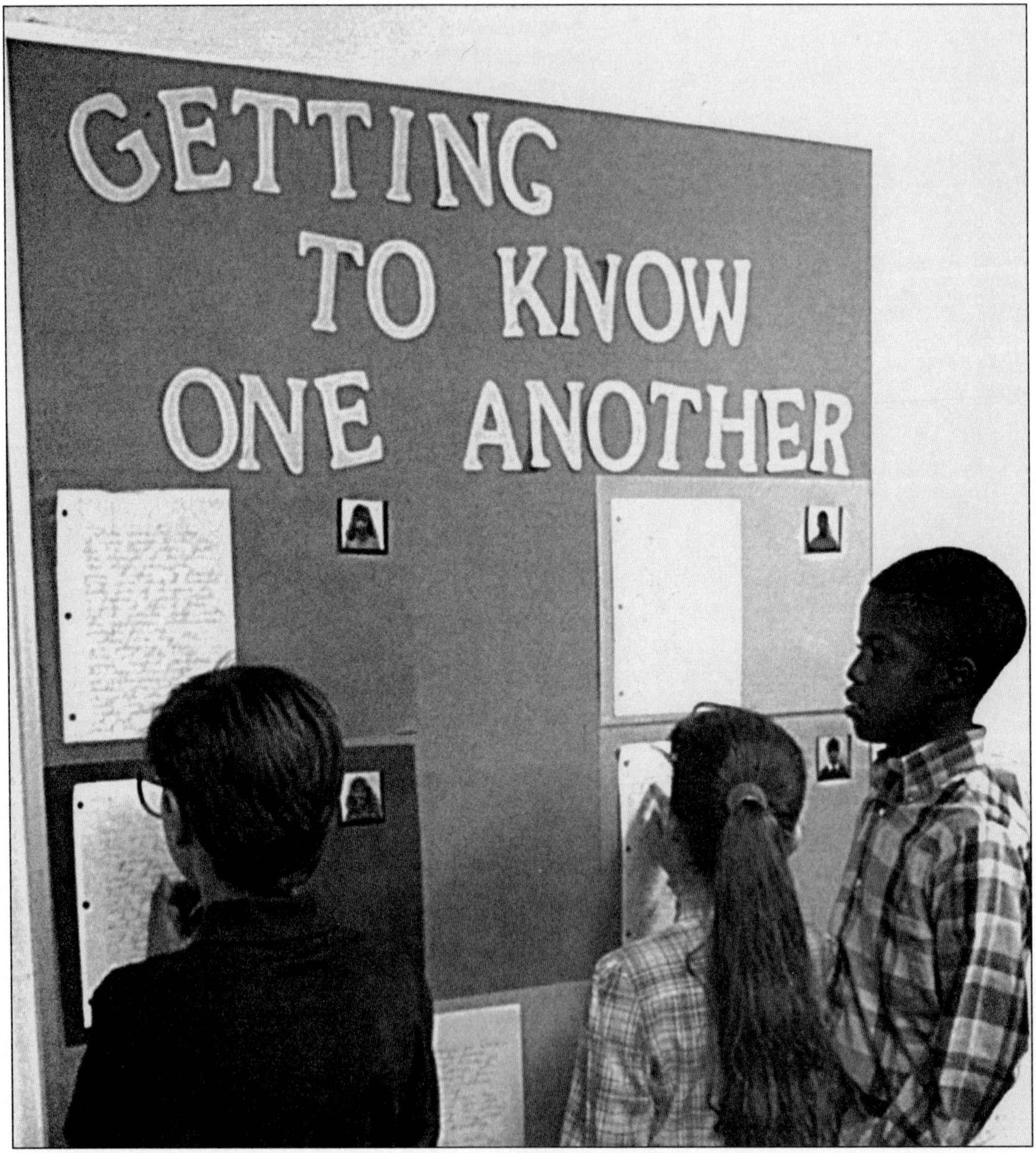
GETTING
TO KNOW
ONE ANOTHER

PART I
INTRODUCTION

WHAT IS social studies? What purpose does this subject serve in the elementary school curriculum? Teachers often ask these questions when they are planning a program of learning experiences for children. Many teachers are bewildered by the complicated problem of combining the proper mixture of reading, writing, math, science, art, music, health, and physical education, as well as numerous other suggested activities. They wonder how social studies can be included in an already crowded schedule, and even more relevant, if the subject is really that important.

Part I attempts to answer these questions by introducing children who come from a variety of backgrounds and bring their hopes, fears, values, and aspirations to the classrooms. Teachers are presented who hold different conceptions of social studies and the way it should be taught. They bring their different backgrounds, values, hopes, fears, and aspirations into the classrooms, as well. Different classrooms and schools are presented to emphasize the fact that the environment within which social studies is taught will affect the way in which it is received.

Next, the various social science disciplines including history, geography, political science, economics, anthropology, and sociology are introduced by social scientists representing each discipline who explain the concepts, method of inquiry, and contribution to social studies of their discipline. The social scientists meet to tackle the problem of environmental pollution and demonstrate how each of their respective social sciences would approach the problem.

CHAPTER 1

WHAT IS SOCIAL STUDIES?

WHO ARE THE CHILDREN?

Children in the classrooms around our nation come in all sizes, shapes, and colors. They come with dreams, hopes, aspirations, hurts, fear, frustrations, and resentment. They come eager to learn and are inquisitive about the world around them—liking people and happy about themselves. But they also come uncertain about learning, fearful of the unknown, and distrustful of people—not sure they have anything to offer.

There's Jessica, a serious-minded child, who doesn't smile much and appears to carry the weight of the world on her shoulders. Right now she lives in a homeless shelter with her mother and younger sister Rachel. She worries about both of them. Her mother is out on the street every day looking for a job, while Rachel goes to kindergarten at another school. She doesn't want the other students to know that she doesn't have a home. She knows how they talked about Justin who was also homeless, but Justin's dad found a job and they've moved to a new apartment. Jessica remembers how good it felt when she lived in a home with her parents and sister before her father died. Rachel doesn't remember, since she is younger and they have lived in numerous shelters over the years. Jessica has difficulty concentrating on her studies and isn't interested in learning about how long the Amazon River is or what is the capital of Brazil. She's much more interested in learning why her family is homeless while the other students aren't. How will Jessica's view of herself and the world around her affect her participation in social studies?

Terrance lives in the "projects." His world is full of violence. He sees the drug deals and the prostitutes. He sees evidence of the money they have and the expensive clothes they wear and the cars they drive. He also sees the guns and shootings. His best friend, Major, was killed last week in his apartment by a stray bullet during a shootout. Terrance likes school and feels safe there but doesn't understand much of what they are learning. He wishes someone would explain why his neighborhood can't be cleaned up and made safe. How will Terrance respond to learning about the world and the way others live?

Then there's Anthony, a bright and aggressive child, who spends most of his time in the classroom acting up, disrupting any group activity. Anthony begs to be noticed. His actions constantly say "Here I am," "See me," "Listen to me." Anthony comes to school clean and well dressed, leading one to believe that his is a caring family. However, there are seven children at home and both parents work. There is never any time to answer Anthony's questions, listen to him, read to him, praise him for successes, or provide experiences outside the home or neighborhood. Anthony knows very little about his city other than that it's full of hurrying, uncaring people. He observes how they push and shove one another on the streets, rushing to catch a bus or be first in line at the food counter. His knowledge of the world beyond comes from watching television where he sees mostly violence. What ideas about the world and himself does Anthony bring to the classroom?

Gwen, on the other hand, is a happy, responsive child. She likes people, school, and herself. Her mother has spent much time with Gwen and her brother, reading to them and exploring with them on trips around our nation and Mexico. Gwen, even though she's only a third grader, realizes that, although people may act differently and dress differently, they have many of the same feelings and problems. She has played with Rosa, a Mexican girl, and knows you don't have to speak the same language to communicate with one another. What view of people and the world does Gwen bring to the classroom?

Robert is a child with a learning problem. He cannot read. This creates difficulties in many of his subjects. What is even worse is the way the children have treated him. Most of the time they refer to him as "dummy." The kids don't understand how badly he wants to learn. How will Robert react to social studies?

Ceci has lived a lifetime in the two short years she has been in school. She is fearful of her own shadow and rarely says anything unless asked a direct question. Ceci is a child who is bused to integrate a school. She remembers the taunts, "We don't want you niggers," "Go back where you belong." She has seen buses shaken and windows broken, people acting frenzied and hateful. The taunts and riots have stopped, but Ceci isn't sure that her teachers and classmates want her there anyway. Sometimes, the comments and looks she receives make her want to go home where she knows people love her and she can trust them. What is Ceci's view of the world?

Roya is a child whose parents came to the United States from a Middle Eastern country. Roya doesn't speak English nor do her mother and the other children in the family. She is aware of how different this new culture is from her own. She realizes that, in addition to differences in dress and food, there are many customs of her country that are not practiced here. She misses the familiar sights and smells, plus she doesn't understand much of what is going on around her. The children in school behave differently toward the teachers and their friends. They tease Roya and laugh at her when she doesn't answer them. How will Roya's view of herself and the world develop?

Carl is a noisy, outspoken child. He comes from a family with a hard-working father who tries to provide for the family the best he can. Carl's father quit high school and has had to work at unskilled jobs all his life. He has some strong prejudices about society and people that he has passed along to his family. Carl's father believes that the many "foreign people" who have moved into this country have deprived him of a good job and the chances he deserves. He takes advantage of every opportunity to point out when "they" have done something unlawful, and that "they" should never have been allowed to come here. He doesn't want his taxes providing welfare for anyone, particularly "foreigners." Carl loudly announces his dislike for these people when his class is studying about cultures in other countries. What view of people and the world does Carl bring to the classroom?

WHO ARE THE TEACHERS?

Teachers as well as children come in all sizes, shapes, and colors. They come with dreams, hopes, and aspirations. They come with values, beliefs, and attitudes about the world and themselves. They also come with different beliefs about teaching and about social studies.

Rita is an attractive young woman who comes from a middle-class value-oriented family. She's had a good education and travel experiences that have exposed her to a wide variety of ideas and places. She has some strong opinions about teaching and people. She's rather cynical about her teacher preparation program believing that teaching is mostly giving the information that kids need. She's quite sure that methods of inquiry and discovery take too much time, and that, more importantly, kids need to know the right answers. Rita is sure *she* knows the right answers.

Rita's view of social studies would appear to be aligned with the conception of knowledge of the past as a guide to good citizenship (Brubaker, Simon, & Williams 1977; Engle 1989). She believes that students need to *know* past history in order to become good citizens. Most of her instruction is teacher directed and students are required to memorize information that will appear on objective tests. Without this information, Rita believes, students won't understand why their society and world is the way it is today. As citizens, they won't know what decisions to make because they won't know what mistakes people in the past have made. Rita has read the article, "Tot Sociology: Or What Happened to History in the Schools" by Diane Ravitch (1987) and agrees that without that extensive history background, social studies becomes a discussion of trivial things that don't really help children become good citizens. Rita uses a textbook, but reads to her second graders historical descriptions of events from primary sources. She doesn't have much patience with children who differ from her idea of a typical child (one who sits quietly and listens to the teacher). She doesn't think much of children from families on welfare because she believes everyone can get a job if they really want one. She doesn't understand children who come from backgrounds different from her own since she has had very little exposure to people from other backgrounds. What effect will Rita have on the Jessicas, Terrances, Roberts, Anthonys, Gwens, Cecis, Royas, and Carls?

Julie is a bubbly and enthusiastic individual. You can tell by the look in her eyes when she greets you that she likes people. She comes from a wealthy family. Her father is a doctor and he has given the family many experiences, including a year in the jungle while he operated a clinic. Julie has volunteered summers to work at the recreation center where she has encountered children from all types of neighborhoods. She enjoys teaching, but often feels that she hasn't reached a certain child. She realizes how difficult successful teaching really is. The children know she respects and accepts them, whatever their backgrounds or problems. They are comfortable in her classroom.

Julie's conception of social studies is one that emphasizes reflective inquiry. She believes that students need to become problem solvers by identifying a problem, hypothesizing a reasonable solution, gathering data to test the hypotheses, and arriving at some conclusions. She believes that being involved in the inquiry process is far more important than memorizing a series of facts. But she wants her students to use facts to solve problems. She assesses their ability to conduct an organized search for information and their participation "in the reflective thinking process" (Brubaker et al. 1977, p. 203). One of the recent problems her third graders tackled was pollution. They first investigated the pollution problem from a historical perspective and learned that there has always been a problem with disposing of waste since people began living together in groups and that this problem has worsened with the larger populations of cities. Some of the solutions the students arrived at were quite drastic but ones they believed were necessary. How will Julie affect the learning environment for these children?

Hugo is a member of a minority group who believes that education is crucial to the improvement of the economic and social situation for all people. He chose teaching because he thought he would be an effective model for minority children. His classroom is a place where children can state their values and opinions without fear of being "put down." He wants children to recognize that people may have differences but can still try to work out solutions together. He cautions children to learn about all sides of an issue before drawing conclusions or making a decision. He knows that some children don't trust him because he is a minority person, but he tries hard to treat all of them with respect.

Hugo, mostly due to his background and experiences, believes in the sociopolitical involvement conception of social studies (Brubaker et al. 1977). He believes that students need opportunities to deal with issues that affect their lives. If they are to become active participants in society, they will need to do more than acquire information. They should learn to deal with conflict, be involved in the valuing process, make decisions, and become active within the school and the community (Engle 1989). Recently his fifth grade class has been investigating hate crimes, since one occurred in their community. One of the criticisms of the socio-political concept is that students will not study information from the past, but Hugo has had his students investigating historical hate crimes including Hitler's treatment of the Jews during World War II, the treatment of the freed slaves after the Civil War and on through to the current situation and even going back to treatment of religious groups such as the Mormons and the people labeled as witches during the colonial period. This study gave his students a better perspective on what is happening in their community today. The students wrote a letter to their mayor and city council with their own solution to the community problem. They volunteered to talk with other community leaders. Hugo evaluates his students through an assessment of their skills and their ability to arrive at reasonable solutions. How will children in Hugo's classroom respond to people and the world?

Lewis is an intense young man from a family within a religious minority. His family has long been involved in community service efforts. He has traveled extensively and has much interest in international affairs. Lewis's educational background includes a strong social science emphasis. He has been on archeological digs in Africa and done historical research in England. He is convinced that the best way for children to learn to be good citizens in the future is for them to learn the methods of inquiry of the various social science disciplines and their conceptual structure. His belief is that students become better citizens if they learn "how to look at the world through the eyes of the social scientists" (Barr, Barth, & Shermis 1977, p. 63). His sixth grade students have completed an ethnography of a small ethnic conclave in their community after having read an account of that ethnic group in their textbook. They also studied the ethnographic techniques of anthropologists. Lewis believes that only through the study of the social sciences will his students become good citizens. He evaluates them on their ability to apply major social science concepts to new situations and acquire social scientists' skills as they conduct their inquiries.

WHAT ARE THE CLASSROOMS LIKE?

Classrooms come in all sizes, shapes, and colors, too. There are classrooms in new, colorful, open-space buildings. There are classrooms in old, traditional, egg carton–style buildings. There are classrooms equipped with a wide variety of materials that make teaching and learning an interesting experience. There are classrooms that are barren and unproductive. There are classrooms where children receive understanding, motivation, guidance, patience, and a learning environment that meets their needs. There are classrooms where children meet with indifference, hostility, and uncaring teachers.

One classroom in a traditional-styled building catches the eye. The building has been repainted with bright colors and the classroom is a soft yellow. Entering the room, one has a good feeling about it. There aren't any terribly neat teacher-made bulletin boards, rather the children's work is displayed. It's obvious that the room is for the children. One bulletin board depicts the cultures the children have been studying this year, showing pictures from magazines and newspapers as well as postcards and artifacts from different countries. The children have pen pals in each country and letters are also in evidence. A globe and several maps are in constant use, and one map depicts the time and mode of transportation used if one were traveling to different countries. Another section of the board displays "How Are We Alike and Different?" and shows pictures of the children and their pen pals with a chart contrasting facets of their cultures, such as school, clothing, houses, games, government, feelings, values, and problems.

Upon entering a pod in a modern open-space school, one is struck by the coldness of the atmosphere. The surroundings include brightly colored carpet and walls, but all the materials seem to be tucked away in the cabinets. There is limited bulletin board space and this is covered with a do's and don'ts chart of rules, a neat display of math sets, and a sterile set of pictures entitled "Our Community." No children's work is displayed and no maps or globes are in evidence. One wonders how social studies is taught in this classroom.

WHAT ABOUT SCHOOLS?

Schools are found in crime-ridden inner cities, as well as inner cities that have been revitalized, quiet suburban neighborhoods, and small-town rural areas. The outside environment of the school has an impact on the children and the social studies program, but the environment within the school impacts them as well. Regardless of where children go to school, the atmosphere and people who greet them each morning will affect how they perceive the world they live in.

As children enter a modern school in an inner city neighborhood, the principal is near the door to greet them with a smile and an honest concern for their well-being. The principal knows the children by name and calls out questions about their after-school activities or how their schoolwork is going. The children walk down the halls in small groups chatting about events in their lives. Even though the neighborhood is often the scene of violence, they know the school is a safe environment. Most of their teachers will greet them in their classrooms as the principal did. The principal has worked with the teachers as a team to develop reasonable rules that children can understand and are willing to follow. Teachers have developed classroom rules with the children, so that they understand the reasons for the rules. Older children in the school have been trained as peer mediators and they work out conflicts that occur between and among children. Very few of these conflicts end up in the principal's office. If they do reach the principal's office, paddling is rarely if ever administered. Work responsibilities in the school may be assigned or a parent conference scheduled. Children know they will be treated fairly and respond well with a limited display of aggressive behavior. What the children are learning in social studies about getting along with people, rules, laws, democracy, and conflicts makes more sense in a school environment that recognizes them as individuals with rights and responsibilities.

Another school in a suburban neighborhood receives the children with quite a different atmosphere. Running and shouting children approach the doors to be stopped by teacher hall monitors who require that the children form straight single lines with absolutely no talking as they go to their rooms. Frequent yelling by the teachers warns the children to be quiet, keep those lines straight, and not to push or run. Some teachers will greet the children with warmth and a pleasant atmosphere, but too many continue the yelling to get them into their seats. School rules are posted on each classroom door and teachers point out those which have been broken. Children aren't sure why certain rules are necessary. No one has explained them. Before much of the school day has passed, several children have been sent to the office for fighting on the playground or disrupting the classroom. Paddling is a frequent punishment and children respond with repeated aggression toward other children. Those children with violence or physical abuse in their lives don't see much difference in the school environment. Children in this school don't become self-disciplined but need constant monitoring to obey the rules (Essery 1992). How will these children respond to their social studies program?

WHAT ABOUT SOCIAL STUDIES?

As indicated by the previous descriptions of teacher beliefs, it is obvious that individual teachers hold different conceptions of social studies and therefore use different approaches to instruction and evaluation. Not all teachers have such strong beliefs as Rita, Hugo, Julie, and Lewis. Some teachers combine conceptions of social studies with a major emphasis such as citizenship transmission and a minor emphasis on the social sciences (Essery 1992). Other teachers have not identified what their beliefs are about teaching social studies.

Our four teachers happen to be together at an inservice meeting that was introducing the new social studies textbook series for the district. Let's listen in on their discussion.

Rita is quite discouraged. She expresses her concern. "I'm really disappointed in our new textbooks. They simply do not have enough historical information included. My second grade book focuses on neighborhoods, as it has been for the last twenty years, but my students know enough about neighborhoods" (Akenson 1989). "They need to know more about the historical development of their country *and* of their neighborhoods."

Julie quickly disagrees with Rita and presents her view. "I don't know what the children are going to do with that historical information. Young children especially can't conceptualize the time when the events took place and they merely memorize the information to give back on a test. Most children think social studies is boring when all they do is learn facts. I'm much more interested in their learning a process of problem solving than acquiring a lot of information they don't understand and won't use."

Hugo jumps in with his comment: "Just learning to solve problems isn't enough. The students need to be dealing with problems that affect their lives and issues that affect the society in which they live. They need to know what to do once they arrive at some type of solution—whether it's writing a letter to the editor or their city councilperson or actually implementing the solution. They are going to be more active and effective citizens now and as adults as a result."

Lewis can't stand by and listen to the discussion without adding his own views. "Our new textbooks don't have any of the basic concepts of the social science disciplines or about the methods of inquiry that social scientists use. Just think if our students were able to understand the basic concepts of economics, sociology/anthropology, political science, and geography, they would be able to apply them in any situation they encounter. Also, by knowing the method of inquiry of the social scientist, they would be able to identify the kinds of problems that Julie has been talking about. Hugo, we can't expect these children to solve the problems of our society now, but maybe with the concepts and skills of inquiry, they'll be much better able to be effective citizens as adults."

Rita argues, "All of you are leaving out that important historical background. Of course, I'll have to supplement our textbooks with other materials, since the books are limited."

Julie responds, "No, Rita, that's not true, our students can't solve problems in a vacuum. They have to have information about the past. The difference is that they are selective about the information and they see a reason for learning it. It's not just a matter of acquiring a chronological parade of facts about a topic. But, Lewis, I can't agree with you about developing miniature social scientists (Engle 1989). Think how people spend their lifetimes acquiring the skills of a sociologist or political scientist. How can we expect children to do that? Also, we don't divide our lives and problems into the neat compartments of the social sciences."

"Oh, Julie! We don't expect that children will develop as sophisticated skills, but rather that they begin thinking like and asking questions as a social scientist might."

Hugo interrupts, "I think you are all forgetting one important factor. Values. Students have to learn to make decisions and those decisions are based on their values. They have to deal with conflict and recognize that not everyone necessarily believes as they do, but they learn to listen to others' views, support their own beliefs, and be an active participant in and out of school. Active learning will make social studies much more interesting to our students."

"Hugo, don't you realize how difficult that's going to be to implement such a program? How are the principal and the other teachers going to react toward students who don't agree with their decisions or how will community leaders react when students write letters or make suggestions about situations in the community?"

Hugo argues, "Well, how do you think we're going to develop active participating citizens if we don't give them an opportunity to make meaningful decisions now? It also affects the decisions they make in their personal lives. I've been reading an article by Shirley Engle (1989) titled "Whatever Happened to the Social Studies" where he points out that we can develop citizens who are robots, learning by being told what to memorize, or we can develop citizens who can think independently and use information to solve problems. Our textbook can be one source of that information."

Lewis points out, "I think all of us recognize that our textbook isn't enough, however we teach social studies, and we'll need to supplement it with other resources."

Julie advises the group, "This discussion has been very helpful to me. I think all of us have a legitimate argument. Maybe we should consider what each of us has said and think about how it might affect the way we view social studies and our approach to teaching. We really should discuss this again after we've had time to think about it."

Defining the Social Studies

Social studies should be more broadly conceived than any one of the previously described positions and thus encompass something from each of them. As one reflects back on the descriptions of the children, teachers, classrooms, and schools, one realizes the impact of the self-concepts, experiences, values, frustrations, resentments, and skills that the individual children and teachers bring to the social studies arena. What then should be the definition of social studies that will attend to the needs of the children, be intellectually sound, and develop necessary skills for effective participation as citizens in society?

The function of social studies should be to assist children in the development of a good self-concept; help them recognize and appreciate the global society and its multicultural composition; further the socialization process—social, economic, and political; provide knowledge of the past and present as a basis for decision making; develop problem-solving and valuing skills; and foster an active participant role in society.

As the children learn more about themselves and other people, they realize that others have similar feelings and problems, and they feel better about themselves. Children are then able to relate more effectively to others. Children dissatisfied with themselves are unlikely to care much about the feelings and concerns of others.

Within almost any classroom will be children with a variety of cultural backgrounds, severe racial or ethnic prejudices, and a multiplicity of value beliefs. In addition, there will be different degrees of motivation, apathy, or disinterest, and different levels of intellectual capabilities and different feelings of self-worth. Hopefully, these children will be taught by teachers who respect them regardless of their backgrounds, capabilities, and value systems, and who try to provide a classroom atmosphere that is open and accepting—an atmosphere that recognizes our multicultural world and realizes that each culture's response to a common problem, however different, can still contribute something unique to the fabric of society. Socialization (the ways people learn about their culture, i.e., roles, norms, values, customs) that occurs within such an atmosphere should give children a more objective view of the social, economic, and political processes of which they will be a part.

Content is selected that will illuminate an understanding of the past. Children cannot make decisions about the present or the future without some basic understanding of how we arrived at the present. This does not mean a chronological assemblage of facts that are soon to be forgotten, but rather a selection of the information necessary to understand current problems such as the decline of the cities, racial strife, or the unrest in the Middle East. Basic understanding also entails acquiring a respect for the cultural heritage of our country and other countries of the world.

The development of problem-solving skills provides a basis for the acquisition of decision-making skills. Children hypothesize a solution to a problem, but then need sufficient information to test the validity and feasibility of the hypothesis. Valuing skills are also necessary in the process since the action to be taken or the solution hypothesized should be guided by value priorities. Children must realize why they value as they do, that others may value differently, and the effect their values have on their actions and the consequences of those actions to themselves and others. Decisions can then be made.

As children are given the opportunity to act on the solutions they conceive, they then see the efficacy of their roles in society. For example, when children arrive at the solution that a crossing guard is needed at a street intersection where several accidents have occurred, they take their solution to the proper authorities and observe the results after the authorities agree to add the guard; then they realize participation can be effective. Fostering this action is a necessity so that it will become a lifelong habit.

Goals established for the social studies from the earlier definition would be:

- To improve the individual's self-concept.
- To recognize the varying abilities of individuals and the worth of each individual.
- To acquire knowledge of and appreciation for the cultures within society.
- To increase awareness of and appreciation for the global society and its multicultural composition.
- To acquire knowledge of global problems.
- To acquire knowledge of past events and their influence on the present and the future.
- To acquire problem-solving and valuing skills that provide the basis for decision making.

- To acquire social skills that increase communication among individuals.
- To acquire knowledge of the economic and political systems for effective participation.
- To foster an attitude that encourages each individual to become an active member of society.

Developing Objectives/Outcomes

Specific objectives/outcomes developed for a social studies curriculum would be based upon the earlier-defined function and goals but with consideration for:

- The experiential background of the students: the attitudes, values, skills, and experiences that the students bring with them.
- The intellectual abilities of the students: the capabilities exhibited by the students.
- The availability of materials: the resources that are available within the school and community.
- The goals of the total school curriculum; the social studies objectives should assist in attainment of the overall goals of the school.
- The societal factors that affect each and all of us: the changes in society to which the curriculum should respond.

A more detailed discussion of developing objectives/outcomes for social studies will be developed in Chapter 4.

SUMMARY

As teachers consider social studies and its role in the curriculum, they must first think about the children in their classrooms. What value beliefs do they bring with them? What are their feelings about themselves and others? What are their prejudices? What are their experiences? What are their abilities and expectations?

Next, teachers must consider themselves. How do they feel about themselves and others? What are their value beliefs? Can they accept children who may hold different values? Will they attempt to impose their value beliefs? What are their experiences? Have they interacted with multicultural groups within the society or do they have a narrow view of culture? Can they accept children who come from cultural backgrounds different from their own? What expectations do they hold for children?

In addition, teachers need to consider their position on the function of social studies. Do they view it as training for becoming social scientists? Do they view it as a vehicle for transmission of culture? Do they view it as reflective inquiry or action and valuing? Or are they in agreement with the position that it is a composite of all these functions, with special consideration for improving the self-concepts of children, developing an awareness of the multicultural composition of society and its global nature, and fostering an atmosphere for acceptance of varying opinions and beliefs?

SELECTED REFERENCES

Akenson, J. E. (1989). The expanding environments and elementary education: A critical perspective. *Theory and Research in Social Education, 17*(1), 33–52.

Banks, J. A. (1990). *Teaching strategies for social studies* (4th ed.). Reading, MA: Addison-Wesley.

Barr, R. D., Barth, J. L., & Shermis, S. S. (1977). *Defining the social studies.* Washington, DC: National Council for the Social Studies, Bulletin 51.

Brubaker, D. L., Simon, L. H., & Williams, J. W. (1977). A conceptual framework for social studies curriculum and instruction. *Social Education, 41,* 201–205.

Butts, R. F. (1980, October). Education for citizenship. *Educational Leadership,* p. 6.

Cogan, J. J. (1989). Citizenship for the 21st century: Observations and reflections. *Social Education, 46*(7), 243.

Edelman, M. W. (1992). The challenges of the 90s: Saving our children. *Social Education, 40*(4), 187–222.

Ellis, A. K. (1991). *Teaching and learning social studies* (4th ed.). Boston: Allyn & Bacon.

Engle, S. H. (1989). Whatever happened to the social studies? *International Journal of Social Education, 4*(1), 42–51.

Essery, M. (1992). *An investigation of preservice and beginning teachers' views of social studies and implementation of social studies instruction.* Unpublished doctoral dissertation, George Peabody College for Teachers of Vanderbilt University.

Jarolimek, J. (1990). *Social studies in elementary education* (8th ed.). New York: Macmillan.

Martorella, P. (1985). *Elementary social studies: Developing reflective, competent and concerned citizens.* New York: Harper & Row.

Michaelis, J. (1992). *Social studies for children: A guide to basic instruction* (10th ed.). Englewood Cliffs, NJ: Prentice-Hall.

Nelson, M. R. (1992). *Children and social studies* (2nd ed.). Fort Worth: Harcourt Brace Jovanovich.

Pallas, A. M., Natriello, G., & McDill, E. L. (1989, June–July). The changing nature of the disadvantaged population: Current dimensions and future trends. *The Educational Researcher,* pp. 16–22.

Ravitch, D. (1987, Summer). Tot sociology: Or what happened to history in the schools. *The American Scholar,* pp. 343–354.

Seefeldt, C. (1993). *Social studies for the preschool–primary child* (4th ed.). New York: Macmillan.

Taba, H., & Elkins, D. (1966). *Teaching strategies of culturally disadvantaged.* Chicago: Rand McNally.

Webster, S. W. (Ed.). (1966). *The disadvantaged learner: Knowing, understanding, educating.* San Francisco: Chandler.

Welton, D., & Mallen, J. T. (1992). *Children and their world: Teaching elementary social studies* (4th ed.). Chicago: Rand McNally.

LEARNING ACTIVITY

Right now, you may be somewhat confused about how you view social studies. Reading about and talking with others about the different conceptions may help clarify what you think. Form five small cooperative groups of classmates with each group responsible for one of the five conceptions (this text only outlined four) as described by Brubaker in the following article, *A Conceptual Framework for Social Studies Curriculum and Instruction*. Read that article and the one by Engle titled *Whatever Happened To The Social Studies?* Within your group, discuss the conceptions and Engle's views, remembering that you will be responsible to explain this conception to another group. After discussion time, reform the groups to include at least one person from each conception in the group. Spend some time sharing each person's understanding of his or her assigned conception and also the counter arguments. After the discussion, take some time to write down in your journal your thoughts about what social studies should be. Plan to keep a journal of your thoughts as you work through the book.

A Conceptual Framework for Social Studies Curriculum and Instruction

Dale L. Brubaker, Lawrence H. Simon, Jo Watts Williams

Dale L. Brubaker is Professor of Education at the University of North Carolina at Greensboro; **Lawrence H. Simon** and **Jo Watts Williams** are Associate Professors of Education at Elon College, North Carolina.

There are many ways in which one can view social studies curriculum and instruction—past, present, and future. One way, which may well be labelled the Social Foundations of the Social Studies, identifies a number of ideological camps and compares and contrasts these camps as they answer key questions about the social studies. This process of conceptual model-building affords the students of social studies the opportunity to become engaged in dialogue about the way things have been, should be, and can be. It is hoped that such discussion will influence one's course of action.

In 1967, this senior author's *Alternative Directions for the Social Studies* provoked a good deal of discussion by identifying two major camps, one of which was labelled the "good citizenship" position, the other the "social science inquiry position."[1] Basically, the two camps reflected the different goal orientations of educationists and social scientists, the former including professors of education and teachers of the social studies.

James L. Barth and S. Samuel Shermis expanded the two-camp model into a model that focused on three traditions: (1) social studies as citizenship transmission, (2) social studies as social science, and (3) social studies as reflective inquiry. Their model was the subject of a provocative article in *Social Education* in 1970.[2]

This article is another extension of the two previously mentioned publications. It is a five-camp model for analyzing social studies curriculum and instruction.[3] The five camps are: (1) social studies as knowledge of the past as a guide to good citizenship, (2) social studies in the student-centered tradition, (3) social studies as reflective inquiry, (4) social studies as structure of the disciplines, and (5) social studies as socio-political involvement. A series of questions guided our inquiry into the nature of the five camps:

1. What provision is made for citizenship education?
2. What assumptions are made about the social and intellectual maturity of the pupil?
3. How is the content of the curriculum selected?
   3.1 What constitutes the body of knowledge for the curriculum?
   3.2 What are the sources of content for the curriculum?
4. How is the content of the curriculum utilized?
   4.1 What is expected of teachers in dealing with the content of the curriculum?
   4.2 What is expected of students in dealing with the content of the curriculum?
   4.3 What is expected of significant others (e.g., professors in academic disciplines, publishers) in dealing with the content of the curriculum?
5. How is evaluation of pupils and teachers with regard to curricular objectives accomplished?

---

[1] Dale L. Brubaker, *Alternative Directions for the Social Studies*, (Scranton, PA: International Textbook Co., 1967). Some scholars felt that the two camps reflected the basic ". . . ambivalence built into the social science-social studies confrontation. . . ." "Report of the Political Science Panel," *Social Sciences Education Framework for California Public Schools* (Sacramento, CA: Statewide Social Sciences Study Committee to the State Curriculum Commission and the California State Board of Education, 1968), 7.

[2] James L. Barth and S. Samuel Shermis, "Defining the Social Studies: An Exploration of Three Traditions," *Social Education* (November, 1970), 743–751. Several doctoral students at Purdue University have written dissertations stimulated by the Barth-Shermis model.

[3] Two dissertations have been based on the five-camp model. Lawrence Howard Simon, "Toward the Development of a Programmatic Language for Social Studies Curriculum and Instruction," University of North Carolina at Greensboro, 1973; and Jo Watts Williams, "A Conceptual Framework for Elementary Social Studies Curriculum and Instruction," University of North Carolina at Greensboro, 1973.

In pursuing these questions within the five-camp model, we surmised that many teachers probably used a mixed strategy drawing from two or more camps. At the same time, we felt that their overall teaching approach would give primary emphasis to one of the camps.

Social Studies as Knowledge of the Past as a Guide to Good Citizenship

Past and present advocates of this position share the beliefs (1) that history should be the major and/or integrating focus of study, and (2) that emphasis on sound knowledge and understanding of the past will serve as an effective guide to good citizenship. Beyond these two areas of agreement, however, there is a good deal of variance of opinion among advocates.

The view that knowledge of the past should play the central role in "social studies" instruction has its roots in the history-geography-civics tradition that emerged during the early history of our nation. "Teaching methods consisted chiefly of having children read passages aloud and recite memorized portions of the text."[4] Although the material to be memorized was treated as factual, it did in fact consist largely of moral prescriptions concerning ". . . the nature of man, his relation to God, and the manner in which he is to conduct his life."[5]

Independence from England and a burgeoning national consciousness introduced a secular religion—Americanism—with new texts that emphasized deeds of American heroes, incidents in the life of the new United States, and partisan interpretations of political events. The Civil War, in turn, gave the greatest impetus to the study of history as an independent subject, with many Northern cities adding United States history as a required subject ". . . to emphasize American accomplishments, with the chief stress on the memorization of facts relating to our national heroes, wars, and political struggles."[6]

Some recent advocates of the "social studies as knowledge of the past" viewpoint, such as the Organization of American Historians, warn us of the dangers of being occupied with "presentism and history instruction that emphasizes concepts rather than facts."[7] Other historians "have become convinced that the use of a social science concept like status, social mobility, consensus, cultural change and alienation can be of great value to a better understanding of a historical event or a personality."[8]

A more extreme position concerning the central role that the acquisition of facts should play in learning about the past has been argued by Max Rafferty, former Superintendent of Public Instruction for the State of California: "Classwork should include in all schools memorization and drill . . . in historical dates and names of significance."[9] Unfortunately, however, ". . . the study of history as an uninterrupted chronological narrative is often boring . . . and becomes the story of 'dry facts' and dates, taught superficially on the basis of inane textbooks."[10] (As Irving Morrissett has communicated to this senior author, "Logically, the emphasis on history and the emphasis on facts need not go together; in practice they have to a very large degree.")

Who, then, according to this position, is the good social studies teacher? It is the person who believes that the study of the past should be the major and/or integrating focus of study so that this knowledge can serve as a guide to good citizenship. Some advocates of this position would argue that

---

[4] R. Murray Thomas and Dale L. Brubaker, *Curriculum Patterns in Elementary Social Studies* (Belmont, CA: Wadsworth Publishing Co., 1971), 8. See, also, Erling M. Hunt, "Changing Perspectives in the Social Studies," in Erling M. Hunt et al., *High School Social Studies Perspectives,* (Boston: Houghton Mifflin Co., 1962), 3–28.

[5] Thomas and Brubaker, op. cit., 7.

[6] Ellwood P. Cubberley, *Public Education in the United States* (Boston: Houghton Mifflin Co., 1947), 399.

[7] "History Teaching Is 'in Crisis'," *Greensboro Daily News,* Greensboro, NC, August 11, 1975, A2.

[8] Mark M. Krug, John B. Poster, and William B. Gillies, III, *The New Social Studies* (Itasca, Ill.: Peacock Publishers, 1970), 37. The ambivalence of historians in relating to concepts and the behavioral sciences is noted and discussed in Dale L. Brubaker, *Social Studies in a Mass Society* (Scranton, PA: International Textbook Co., 1969), 117–142.

[9] Max Rafferty, *Suffer, Little Children* (New York: The Devin-Adair Co., 1962), 136.

[10] Krug, Poster, and Gillies, op. cit., 162.

the teacher must move beyond this belief to explore creative and imaginative ways of teaching about the past, whereas others leave you with the impression that learning must be a tough intellectual disciplining process whereby a drillmaster puts his students through their paces by memorizing facts. Still others would provide the student with a mishmash of facts and generalizations that focus on the past. Many social studies textbooks demonstrate this latter approach.

Major criticisms of the "social studies as knowledge of the past as a guide to good citizenship" position are as follows:

1. The attitude toward authority(ies) taught by those who want to drill facts into students' heads creates bureaucrats who are expected to comply with commands from those higher up in the hierarchy. This attitude is reinforced by the assumption that (a) all ends are measurable, (b) there is consensus for reaching such ends, and (c) the causal relationship between means and ends is readily and concretely demonstrable.[11]
2. Studies in learning indicate that we quickly forget the many facts formerly memorized.[12]
3. Facts are not sacrosanct. Scholars disagree with respect to the validity of many facts, and facts quickly become dated with new findings.
4. Students are present-oriented and find most approaches to studying the past boring and irrelevant.
5. Students should be considered as citizens now, rather than as preparing for future citizenship by studying the past. New realities, such as economic and political power for youth, must be considered in this regard.[13]

Social Studies in the Student-Centered Tradition

Although the origins of the student-centered tradition were in the decades immediately following the Civil War, the tradition is best illustrated by the progressive education movement which flourished during the first half of the twentieth century.[14] As suggested by its title, at the heart of the tradition is the student who should be nurtured in his natural growth. He or she is viewed as the source of all content in the social studies program, with curriculum and instruction based on his or her nature, needs, and interests. The whole person, not just the cognitive person, should be the concern of the social studies educator. Knowledge is therefore instrumental and secondary, for it is useful only as it serves the student's interests and needs.

The classroom is expected to be a "miniature society" with the student acting as a citizen in this *simulated* society. Advocates of this curricular focus believe that students pass through a variety of developmental stages, and that their growth rate during these stages is not uniform with respect to any personal characteristic. Nevertheless, students of all ages are assumed to have a sufficient measure of social and intellectual maturity to play a central role in determining what educational experiences are most appropriate for them.

The content of the student-focused social studies curriculum begins with the personal experiences of the student in his or her total environment. Vicarious experiences of the person are also included. These experiences are then springboards into other new areas of interest for the student. One can see that emerging curriculum was of considerable importance to the student-centered educator. The "expanding-communities-of-man" curriculum model, often associated with Paul Hanna, illustrates the student-centered curriculum.

According to this position, the good teacher is one who teaches the whole student, rather than just teaching facts or academic disciplines. This teacher can work with the student in order to integrate the various learnings that emerge from new experiences into the everyday living of the student. Accordingly, evaluation of the student should be a shared, subjective assessment of pupil progress in light of the total development of the person. This

---

[11] Dale L. Brubaker and Roland H. Nelson, Jr., *Creative Survival in Educational Bureaucracies* (Berkeley, CA: McCutchan Publishing Co., 1974), 66.

[12] John DeCecco and Arlene Richards, *Growing Pains: Uses of School Conflict* (New York: Aberdeen Press, 1974), 36.

[13] John DeCecco has strongly supported this position in his writings on social studies education. See, for example, ibid., 43–86.

[14] Lawrence Cremin, *The Transformation of the School* (New York: Vintage Books, 1961), viii.

should include a subjective determination of change in the student's personality, social attitudes and skills, and his or her physical well-being.

Some of the criticisms of the "social studies as student-centered" position are:

1. It is too self-centered and does not teach the student to be responsible for social action outside the school.[15]
2. Related to the first criticism is the fact that the student-centered curriculum and experimental schools that practiced this curriculum wanted to protect students from the hard realities outside the school by limiting enrollment to "nice" people. Students were not encouraged to wrestle with problems in their natural environment; so these schools became antiseptic islands in the midst of agonizing social problems.
3. Student-centered educators tended to "go off the deep end" and emphasize the student's present interests at the expense of important learnings of others in the past. Afraid to impose anything on the student, the educator failed to transmit a rich and varied culture from the past. Student-centered education therefore had a tendency to become "wishy-washy" and aimless.

Social Studies as Reflective Inquiry

Industrial and technological advances in the United States have provided American youth with more and more cultural alternatives. There is a diminution of culturally fixed mores and values—with traditional values, founded in Puritan morality, the work-success ethic, and individualism and achievement being supplanted by emergent values based on sociability, consideration for others, happiness, and conformity.[16] Given these cultural realities, social studies educators must be responsible for creating conditions whereby students can inquire into beliefs, values, and social policies, as well as assess the consequences and implications of possible alternatives. Social studies as reflective inquiry provides a means for students to participate in the inquiry process.

Above all, social studies as reflective inquiry emphasizes process over product. Its main concern is with students learning a generalized method of problem solving. That method would include sensing a problem, articulating it, hypothesizing a plausible solution, gathering data, testing the hypothesis, and drawing appropriate conclusions.[17] These acts would not necessarily be in sequence; and shortcuts might be taken, as, for example, when one plays out a hunch.

With this view of social studies curriculum, citizenship is defined as a process of decision-making within the socio-political framework afforded by our form of democracy.[18] In selecting content, no one set body of information is considered essential; rather, the emphasis is upon an organized, directed search. The teacher's role is that of fellow inquirer who invokes doubt in behalf of the inquiry process.

In order to assist teachers and students in the inquiry process, publishers have been challenged to produce many and diverse multimedia packages. Some publishers have successfully met this challenge, while others have simply introduced the label "inquiry" in their textbook titles and advertisements.

Student progress, as might be expected, is evaluated rather subjectively by teachers and students based on their participation in the reflective thinking process.

Criticisms of the view of social studies as reflective inquiry have come from many quarters. Such criticisms include the following:

1. Although students should be engaged in the reflective thinking process, they should go beyond thinking to acting on behalf of their beliefs

---

[15] George Counts, *Dare the Schools Build a New Social Order?* (New York: John Day Publishing Co., 1932).

[16] Byron Massialas and C. Benjamin Cox, *Inquiry in Social Studies* (New York: McGraw-Hill Book Co., 1966), 7. Correspondent Theodore White argues that the Nixon men were basically men of the old culture who did not adjust to the cultural changes of the sixties; the result was a credibility gap between the White House and the citizenry. This thesis is a provocative one for the social studies educator to consider. Theodore H. White, *Breach of Faith* (New York: Atheneum Publishers, 1975), 331.

[17] John Dewey used the term "reflective thinking" to describe his problem-solving model. John Dewey, *How We Think* (Boston: D.C. Heath and Co., 1933), 106–118.

[18] Barth and Shermis, op. cit., 748–749.

in the school and outside the school. In fact, thinking about a problem can sometimes leave the student with the mistaken impression that he or she has actually done something about the problem.
2. Not enough attention is given to the emotional side of learning, for there is a definite bias toward scientific reasoning. Leaders in society simply do not act as professors say they should. Scientific reasoning is too antiseptic.
3. Learnings from the past are often ignored.

Social Studies as Structure of the Disciplines

Increased involvement of social scientists in the social studies occurred in the sixties as a result of government and private funding. Social scientists' principal concern was with students learning the basic concepts and methods of scholarly inquiry in their respective disciplines.[19] It was argued that concepts would serve as "handles" that would help the person organize newly acquired learnings wherever such learnings were possible.

Support for the "structure of the disciplines" approach came from psychologist Jerome Bruner, who asserted that ". . . there is no reason to believe that any subject cannot be taught to any child at virtually any age in some (intellectually honest) form."[20]

With this view of the social studies curriculum, students are not considered citizens in the present. Rather it is argued that the structures learned and the inquiry methods used will transfer to the student's adult life so that he or she can discharge his or her duties as a citizen.[21] One may infer from the "structure of the disciplines" position that it would be presumptuous to expect the student to build his or her own structures, for university academicians have been specially educated to engage themselves in this process.

The good teacher, according to this position, is one who keeps abreast of the most recent research and can effectively teach the structure of the disciplines and their methods of inquiry. The teacher is aided by various media designed to teach structure of the disciplines.

The student is evaluated on the basis of his or her ability to define and apply key organizing concepts in different situations. He or she is also expected to ask the kinds of questions asked by scholars in the various disciplines.

Although the "structure of the disciplines" approach has had a significant influence on social studies curriculum and instruction in the sixties and seventies, criticisms such as the following have been directed at the position:

1. Citizens in the world do not divide their decision-making into various disciplines. The gas station attendant, for example, does not say to his customer, "For the next few minutes I would like to talk to you as a sociologist would, after which I will talk to you as a geographer would," etc. "Our students," some teachers say, "are not going to be university professors."
2. Emphasis on scholarly activity in the disciplines can actually serve as a substitute for action in the world outside the school. Students' feelings are often left out of the curriculum in universities in the name of objectivity. Today's generation of students will insist on the importance of affect in their decision-making, and the "structure of the disciplines" approach too often does not accommodate such affect.
3. Students should be actively involved in building their own learning structures. It is too easy to substitute the memorization of concepts for the memorization of facts.

Social Studies as Socio-Political Involvement

The individual's attempt to face conflict squarely is central to the "social studies as socio-political involvement" position. In order to deal with conflict-ridden situations, one must feel confident that one's own beliefs are realized in one's actions. Credibility, as reflected in others' faith in oneself as a person

---

[19] Some historians have argued that many, if not most, of their colleagues are uncomfortable with conceptual approaches. See Edwin Fenton's statement in Irving Morrissett, ed., *Concepts and Structure in the New Social Science Curricula* (New York: Holt, Rinehart and Winston, Inc., 1967), 52; and Mark M. Krug, *History and the Social Sciences* (Waltham, MA: Blaisdell Publishing Co., 1967), 47.
[20] Jerome S. Bruner, *The Process of Education* (Cambridge, MA: Harvard University Press, 1960), 47.
[21] Barth and Shermis, op. cit., 747–748.

and leader, depends on this.[22] The teacher of the social studies and social studies students must therefore be actively involved in the valuing process; and for a person to hold a value, he must act repeatedly in behalf of his professed belief.[23]

How does the student learn to be an active citizen? He learns *now* in his immediate environment. He or she can be active as a decision-maker in his or her school and community(ies) outside the school. The good teacher, according to this position, is one who facilitates this involvement and is personally active himself. Students are encouraged to disagree with each other and with the teacher, but the highest compliment they can pay their teacher is that he acted in behalf of his professed beliefs. Of course, active involvement will at times be controversial, but the rationale for living one's professed beliefs is clearly in our democratic heritage. It is also true that a lack of a working knowledge of politics (conflict resolution and reconciliation) and a certain temerity on the part of many teachers add to the controversies when those who teach social studies initially try out socio-political involvement.

A critical assumption of this position is that students are capable of socio-political action. Their sophistication levels will vary, of course, and the teacher will have to make clear his own responsibilities because of his role in the socio-political systems of which he is a part.

All of the reflective inquiry techniques, such as simulation games and case studies, can aid students' involvement; this depends, however, on the teacher making a conscious effort to link teaching and learning in the classroom to community(ies) outside the classroom. Significant individuals from such communities can help the student.

According to this position, students can be evaluated on the basis of their participation in the reflective action process. This will create controversy in the school at times, for students are presently involved and evaluated in their roles as incipient scholars. Teachers should be evaluated for their success in actively involving students in reflective action in class, in the school, and outside the school.

The "social studies as socio-political involvement" position has emerged in recent years in response to cultural change in our nation. As such it is very controversial and has been criticized for many reasons, including the following:

1. Colleges and universities have not prepared teachers for this approach to social studies instruction.
2. The school as a socio-political system simply will not tolerate students as active citizens, nor will the communities outside the school.
3. Students already vent their emotions too much. Allowing for greater expression of emotions will be detrimental to schools and learning.
4. This position too easily tends to neglect the great learnings of the past. It tends to be anti-intellectual.

Conclusion

The rhetoric of any era in a nation's history tells us a great deal about people and events. Much of the terminology of our age points to distance between people and their beliefs. In fact, one might describe recent history in the United States as the period of "gaps": the generation gap, the credibility gap, the leadership gap, etc. A more balanced view, however, is that important progress has been made in bridging these gaps. At any rate, the challenge to those of us interested in social education has never been greater. In order to meet this challenge, we must involve ourselves in vigorous dialogue and reflective action in behalf of our beliefs. We hope that this article has been helpful in stimulating thinking and action concerning ends and means for social studies curriculum and instruction.

---

[22] Theodore White's thesis in *Breach of Faith* is that former President Nixon failed to honor the trust people placed in his leadership. White, op. cit., 322.

[23] Louis Raths, Merrill Harmin, and Sidney Simon, *Values and Teaching: Working with Values in the Classroom* (Columbus, Ohio: Charles E. Merrill, 1966), 28–30. There are several articulate spokesmen for the social action position, including Anna S. Ochoa, Patricia L. Johnson, and Fred M. Newmann. Ochoa and Johnson have prepared papers and speeches on a social action curriculum. Fred M. Newmann's *Education for Citizen Action* (Berkeley, CA: McCutchan Publishing Co., 1975) may well become a classic work on social action for secondary school students.

Whatever Happened to the Social Studies?

Shirley H. Engle

There are two quite opposite ways to educate citizens of a state. One method assumes that the role of the citizen is to be a follower, one who conforms to the governance of the state, one who accepts whatever lot falls to him or her in deference to the person who is in power, one who defends the state unquestioningly whenever called upon to do so. This role is the relationship between the state and a citizen in all autocracies, whether of the right or the left.

The other method assumes that the role of the citizen is to participate in the governance of the state, even to work to change the policies of the state. The good citizen is seen as a friendly and well-informed critic of the state. This conception of the role of the citizen fits better the relationship of the state and its citizens in a democracy.

This distinction seems to be poorly understood by many citizens of this democracy and even by many, if not most, social studies teachers, for many of the things we do in school in the name of citizenship education logically fit the needs of an autocracy better than those of a democracy. The authoritarian nature of citizenship education in this country has been attested to by every study of the social studies that has been made in recent years. Democratically oriented citizenship education seems to be the exception rather than the rule in our schools. Among the common practices that logically fit autocracy better than democracy are the slavish use of the overly simple, single-version textbook to be memorized rather than questioned, the obsession with so-called correct answers to be held in memory in lieu of a genuine search for true answers, the dominance of teacher talk usually in the expository mood to be taken as gospel, and the almost complete avoidance of the controversial: This is really a poor arsenal of tools if democratic citizenship is our goal.

As Gunnar Myrdal pointed out years ago, nothing is better calculated to maintain the status quo in a society than the straight exposition of history while leaving out the assumptions, the caveats, and the qualifiers that all historians make in writing history,[1] and, it might be added, without a sense of the problematic that invests all historical study. There is little about this process that produces the critical and independent minds that democracy requires. Nor has this process that dominates social studies teaching today changed very much in the seventy-five years since the social studies movement began.

Studs Terkel hit upon the important distinction between citizenship education in an autocracy and citizenship education in a democracy when he commented on the recent celebration of the one-hundredth anniversary of the Statue of Liberty. He noted what he called the obsessive regard for patriotism. Where, he said, was the recognition of the critics in our society, many of whom came into our country within the very shadow of the statue that we celebrate and many of whom were perhaps more responsible than the so-called patriots for building the enduring strength of this nation? Is criticism becoming out of style? With some, was it never in style? It is easily observed today that critics have a hard time of it in schools and out. Rather than being respected as they should be, they are frequently silenced, reviled, and persecuted, often by the government itself, and even by school teachers. It is a chilling thought that critics are so easily mislabeled as communists and unpatriotic even by some leaders in our government. Is it possible that there is a relationship between the undemocratic attitude toward the critics in the public domain and the authoritarian mold of so much that passes in our schools for citizenship education?

Contributing to our failure to develop citizenship education appropriate to a democracy is confusion in our thinking in at least four matters important to such development.

1. We continually confuse the study of a discipline, or perhaps I should say the study of human phenomena after the manner of a discipline, with teaching a discipline in the strict expository mode

---

[1] Gunnar Myrdal, *An American Dilemma*, 2 vols. (New York: Harper and Brothers, 1944), 2: 1041–57.

in school. They are very different processes with different outcomes. The first may contribute to the development of critical ability that democratic citizens need; the second contributes more to the development of the unquestioning minds upon which autocracy thrives. Even some of the best friends of disciplined study violate this distinction. For instance, the history professor who, as a scholar, studies his field with great objectivity, holding to any conclusions he may reach as a result of his study with great tentativeness, treating even accepted conclusions as if they were hypotheses rather than facts, forever arguing his position with other professors and frequently accepting the fundamental changes in what he claims to be true, once he has laid aside his scholarly eyeshades and comes before his class in History 101 as Herr Professor, lectures as if he knows all the answers, not once recognizing the assumptions and caveats that underlie all of his conclusions and infrequently, if ever, suggesting that there might be other scholarly acceptable versions or interpretations of the events he purports to describe and interpret. Sitting in his class, no doubt, there are future high school history teachers who will go out to their high school classes and teach history as it was taught them without warning their students that there may be errors in what they are being taught. Gross errors of historical interpretation have persisted in textbooks for years, and teachers go on teaching them as true. But more important, students have not learned how to use historical study. Thus teaching history becomes almost a negation of the scholarly study of history. But the important thing to note, for citizens of a democracy, is that whereas disciplined study may hold out the possibility of teaching students to be critical, and it may teach them how to be critical, the straight exposition of history may teach them just the opposite, to accept as true whatever they are told by authorities. It may render them incapable of criticism.

Lest you think I am being too hard on historians and history teachers, I will say that it is my opinion that economists and economics teachers may be the worst offenders in this matter. A field riven by disagreement among scholars is frequently reduced to one version as it is taught in Economics 101 and in high school economics, the gospel according to Adam Smith, who would probably turn in his grave at the oversimplification and distortion that have been imposed on his ideas to fit not scientific but political ends. If the study of disciplines is to contribute anything to citizenship education in a democracy, it must be taught honestly, warts and all, not as a vehicle for imposing a particular political bias on students. Even better, disciplines should be used in thinking about and, perhaps, solving social problems.

All of this is not to say that there is no usefulness in exposition. Quite the contrary; exposition is absolutely necessary in the transmission of information. Its usefulness depends, however, on how information is used. If merely "received into the mind," memorized, as "inert ideas" as Alfred North Whitehead suggests, "without being utilized, or tested or thrown into fresh combinations," it is "not only useless" but "above all things harmful."[2] To be useful, information transmitted by exposition must be immediately used in thinking about or solving some important question or problem. Confusion in our thinking between this intellectually demanding process and the slavish use of exposition to transmit information merely to be held in memory is the root of the problem.

2. A second mistaken idea that persists in our thinking is that the social sciences and history, taken together or separately, are sufficient content for citizenship education. There are so many things wrong with this idea that I cannot possibly explore them all within the limits of this paper. The insufficiency and, in some respects, inappropriate nature of a citizenship education program based solely on the study of the social sciences and history, even if these are studied as disciplines should be studied, was brilliantly laid out years ago by Fred M. Newman, who argued persuasively that the very questions that social scientists study are different both in kind and in scope from the questions with which citizens must learn to cope.[3] Importantly, the questions with which citizens must deal always ultimately

---

[2] Alfred North Whitehead, *The Aims of Education* (New York: The Macmillan Company, 1929), 1.
[3] Fred M. Newman, "Questioning the Place of Social Science Disciplines in Education," *Social Education* 31 (November 1967): 593–596.

involve questions of moral judgment toward which the study of the social sciences has little to contribute. In fact, the models for making moral judgments are more likely to be found in literature, art, music, religion, journalism, and philosophy than in the social sciences and history. Of course some historians behave more as moral philosophers than as scientific historians, a fact frequently overlooked in the expository teaching of history.

As Henry Steele Commager pointed out, it is much more important to judge history than to remember it.[4] For instance, it is probably more important for young citizens in a democracy to learn how to cope with such questions as "Were John Brown and his followers of Harper's Ferry fame right or wrong in what they did there?" and "Were the events that surrounded the Hay Market Square affair matters of which we should be proud or ashamed?" than it is to know only what took place during these famous episodes in history. These are the kinds of questions that are of central importance to the democratic citizen, but they are questions into which an exclusive study of the social sciences and history does not take us.

3. Increased recognition that the development of problem-solving ability is critical to the development of citizenship in a democracy has been dissipated by confusion over the nature of a social problem and lack of clarity about how a social problem is studied and resolved. Questions that may be answered, if superficially, by reference to authority such as a textbook or the teacher's word are confused with problems. *Inquiry,* a word much in vogue of late, is frequently reduced to the process of looking superficially for the answers to such questions. The study of social problems has been confused with studying about social problems, including ready-made solutions. Even the famous Committee of 1916, with its concern for the study of social problems, made this error. Questions become problems only if there is genuine doubt about the answer. Inquiry may occur only if there is genuine uncertainty between alternate solutions or if no immediate solution is in sight. Social problems exist when there are real perplexities about what to believe or how to behave or what course of action to follow. Social problems invariably involve judgments of the facts of the case to resolve conflicting values. To work out at least tentative accommodations to such problems, citizens of a democracy need all the skill they can muster. The complex nature of social problems and how one teaches students to deal with them is most ably treated in *Teaching High School Social Studies,* by Maurice P. Hunt and Lawrence E. Metcalf.[5]

4. There is confusion about how problem-solving ability is learned. The idea persists that children cannot engage in problem solving until they have learned and hold in memory all or most of the facts involved. This is an extremely doubtful proposition that flies directly in the face of how scholars—and for that matter any thinking adult—go about problem solving. Hunches are made on the basis of a relatively small amount of loosely organized information, and these hunches serve as guides for gathering other information that either supports or disproves the hunch. At a later stage, hunches may become more definitive hypotheses to be tested. There is little reason to believe that children do not think very much as adults, and there is good reason to believe that they can become quite good at it, certainly by the middle school years. A second idea persists that problem solving is learned by reading and talking about how it is done, that is, by formal instruction in problem solving. Although such instruction may have usefulness, Jerome Bruner, famous student of problem solving, was probably right when he said,

> It is only through the exercise of problem solving . . . that one learns the working heuristics of discovery; the more one has to practice, the more likely one is to generalize what one has learned into a style of problem solving . . . that serves for any kind of task encountered. . . . I have never seen anybody improve in the art . . . of inquiring by any means other than engaging in it.[6]

Now let us turn more directly to the nature of the social studies today vis à vis these misconceptions. The social studies originated out of the concern of a

---

[4] H. S. Commager, "Should the Historian Make Moral Judgements?" in *A Sense of History,* ed. American Heritage Staff (Boston: Houghton Mifflin Company, 1985), 471.

[5] Maurice P. Hunt and Lawrence Metcalf, *Teaching High School Social Studies* (New York: Harper and Brothers Publishers, 1955).

[6] Jerome S. Bruner, *On Knowing* (New York: Atheneum, 1965), 94.

very few scholars, teachers, and citizens that the teaching of formal disciplines, primarily history and geography, as practiced in schools up to the early 1900s provided an inadequate, even if an appropriate, preparation for democratic citizenship. With the publication in 1916 of *Report of the Committee on Social Studies,* which seemed to declare the independence of citizen education from college entrance requirements and from the study of formal disciplines, two quite different lines of reform, both calling themselves social studies, were set in motion. One conceived of the nature of citizenship education as being primarily that of transmitting the appropriate knowledge and good habits to children. This was really not much of a break from the past, for teaching subjects more or less based on disciplines continued to be the mode of citizenship education. Education continued to be conceived as being a hierarchical process, the all-knowing elders, scholars, textbook writers, teachers, and parents imparting their superior knowledge to youth who were supposed to learn from this process everything they needed to know to be successful adults and good citizens. There was little room under the concept for learning to deal with either the unprecedented change or the equally impressive problems with which adults in this same time period were trying to cope. It was a design for static education for a dynamic period, a design for maintaining the status quo.

Curriculum reform in this light was a matter of getting the information thought to be of the most use into the curriculum by reorganizing the rubrics into which information was to be included, adding new subjects, modifying old subjects, changing the order in which subjects are to be taught, updating content, cramming as much information into the curriculum as possible, and inventing new gimmicks for enticing children to learn that which they had no immediate felt need for learning.

In this vein, we have tried to organize the teaching of the disciplines in all kinds of orders, sequences, and cycles; we have tried to organize teaching around concepts, generalizations, problems, and values; we have tried fusion, integration, orchestration, and correlation of social science disciplines; we have tried cases, projects, and contracts as organizing principles; we have prettied up our textbooks with maps, pictures, diagrams, graphs, charts, and a dozen other kinds of paraphernalia; we have thrown in audiovisuals and now computers. Even now the field is deeply engaged in the study of a new scope and sequence expected to resolve all the problems of educating citizens. To what end has all this, which is by all odds the prevailing approach to curriculum reform in our schools today, brought us? The dissatisfaction with the outcomes of citizenship education is about as great today as it was in the 1920s, if not actually greater. We are confronted, as before, with indifferent students, apathetic and nonparticipating citizens, and colossal ignorance of the issues that confront our nation.

Paradoxically, the NEA Commission on the Social Studies of 1916, from which this line of development emanated, claimed to have been influenced by John Dewey's teaching. But either they never understood Dewey, which is quite possible, or they were too heavily influenced by the scholars in the disciplines who continue to insist to this day that the study of disciplines is the sure road to good citizenship. In any case, what came out of the Report of the Commission was a subject matter curriculum, and this is largely what schools have followed ever since. Even social problems, which the commission proposed should be studied, were treated merely as topics with ready-made solutions as proposed by the scholars rather than the real problems that they were. In this same vein, as late as 1985, a committee of experts—set up under the auspices of the NCSS to explore what should be taught in schools about nuclear power—spent its time discussing what is safe to teach children about nuclear power rather than how children can be involved in studying the problem of nuclear power, certainly a problem for adults as well as children.

A second group of reformers better grounded in Deweyan thought took their cue for the content of the social studies from democracy itself, which requires citizens with independent minds rather than robots, and from young developing citizens as they struggle to understand and find their identities in a democratic society.

These reformers believed that the questions children ask together with the questions they can be encouraged to ask was the proper starting point for citizenship in a democracy. They strove to substitute student-posed questions for teacher-posed questions. They strove to substitute thinking about and through problems with which children could identify or be helped to identify for what they saw as senseless memorization of facts unrelated to anything that children could see or be helped to see as a problem. They saw skill at problem solving including the command of disciplines together with a questioning attitude as the attributes of citizenship education most consistent with democracy. They were disdainful of the lock-step, from-the-top-down, teacher-dominated, subject-loaded, memoriter curriculum that persisted in schools as better suited for producing citizen soldiers than independent minded democratic citizens.

Working along these lines a number of programs were developed in the 1940s, 1950s, and 1960s that focused on the study of problems and the development of problem-solving ability while eschewing the formal or memoriter study of disciplines. The best of these, taken together, held out the promise of developing a social studies that was logically related to the need of a democracy. Among the works produced in this vein, a book by Lawrence E. Metcalf and Maurice P. Hunt, *Teaching High School Social Studies,* was, in my opinion, by all odds the most imaginative and carefully crafted work in the field. As we all probably know, after a brief period of euphoria, in which the book was highly acclaimed by some and widely discussed in the field, for it was a book not easily dismissed, it fell into disuse and like most of the other works of its kind was never widely used in schools.

Why? Why has most or all of the work intended to transform citizenship education into an intellectually demanding and thoughtful process, as did Dr. Metcalf's work, been rejected by the profession of teachers? Why has most or all of the work crafted to develop independent thinkers of the kind democracy requires been largely rejected by the profession? Why have most or all of the programs based on teaching or learning principles consistent with the development of critical minded and open-minded citizens been rejected in favor of associationist principles even by university professors of education? Why have the only programs that have had any real validity as social studies even as defined by the Commission of 1916 been rejected in favor of the largely memoriter study of single-version textbooks based on disciplines?

There are a number of reasons for this intellectual aberration. Some of the reasons are fairly obvious and with a little good sense could be easily corrected; others, far more subtle and pernicious in nature, lie deep in our cultural biases and are not so easily dealt with.

It is fairly obvious that teachers are themselves the product of a system of education that even in the university places the emphasis on memory, with little opportunity to criticize, argue with, or think about either the truth or the meaning of what they are learning. Can teachers be blamed for teaching as their university professors teach? There is far too little opportunity in university classes—and the social sciences and history are frequently the worst offenders—to learn how to verify the facts being memorized, or how to deal with questions that have no clear-cut answers, or how to think through problems that cut across subject matter lines, or how to make the moral judgments that are involved in nearly every really important question. The preparation that teachers receive leaves them incompetent to deal with controversy and uncertainty. This is clearly a fault of university education, particularly of how scholarly disciplines are taught in universities.

Lower-school teachers hard-pressed at best to make it through the day where they must frequently teach five or six classes and meet 150 or more students, with only the models provided by their university professors to follow, and not really knowing how to deal with uncertainty or with open questions that do not have answers, and not knowing how to think through a problem where answers are seldom final, take the easy way out, a way with which we are all too familiar. By sticking to the straight exposition of the textbook, asking only trivial questions, avoiding controversial questions and discouraging students from asking them, discouraging students from expressing doubt or hypothesizing about anything, avoiding other possible versions of events and skirting moral issues within questions, the teacher can feel secure, in complete control of the situation, and can get safely through another school day and, incidentally, unwittingly serve the purpose of turning out passive, uncaring, uninvolved, conforming citizens, just the kind democracy can well do without. They can also avoid trouble from a meddling public.

A contributing factor here is the textbook industry, which thrives on the expository mode. Using the expository mode, textbook companies are able to produce millions of copies of a textbook, all exactly alike, and in the process, make a handsome profit. Textbook companies are challenged beyond their capabilities by an open-ended curriculum that raises unpredictable questions and is taught in the hypothetical mode, as our brief encounter in the 1970s with the "new social studies" demonstrated. Thus we have teachers who shun the uncertain waters of controversy and textbook companies that make millions out of producing uniform, single-version textbooks allied against the open, questioning curriculum.

There is, however, a deeper and largely unnoticed reason why teachers behave in this way. There is an ancient belief, long predating democracy and buried deep in the folkways, that education consists of the elders instructing the youth in the wisdom of the tribe. As Margaret Mead has dramatically demonstrated, this process filled very well the needs of youth in primitive societies where change was almost nonexistent.[7] But this conception of education has clearly outlived its validity. Today, change comes at a dazzling pace, and less and less distance separates adults from youth in experience and wisdom. Such an idea is clearly out of tune with democracy, to which change and progress are endemic. Still, it is an idea that persisted among many adults and many teachers. Many parents, even those who ought to know better, expect their children to be *taught* in school rather than in any true sense to be *educated*. Many teachers see transmission of knowledge as their primary task, and even those whose own lives are beset with problems would deny children the right to think about their problems. Such an attitude toward education as being an open and shut matter clearly runs counter to the idea of a democracy where people, including children, are more appropriately seen as working out their problems together.

But there is a far more pernicious reason why the teaching of independence of thought and problem solving are resisted in this country. It is the persistence of the belief that the ordinary people cannot be trusted to rule themselves, that some kind of upper or privileged class must always hold the reins of governance. Such reasoning will quickly be recognized as the kind by which kings and tyrants, sometimes with the ready acquiescence of the oppressed, have always justified their privileged position in society; but as James MacGregor Burns has pointed out in his books *The Deadlock of Democracy* and *The Deadlock of Democracy Revisited,* we in America have always tended to equivocate on this question, emphasizing at times Republicanism and at other times class rule. Thus in the heat of the movement for independence we were able to produce the Declaration of Independence, an immortal statement for democracy, and later, the Bill of Rights embodied in the first ten amendments of the Constitution, which clearly followed republican principles; but at the same time, the Founding Fathers, looking over their shoulders at Shay's Rebellion, crafted a framework of government in the Constitution that limited voting to people of property, protected slavery, and guaranteed the preeminence of property over human rights.

As Samuel Bowles and many others have pointed out, public education has not guaranteed an open society where any citizen can rise from the lowliest background to the highest position according to his or her ability, as was the promise of education in a democracy. The rich, while sending many of their own children to private schools, have supported public education, sometimes grudgingly, not because it held out the possibility of producing independence of mind, but because it taught such good habits to the newly arriving immigrants as punctuality, a work ethic, work skills, obedience to rules, and patriotism to the nation, all traits that were believed to ensure a dependable and obedient work force. Public education today seems to have more to do with maintaining the class structure than with opening up opportunity.[8]

---

[7] Margaret Mead, *Coming of Age in Samoa* (New York: W. Morrow and Company, 1928); *Growing Up in New Guinea* (New York: W. Morrow and Company, 1930); Joan Gordon, ed., *Margaret Mead: The Complete Bibliography, 1925–1975* (The Hague: Mouton, 1976).

[8] Samuel Bowles, "Getting Nowhere: Programmed Class Stagnation," *Society* 9 (June 1972): 42–45.

Throughout our history efforts to move the nation toward greater republicanism—though in some measure successful as with the abolition of slavery, adoption of the principle of progressive taxation and other progressive reforms of Theodore Roosevelt's day, the welfare state legislation of Franklin D. Roosevelt's time, the civil rights movement and extension of voting rights in the 1960s—have always been followed by a period of reaction in which gains previously made for republicanism are limited or even taken away.[9] We seem to be in just such a period right now. Basic democratic principles such as progressive taxation, separation of church and state, freedom of speech and the press, the right of privacy in the home, the right to assemble and express grievances, even the right to vote are under attack from powerful factions of the far right. Frequently allied with fundamentalist religious groups who seem to prosper on ignorance, they are ready to control the press, to dictate what the schools may and may not teach, and to deny to the schools the right to discuss controversial issues in any balanced fashion. At the same time they oppose any measures that would limit what the wealthy may spend to influence government policy. According to a distinguished student of democracy, John R. Schmidhauser, professor of political science at the University of California at Los Angeles, the representative function today is so weighted on the side of the powerful that it is detrimental to any evenhanded resolution of contemporary issues.[10]

For whatever reason, lust for wealth and power or lack of understanding, more of our citizens than we would like to think are really hostile to democracy. They do not want the schools to teach their children to think. And many teachers cave in to the pressures emanating from such citizens. These find the subject matter curriculum a safe haven from controversy. Dr. Metcalf's book was not only a great book, but, as befitting a democracy, it was a book full of risk for those who dared to use it.

It is for this assortment of reasons, great and small, that a social studies genuinely committed to the education of citizens for a democracy has never flourished in the land. As Professor Burns suggests, democracy in this country is still up for grabs.[11] It should be clear that a social studies more along the lines of Dr. Metcalf's work is crucial to its survival.

---

[9] J. M. Burns, "The Deadlock of Democracy Revisited," *The Center Magazine* 19 (July–August 1986): 2–49.

[10] J. R. Schmidhauser, quoted in Burns, "Deadlock," 11.
[11] Ibid., 19.

CHAPTER 2

THE SOCIAL SCIENCES

WHAT ARE THE SOCIAL SCIENCES?

As an individual, you are different from any other person in the world. Your fingerprints are not like any other person's and your voice is uniquely your own. But there are things about you and things you do that are the same or similar to other peoples the world over. Most everyone you know has feelings, ideas, and problems similar to your own. From the earliest time that people lived on the earth, they have provided clues about themselves and their activities. Most of these human activities have resulted from people living together in groups. People had to communicate with others so a language developed. People had to find ways to clothe and shelter themselves and to provide food. The physical environment required that people learn to protect themselves from heat, wind, or rain and to adapt themselves or the land when possible. As people satisfied their needs, they found ways to enjoy life through music, art, or games.

Living together in groups, people were confronted with problems. How could many people live together without fighting? Who would do the work? Who would be given the power to rule the people? Could one person take another person's life without being punished? Who would decide the punishment? These and many other problems resulted. The larger the number of people living together, the more problems seemed to occur.

In our modern world, we find this is also true. As people concentrate living in larger cities, the more problems they face. Many of these problems are difficult to understand and solve. The social sciences study the actions of humans engaged in the process of living in an attempt to explain why people behave the way they do. Each social science is identified as a discipline which is a body of knowledge about a subject, the individuals who investigate it, the methods of inquiry used by them, and the desired outcomes of the inquiry. Each of the social sciences (history, geography, political science, economics, sociology, anthropology) views humans from a different vantage point and uses similar methods of inquiry to acquire its knowledge. This knowledge about human actions forms the basis for the content of the social studies.

This content is structured around organizing concepts in each of the disciplines. What is a concept? Possibly one of the difficulties in explaining concept is inherent in this definition: "A concept is something conceived in the mind—a thought, an idea, or a notion" (Moore 1970, pp. 112–113). Parker (1988) states: "concepts—ideas about what something is . . . a concept is an idea that exists through its examples" (p. 71). In the first definition, the individual conjures up a way of thinking about "that something," while the next one indicates that the individual must be involved in thinking processes—becoming aware of examples of the concept. This process is known as conceptualization. It is an ongoing process that operates as the individual encounters new examples with the concept. Thus the "mental image of any given concept will vary according to the background or experience of whoever is conceptualizing" (Beyer 1971, p. 126).

Concepts are stated in a number of forms: concrete or abstract; broad or narrow; single words, or phrases. Some concepts are concrete, for example, "man," while others are abstract, for example, "government." Some are so broad that they are difficult to conceptualize and must be broken down in order to be understood, for example, "culture," while others are so narrow they are of limited use, for example, "homes." Single words such as "work" are concepts as well as are phrases like "division of labor."

Why are concepts so important? Concepts permit individuals to organize the information or data they encounter. They place the information in categories or groups and by so doing recognize the relationships within the data. They ask questions about the data and gain meaningful insights. In the formation of the individual's conceptual framework, openings remain available for new information to be placed as it is encountered.

How are concepts acquired? The individual must formulate a mental image of a concept. Through repeated encounters with the concept, the individual learns its attributes, what is and what is not an example of the concept. Therefore, experiences must be provided where there are opportunities to encounter the concept in different situations.

The content of the social sciences is built upon facts, concepts, and generalizations. Facts are pieces of information that have been gathered by the social scientists and proven to be true. For example, the historian, by searching through various primary documents, has verified that the first voyage of Columbus to the New World occurred in 1492. This then is a *fact*. Columbus sailed on that voyage in 1492 before maps of the world were known. Another fact would be that Columbus was seeking India. He was uncertain how he would be able to reach what he was seeking. He sailed into uncharted waters.

These facts, when interrelated, begin to build the idea of the *concept* of explorer. An explorer takes risks, seeks something new, and is willing to face the unknown. As other facts are acquired about the voyages of Columbus, other attributes of an explorer are recognized. When children encounter the concept of an explorer in a new situation, they can identify it. Also, in the new situation, they may acquire more facts about an explorer and add this to their concept.

Generalizations are made after encountering several instances of explorers. For example: After reading about the voyages of Columbus, Marco Polo, and the space explorers, the generalization might be: Explorers seek to find out about the unknown.

Different social scientists might secure facts using different methodologies. For example, a political scientist is attempting to learn about the voting patterns in the most recent election in a certain geographical area. Information is available indicating the percentage of eligible voters who voted. The fact then is: Fifty percent of the eligible voters voted in the recent election. If the political scientist wants to know more about the people who voted for a certain candidate, interviews of a random sample of voters will be necessary. Of the people interviewed, 90 percent of the poor of all races and ethnic groups voted for candidate A, while 75 percent of the more affluent voted for candidate B. These are facts. The political scientist may draw a generalization from this information. Poor people believe that candidate A will provide better support for them.

How do concepts and structure or conceptual framework relate to the social sciences? Much discussion centers around the structure or conceptual framework of the social science disciplines. The discussion involves an identification of the concepts of the disciplines and the role of these concepts in teaching. It also involves determination of what learning experiences allow students to acquire knowledge of a discipline's conceptual framework.

What concepts and methods of inquiry do each of the social sciences contribute to the social studies?

History

History has been identified as the awkward social science (Ward 1971). Often, it is stated as history and the social sciences. The narrative aspect of history is questioned as a scientific method of inquiry.

> The narrative, story-telling aspect of history is too easily treated as simply entertaining, or else didactic. But good history tells its stories about people and events in a spirit of inquiry so as to help each listener or reader do his own critical thinking about what really happened and why, and what is meant. Precise details, dates, and quotations from sources are only parts of a painstaking procedure for testing the truth by going through the story of precisely what happened. (Ward 1971, p. 28)

Mark is a historian who attempts to find the pieces of that story; he searches out information from two sources. A primary source such as a document, original letter, diary, log, or law is vital to him. Secondary sources such as accounts of events written in newspapers, and interpretations of the events by other authors, will give him additional insights. However, Mark may not use all the information he has collected. As he organizes it, tests it, and reconstructs the facts, he will extrapolate, using the biases within his frame of reference. Therefore, to understand fully a historian's record of the past, one must know his or her particular frame of reference. For example, does Mark view most events from an economic or a political point of view? If it is economic, then he would tend to look for pieces of information that would support that point of view. In the process, other important facts might be overlooked. Since history should record all aspects of events, whether social, cultural, geographic, economic, or political, history is often viewed as a foundation or component of all the social sciences. As a result, the major concept of history is *time,* while other concepts discussed in history are drawn from the other social sciences.

The contribution of history to social studies is its accumulation of knowledge of the past, which provides meaningful insight into what is happening in the present and what to expect in the future. It can be the explanation of the cause-and-effect relationship of events. Events do not occur in a vacuum—something must precipitate them and something else will be affected by them. Recognition that what is happening today is history and that it will be recorded is important.

One of the difficult tasks of the teacher is the selection of historical knowledge. Neither is it possible nor desirable for students to learn the accumulated facts of history in some topical or chronological order. Rather, it is suggested that those facts or events be selected which are relevant to key questions of today, creating a postholing effect (Ward 1971). *Postholing* is the study in depth of selected events in history. However, it is crucial that connections be built between the postholes so that an understanding of how the facts or events are related occurs. Students should investigate several accounts of an event so that they can use their own inquiry tools to determine how the pieces of information fit together.

Geography

Geography is concerned with the earth as the home for humankind. Geographers attempt to find out as much as they can about the earth. They are first interested in "place"—place in relation to a specific place like Chicago, Illinois—as well as in regard to classes such as mountain, desert, or farming areas. The second group is often referred to as a region, which is an area identified by the specific criteria of its class.

The concepts most frequently used in geography are location, position, situation, site, distribution, and arrangement. To *locate* or find a place on the earth's surface requires relating it to other known places. Its actual *position* is determined by the lines of latitude and longitude. *Site* refers to the location of a given place with its local interval features or resources; *situation* refers to that location as related to other places. *Distribution* means where people live over the earth, and *arrangement* refers to how things are placed where people live.

How do geographers go about their inquiry? Claudia is a geographer and one of the most frequent methods used by her is mapping. After selecting an area or topic to study, she will make a detailed map of it. She might study the desert areas of the world, comparing their characteristics and determining their similarities and differences. Other geographers might map a specific place to determine its characteristics and the relationship of those characteristics. What type of information does Claudia learn about a place? After determining its exact position by means of degrees of latitude and longitude, she refers to its central location or the relationship of it to other places in the world. "Central location signifies being accessible to the flows of people, goods, and ideas" (Brock 1965, p. 31).

Next, she may study the physical features of the area, climatic factors, density of population, natural resources, land use, agricultural products, industries, exports, and imports. In addition to the above information, she may collect facts about the culture such as birth/death rates, religious influences, and family traditions. Once the information is collected, she tries to determine how factors are related. For example, a question she might ask is: How can a limited land space support such a high density of population? Is the climate a factor? Does it permit more than one crop to be grown each year? What about the soil? Do the chemical industries in the area produce fertilizers to increase the productivity of the soil? Does the area have easy access to other areas in the country that will supply it with food? Do the people have the necessary skills to develop the area's natural resources? How has the family tradition influenced the development of small factory units or are they a result of the lack of raw materials? It is obvious from these questions that she is attempting to learn how the various factors of an area—physical and cultural—interact.

Therefore, the contribution of geography to social studies is the interaction of the relationships between people and places. How do people affect the places where they live and how do places affect how people live? Once again students are not expected to learn all the facts about these places, but rather how to obtain the information that is needed when studying a key question. The students will use all types of maps, globes, and data to learn about places.

Political Science

The attempt of people to bring order to their lives is the concern of political scientists. Marcus studies methods of organizing society in terms of authority at all levels—from family, religious, and social groups to the national level. He seeks to discover why people extend legitimacy of authority—

whether by custom, morality, or legality. He is concerned with the functions and levels of the political system that extend to all people in society. Political parties, lobbies, and individual powers that provide decision-making policies are of interest to him.

Concepts within political science that are necessary to its understanding include political system, political socialization, authority, legitimacy, power, political behavior, and public policy. The *political system* is that system of social control at the top of the hierarchy. *Political socialization* is the process by which individuals acquire their attitudes and knowledge about the political world. *Legitimacy* is the acceptance of the people that the political system has final authority over affairs of society. *Power* is the ability of individuals or groups to influence the behavior of others. *Authority* is the legitimate right of individuals to exercise power over others. *Political behavior* is the way in which individuals exercise their rights. *Public policy* is defined as decisions which carry out and enforce the wishes of the influential in the political system. These decisions include laws, treaties, executive rules and orders, local ordinances, and administrative decisions.

What forms of inquiry does Marcus use? In recent years, many have become intent upon building a science of political phenomena to express political behavior in terms that have predictive value. One application of the behaviorists' theory is evident in the study of voting behavior. The behaviorists attempt to discover who votes and why, and to generalize from these findings. They do not simply analyze the votes recorded, but rather interview voters several times during the political campaign and after it to determine their political attitudes and how they make political decisions.

Another form of inquiry is the case study, in which Marcus may examine a specific unit of the political system or a particular event. An example might be the passing of a law. The case study would be comprehensive, examining all aspects of the particular law beginning with its historical background. Questions Marcus might ask are: What happened to cause legislators to propose the law? Were they influenced by lobbyists? Were the voters responsible? How much opposition was there to the law? Who expressed the opposition? What is the impact of the law? When the study is complete it gives a realistic, descriptive picture of a certain aspect of the political system. From the study, new insights are gained about the political process. However, generalizations cannot be drawn from it since it represents the study of a single law.

Marcus is also interested in comparative studies. He is interested not only in comparing political systems around the world, but comparing institutions such as parties or legislatures within a political system. As an example, he would try to find out how countries vary in politically socializing the members of their society. In such a study, the attempt would be made to determine where children in the societies acquire their political knowledge and attitudes. He would interview individuals within those societies, make observations, and study documents, laws, and the media to determine what most influences the child's political attitudes: parents, peer group, school, government, or media.

The contribution of political science to social studies, then, is to provide basic information concerning processes, behavior, and institutions of political behavior, political relations among nations, and public policies and ideas about government such as democracy, justice, and equality. Children learn how political events impact on their lives as well as being socialized to participate within the political system.

Economics

An economist's major concern is the ability of people to adjust their unlimited wants to their limited resources. Riah, as an economist, is interested in people's use of these resources, both human and physical, in producing goods and services and distributing them among the people. She seeks to answer questions of what, how, when, and for whom to produce.

> Different societies produce different economic systems. A primary task of economics is to explain both the essential similarities and the nature of the differences in the economic life of different people, so that man may be better able to understand the conditions under which he lives and the alternatives that are open to him. (Martin & Miller 1965)

The economic system of the United States is organized on the basis of the market system of making and spending money. Producers pay for resources and the services of people to make the products. People use the money they make in providing services to buy the products they want. This is a simplistic view of a complicated process of decision making and goal establishing by a society. If the goals of a society (for example, full employment) are not reached, economists attempt to explain this failure and to suggest solutions for fulfillment. Much economic information involves facts and figures, which are measurable and objective. However, the search for answers to economic questions also involves factors such as judgments of conflicting interests and goals, which are subjective. Riah contributes knowledge of economic activity in terms of the individual as well as how the system works and the problems encountered.

The most basic concepts in economics are scarcity, specialization, interdependence, market, and public policy. *Scarcity* means that a choice must be made in the allocation of material resources—there is not enough of a particular resource, whether money, time, or gas, to put it to all the uses that people want, and they therefore must make choices. *Specialization* refers to making the choice of completing only one type of task. Sandy does only the cooking, while Ross does the cleaning, or the factory worker drills the holes in the steel plates while another installs the bolts. A *market* means there is need for goods or services that have been produced or provided. *Interdependence* demonstrates that the individual cannot produce all the things needed and is dependent on others for goods and services. *Public policy* is the decision-making process that determines what will or will not be produced.

Riah collects, compiles, and analyzes data about economic systems. She may do historical studies to determine how the economic system developed and is changing. Another type of study would be the investigation of economic institutions such as consumers, businesses, governments, or markets. She might ask the following questions: What and how much are consumers buying? Who is employed and why? What type of industries are flourishing? What type of economic programs will the government support?

Also, Riah studies the efficiency of the economic system to determine if economic development is as rapid as it should be under the current conditions. She attempts to forecast what the future economic activity will be: Will the market go up or down? Will certain industries expand more than others? She uses the facts of production, employment, tax cuts, and so on, to hypothesize what future economic conditions will occur.

The contribution of economics to social studies provides knowledge about how societies decide to use and allocate their resources, how economic systems develop and operate, and the problems encountered by individuals and the systems as they try to satisfy their wants. Children will recognize how limited resources will cause them to make decisions about how their resources will be used.

Sociology

The interactions of individuals with one another and their associations are of concern to sociologists. Rachel is interested in people's membership in groups such as the family, school, church, and government. She studies groups—their internal organization, their maintenance processes, and the relations between members. She attempts to determine the influence of these groups upon their members—to recognize the behavioral changes exhibited by the members.

Rachel contributes knowledge of social institutions (where people have organized in groups). She studies their members, behavior, objectives, norms, roles, values, authority, and location. She describes the social processes, from the simplest interaction to socialization, cooperation, competition, and conflict. She attempts to explain why members of a group behave as they do.

Sociologists are restricted in their inquiry to the information they can observe among and within groups and to that which people are willing to tell them. Many private aspects of human behavior are unavailable to them unless people reveal them through questionnaires, recordings, or interviews.

The major concepts in sociology include group, institution, role, norm, value, socialization, and society. A *group* is a number of people who are together to attain a goal or because they adhere to a set of organized meanings and values. An *institution*—like a church, school, or government—has a formalized set of interrelated roles established to reach certain goals. A *role* is the part an individual plays in an institution or group, for example, the minister in a church or the leader of a gang. *Socialization* is learning that role. A *norm* is the type of behavior expected of an individual in a role. *Value* is what is important to an individual or group. *Society* is a set of interdependent groups or institutions that are self-sufficient.

Rachel utilizes a scientific method of inquiry. After establishing the need for the answer to a problem, she determines if there are any historical data or results from other studies that will help her hypothesize the possible answer. Once she has developed her hypotheses, she will go about collecting data to prove or disprove them. For example, suppose there are problems in the neighborhood schools over what appears to be integration. However, Rachel may believe that problems occur because there is a mixture of socioeconomic groups rather than of racial groups. Her theory may have been developed as a result of research from other studies or some historical precedents that have been set. She will use tools such as questionnaires and interviews to determine how the people feel about integration. She will want to learn how the children, teachers, and administrators perceive the effects of integration. She may begin by sending out questionnaires, but will generally follow up with interviews of a sample of the people so that it will be easier to interpret their responses. She will also interview people in the communities—including parents, local government officials, and community leaders—to develop a more complete picture of the feelings within the neighborhoods. After the results have been compiled, she may seek to do the study again in another similar community so that she may generalize from the findings. In other words, sociologists try to predict how people will react if placed in a certain situation with a certain group of people. Sociology contributes to the social studies an understanding of how institutions develop and how people interact within them. Children learn about these institutions and how they affect their lives.

Anthropology

Anthropologists view people as they adapt to their environment. These adaptations become their culture—customs, laws, beliefs, physical characteristics, and language. This accounts for the many different cultures that have developed dependent upon those adaptations. Anthropology is a relatively young social science which was primarily concerned with non-Western cultures, particularly with small communities, which enabled anthropologists to study all aspects of a culture. However, more recently anthropologists have begun to study complex modern societies including community studies in Japan, Europe, Mexico, and inside the United States.

Some of the basic concepts in anthropology include culture, custom, ethics, race, traditions, law, and beliefs. *Culture* is the overarching concept in anthropology with the others subsumed under it. Culture is the learned behavior of a group of people. Another way of describing culture would be that which is added to the environment. *Custom* is the usual or accepted behavior or practice among a group of people. *Ethics* are the decisions within a group about what is right and wrong. *Race* identifies large groups of people having clearly distinguishable features that differentiate them from other groups of people. *Laws* are the formal sets of rules that a group agrees upon and establishes as a code of behavior. *Beliefs* are the accepted truths we hold without positive proof. *Tradition* is the handing down of beliefs and customs from generation to generation.

Some anthropologists search for the artifacts of early cultures, attempting to date their existence and trying to formulate an understanding of their structure and general characteristics. Their method of inquiry would be an archaeological dig for the remains of the early culture. The anthropologist analyzes and classifies the information collected.

Roger, as an anthropologist, uses another form of inquiry which is the field study. He would go to live with the group of people he is studying. He would observe the people, conduct interviews, and participate in the activities of the culture. This type of study is an ethnography, where Roger will acquire knowledge about the sources of words in the language, customs of marriage and religion, and behavior patterns of members of the culture. He will attempt to learn about all the aspects of the culture and how each piece fits together to form a holistic view. In this way, anthropologists are different from the other social scientists, who may study only one aspect of the culture, such as the laws or physical environment.

Suppose Roger is interested in doing an ethnography of a community. Here are some of the questions he might ask: What are the customs of the community? Who participates in the weddings and funerals? Who helps out when someone is sick? What is the role of the family? Are parents strict with their children? Do the young people remain in the community? Are there community activities such as picnics, parades, and races? Are there any superstitions or tales of strange events in the community? Roger would not necessarily ask people these questions, but as a result of living there over a period of time, he would observe the behaviors. Anthropology's contribution to social studies gives us an understanding of how cultures develop and why they may be different. It helps children understand how and why people may have a different culture from theirs.

Table 2.1 illustrates the major concepts and methods of inquiry of each of the social sciences. In addition, it identifies how each of the social sciences makes an important contribution to the social studies.

SOCIAL SCIENTISTS MEET TO DISCUSS POLLUTION PROBLEMS

Our group of social scientists is assembled to discuss an important problem that is facing our world, "How Can the Pollution of Our Environment Be Controlled?" Each of the social scientists will discuss the perspective that he or she brings to the problem.

Mark, as a historian, knows that disposing of people's waste products is not a new problem. He states, "As early as the Stone Age there is evidence of open sewers dug from house to house in the villages. The early problem was not

TABLE 2.1 Major Concepts, Methods of Inquiry, and Importance of Each of the Social Sciences

ANTHROPOLOGY

Major concepts
similarities and differences of physical and cultural characteristics of man
relationship of aspects of a culture to whole of a culture
culture, custom, ethics, race, traditions, law, beliefs

Method of inquiry
archeological excavations
field studies

Importance
describes the variety of human behavior and aids in the understanding of different cultures

SOCIOLOGY

Major concepts
group life-institutions; small, voluntary stratified groups
relationships among groups
individual's role in the group norm, value, socialization, society

Method of inquiry
observation
theorizing
testing theories through questionnaires and interviews

Importance
deals with social forces in our lives and the forces in the lives of others applicable to us

ECONOMICS

Major concepts
human wants are greater than available resources
scarcity, specialization, interdependence, market, public policy

Method of inquiry
definition of problems
analysis of causes
prediction of effects

Importance
deals in economic reality—an important part of everyday living

HISTORY

Major concepts
understanding of the events of the past and how they are related to the present and future time

Method of inquiry
collection of available information
testing of information

Importance
aids in understanding of the past, helps show mistakes, and possible ways to avoid them in the future

GEOGRAPHY

Major concepts
likeness and difference of earth's surface
relationship of physical environment to humans
origins and composition of a group of people as a result of its geography position, site, distribution, arrangement

Method of inquiry
regional method—one region is subdivided into climate, vegetation, land forms
mapping and direct observation

Importance
aids in understanding the relationship between man and his surroundings and in understanding physical features of the earth

POLITICAL SCIENCE

Major concepts
public processes of political systems
ideas and doctrines about government
political socialization
authority, legitimacy, power, political behavior, public policy

Method of inquiry
case study
historical development
comparative study

Importance
encourages active participation in the political process and clarifies cognitive images of governments

SOCIAL STUDIES

one of concern for polluting the air, water, or earth, but whether it was a nuisance to other people. 'Use your own property in such a manner as not to injure that of another' is a law repeated from Roman times. Before countries were heavily populated, this was not much of a problem. Homes and factories could be built such a distance away from other people that waste products would not be bothersome. However, with the coming of the Industrial Revolution, increased population, and people living more frequently in villages and cities, pollution became more of a nuisance.

"In England, a Towns Improvement Clause Act of 1847 required local authorities to discharge their crude sewage into rivers. However, with the additional industrial wastes being dumped into the rivers, it soon became obvious that some other method of sewage disposal was necessary. There were serious outbreaks of influenza and typhoid as well as an overpowering smell."

> The streets of this city are now in a condition of filth without parallel in the memory of this generation. We do not refer to the mud created by the week's rain. This is trivial and temporary. But the accumulation of garbage, ashes and all pollutions, the choked gutters, the reeking and deadly odors, in most of the back and side streets, is intolerable.

Mark reports that this article appeared in the *New York Times* on May 10, 1863. He continues, "With the increased population, it is obvious that we no longer can rely on the idea that any pollution will not affect other people. Population doubles, production triples, and waste products increase at the same rate. There isn't any location where pollution will go unnoticed, so that we are neighbors one and all." Therefore, Mark asserts, the solutions should be global ones.

One of the difficulties in controlling pollution is knowing what is harmful and the quantity that can be absorbed into the environment without disastrous results. Mark suggests, "Those substances not found in nature, unless they are inactive, will cause changes in the environment and should be avoided. Those substances found in nature should be maintained at levels that will not be expected to cause biological change." He goes on to claim, "All human activities that release waste matter by reason of man's extraordinary proliferation and productivity are likely to upset the balance of nature. Historically, our laws have set a precedent not to release wastes that will be harmful to our neighbors. Therefore, the solution suggested is not a national, but an international one, of no-release of dangerous pollution." Mark knows such laws will be hard to enforce.

Claudia, having studied the earth's surface, does not look at the problem in terms of specific pollution, but rather the overall effects of pollution on the earth. "How is man changing the environment by the enormous waste products he deposits in the air, water, and earth?" One of the long-range problems that concerns Claudia is the effect of pollution on climatic changes. Can continued pollution of the earth cause irreversible changes in the climate? Not all geographers agree.

Claudia states, "The manner in which a geographer measures climatic change is by the temperature of the atmosphere taken at the earth's surface over the whole earth. The temperatures are averaged over a year's time. Between 1880 and 1940, the average temperature increased by 0.4° C. During the last 25 years, it has decreased by 0.2° (McDonald 1970). How does this affect humanity? When the temperatures were increasing, the ice boundaries moved northward and the south-central regions of Eurasia and North America became drier. With the decrease in temperatures there has been a southward movement of ice boundaries and increased rain in these previously dry regions. The North Atlantic has an increased ice cover, which prevents Icelandic fishermen from completing their usual fishing season, but increases the rains in India, which improves the wheat harvest." What Claudia still cannot answer is whether these climatic changes were a result of humanity's technological advancement and pollution of the environment, or natural phenomena. She further comments, "There are several ways human pollution could be changing the earth's atmosphere: burning of coal (fossil fuels), which increases the carbon dioxide in the atmosphere (which some geographers believe has caused a great hole to form in the ozone layer that will lead to global warming [Bookchin 1989]); urban pollution from industry, automobiles, and home heating units, which decreases the ability of sun to travel through the atmosphere (transparency); and an increase in the amount of dust in the atmosphere from improper agricultural practices. The most concern is focused on the increasing particle pollution of the atmosphere. The small particles of dust and smoke decrease the amount of solar radiation to reach the earth. Also, these particles aid the formation of fog and low cloud cover, which in turn reflects some of the sun's energy back into space. Airborne dirt, dust, and soot dropped by 63 percent between 1970 and 1988 due to stiffer emissions control and cleaner fuels ("Living with Our Legacy" 1990). This action may prevent the continual cooling of the earth's atmosphere which could produce another ice age. Remember, this is something we as geographers think might happen, but of which we are not certain. However, since it is a possibility, we suggest there are certain precautions that can be taken. Worldwide recognition, in each of the countries and the United Nations, should be given to the long-term significance of human-made alterations in the climate. Meetings on the environment such as the one in Brazil in 1991 should be held. Worldwide programs to monitor the atmosphere to check for carbon dioxide, particle, and water content should continue. The satellite programs should be developed to monitor the cloud cover and heat balance of the atmosphere on a global basis." Claudia recognizes the immediate concern of people over pollution, but believes there should be greater concern over the long-range effects that may be permanent.

Marcus, as a political scientist, would approach the pollution problem with legislation. He would suggest that laws be passed to control the pollution problem. Laws would be written so that companies or individuals who are polluters would pay a fine if they broke the law. For example, the federal government passed the Air Quality Act of 1967, which set standards for the amount of air pollution permitted. The Clean Air Act was revised in 1989 to reduce high ozone levels, cancer-causing pollutants, and other toxic substances (Bookchin 1989). Obviously, all air pollution cannot be stopped immediately, nor will it ever be possible to stop it completely. The law gives the polluters a time limit when they must reach a certain level of pollution control without being fined. The Department of Health and Human Services is the government agency that must see that the laws are enforced. The enforcement of these laws is accomplished with the aid of state and local governments. Some states may pass laws that are more strict than the ones passed by the federal government.

Marcus cautions, "Since the people of the United States elect their representatives to make the laws—whether at local, state, or federal levels—the political scientists feel that the lawmakers will be forced to pass laws which will control pollution or the people won't reelect them. However, there are some political scientists who say that because lawmakers represent a group of people from a certain area, they are forced to make decisions about pollution that might be best for their area, but not good for overall pollution control or for the nation. Let's say a certain state has a large airline industry that wants to make planes that fly faster than the speed of sound. The airline industry is important to people of the state since it supplies them with jobs. Ecologists claim that too many planes breaking the sound barrier will not be good for the environment. When a law comes before Congress on whether the industry should be given financial support to continue building the planes, how will the representatives from that state vote? Will they vote to finance the planes because they believe they won't hurt the environment? Or will they vote to finance them because they know people back in their state need the jobs the airline industry can provide? In other words, are they more concerned about the environment or being reelected by the people back home?"

He continues, "Another example would be when industries in one state are polluting waters that affect other states' water supply or recreation areas. Should the state lawmakers pass laws that will protect its industries or pass stricter laws which may be expensive for the state's industries but will protect the other states' water supply and recreation areas? These decisions are difficult for the representatives to make, not only on the basis of whether they will be reelected, but also because it is impossible for individual lawmakers to know what will be the total effect of an environmental law.

"Some political scientists believe that all available information about a pollution or environmental decision should be fed into a computer, and then the computer can indicate what would be the probable results everywhere, not just in one area of the action. Not only would the lawmakers or representatives have access to the information, but the people who elect them would also be able to go to centers where the information from computers would be available." Marcus feels it is important that the public be well informed about environmental factors if they are to make intelligent decisions in elections.

Riah agrees with the economists who claim that pollution can be reduced by producing fewer goods or a different variety of goods, by recycling more of what has been produced (the United States recycles 11 percent of its waste "Living with Our Legacy" 1990) or by changing the form of wastes or the manner of their disposal. Riah comments, "The American people have worked hard to improve their standard of living through the production of goods. It is unreasonable to believe that production can be cut without causing a high rate of unemployment. We try to keep the unemployment rate down, but the more people work, the more goods they produce. However, it would be possible to cut down on the number of hours per week that people work and also encourage people to retire earlier. Cutting production may be a doubtful solution to the pollution problem." Bookchin (1989) tells us that "growth is eating away at our biosphere at a pace unprecedented in human history" (p. 21).

Riah feels that changing the form of wastes or their disposal seems to be a more possible solution. Riah approaches the pollution problem in terms of the money to be spent for the control of wastes and the amount of value that would be received as a result of it. Will the costs exceed the benefits or benefits exceed the costs? How can Riah go about determining these amounts? As an example in air pollution, what damages result from it and how can we figure them? She tells us, "Different economists have different ways of figuring the damages. For many years the cost of damages from air pollution was based on cleaning costs that had been figured in the Pittsburgh area. Pittsburgh was one of the first cities to recognize the need for pollution control. The steel mills were polluting the air and causing extensive damage to plants and the paint on houses. Using this figure of $20 per person per year, the cost for the United States came to $11 billion (Rose 1970). What this did not include was the effect of air pollution on health. When costs for health are figured, hospital and doctor bills and the amount of wages lost by people who cannot work due to respiratory diseases are included. There is disagreement over health costs since there is some question as to whether air pollution is the only cause for the respiratory diseases. However, only 25 percent of respiratory diseases were blamed on air pollution."

She continues, "Another group of economists uses property values to estimate the damages of air pollution. Property value means the amount it would cost a person to buy or rent the property. They find that as the level of air pollution goes up, the value of property goes down."

Riah states however, "On the other side of the problem, how much would it cost to control the amount of air pollution to reasonable levels? The National Air Pollution Control Administration has worked out the cost of control and estimates that the cost of air pollution control would be less than the benefits that would result in just the property value increases.

"Now the question is, who should pay for the air pollution control—the industries that cause the pollution or the people who buy the products? The suggestion is made that measuring devices be placed on smokestacks, and industries would then pay a fee for the amount of pollution they discharged into the air, forcing them to control their pollution or pay heavy fines. This pollution control cost would then be passed on to the person who buys the products. Another example of this occurs when car manufacturers place pollution control equipment on cars, thereby increasing their cost to the buyer."

Riah reminds us, "Another serious pollution problem is that of solid wastes—garbage. Each person in the United States throws away eight pounds of garbage a day. What can be done with it? Once again, the economist looks at the problem in terms of costs of disposing of it and the benefits derived from it. There are certain areas where solid wastes can be used for landfill, which could then provide recreational areas. The economist determines whether the cost of hauling the garbage to the location will be less than the profits from the recreation area. The next approach is the solution of the pollution problem from a financial standpoint—can we afford to permit pollution to continue? Can we pay to have it stopped? Who will pay? Economists see a sharing of the costs—the polluters, such as industries, paying for the controls as well as the consumers paying when they buy the products."

Rachel, as a sociologist, suggests, "Primarily, sociologists would be concerned about how the institutions of our culture have caused or effected the pollution of the environment. For example, are there certain religious teachings that have influenced people's behavior toward the environment?"

She continues,

> Does economic motivation cause certain groups to display less concern for the environment? Some sociologists suggest that the desire for a better life increases the demand for goods and services. The result of this affluence is an exploitation of the resources to produce the goods plus additional waste from the consumption process. (Moncrief 1970, p. 510)

Rachel comments, "The social institutions have not been able to make adjustments to this stress." Rachel as a sociologist and Roger as an anthropologist share many of the same ideas.

Roger poses the question: "How do you persuade people to change their ways of living which have led to the present plight of the environment?" Both anthropologists and sociologists would view the pollution problem as indicated by the above question. Why would they view it as a need to change living patterns? They study cultural patterns and the way groups behave in society, and would try to discover what elements in the cultures have created the current pollution problems. "We are convinced that the pollution problem is a cultural problem and not a natural one. For example, as we look at the settlement of America, we find that the country was so rich with natural resources that the people quickly grew to believe that these resources could never be depleted. Actually, some of the resources we now prize were looked upon as nuisances. When the farmer wanted land, he cleared it of valuable trees and sod. Water was often a resource to be feared and controlled. Wildlife was a source of food, but often became a nuisance by destroying crops. As the people moved westward, these resources proved to be a challenge to their survival and once again they were looked upon as inexhaustible."

Roger continues, "Other events occurred at this time which affected the political, social, and economic development of this country, and eventually the pollution problem. The French Revolution began the widespread form of democratic government. This provided for the redistribution of the means of production and resources among the people. Right from the beginning in America, the ownership of the land and the natural resources belonged to the people, and the decisions on the use and abuse of the natural resources are still being made today by millions of people.

"Another event was the Industrial Revolution, which increased considerably the amount each worker could produce. With the development of factories, there began a concentration of population from the farmlands into the industrial cities. There was an increase in the wealth of a large portion of the population. This increase in wealth brought about a greater demand for goods and services. And as can be expected, increased production also increased the amount of waste products. Unfortunately, the concentration of people in the cities made the disposal of these wastes much more difficult.

"Rachel and I feel that these three aspects of our culture have brought about the environmental crisis: The first is the feeling that our natural resources are here to be used and we cannot harm the environment to the extent that it can't be remedied; the second is the fact that decisions about pollution and natural resources are to be made by the people in terms of what they own, and also by voting for the regulations that will stop pollution. There is a wide range of concern about the environment. If the regulation appears to cost too much, such as a tax raise for the improvement of a local sanitation plant, many voters will not support the action. Some of the laws that have been passed by the national government to protect natural resources have not been strictly enforced."

Rachel states, "The third factor is the importance that is placed upon the value of technology. Many people believe that with our advanced technology we can accomplish anything, even save our environment. It is believed if we are capable of building a space station, then we should be able to use that same technology to solve our pollution problems. Also, that same technology has given us a higher standard of living and the desire for a better life, a common goal of all societies."

Roger summarizes, "As anthropologists and sociologists we see as solutions to these problems created by our cultural patterns, an understanding by the majority of Americans (or any democratic industrial nation) that natural resources, air and water included, are exhaustible and pollution must be controlled. The reliance on technology to find the answer to the problem must be revised. Certain technology damages the environment more than what it produces is worth. Since decisions about pollution are to be made by the people, then they must be informed of the effects of their affluent way of life and of the necessary steps that must be taken to correct it."

Judging from the discussion of the social scientists, each views the pollution problem from a somewhat different perspective. However, also noted is the fact that each perspective, thus each social science discipline, makes a contribution to the total understanding of the problem and the possible solution.

Throughout the preceding discussion of the contributions of the social sciences, the tremendous overlapping of the subject areas is obvious. As a result of this overlapping, combinations of the sciences appear, such as social psychology, cultural geography, political sociology, cultural history, and economic geography.

Table 2.2 presents the concepts, information, and generalizations from each of the social sciences as it relates to the problem of pollution.

TABLE 2.2 The Concepts, Information (Facts), and Generalizations from Each Social Science as Related to the Topic "Environmental Pollution"

ANTHROPOLOGY

Concepts
cultural patterns

Information
Cultural patterns that have caused our problem
Natural resources are here to be used and the environment will not be harmed
Decisions about pollution and natural resources are made by people in terms of what they own
Technology can save the environment

Generalization
Cultural patterns will need to be changed to reduce pollution

SOCIOLOGY

Concepts
groups—institutions: social, economic, and religious

Information
Institutions—social, economic, and religious—may cause or affect the pollution of our environment
The desire for a better life increases the demand for more goods and services
Social institutions have not been able to adjust to the stress of these demands

Generalization
Institutions both cause and solve the problem of pollution

ECONOMICS

Concepts
production
consumption
unemployment
costs

Information
The high production of goods causes more pollution
The standard of living causes people to consume more goods
Decreasing production will cause unemployment
Costs of pollution control would be less than the benefits

Generalization
Producers and consumers will have to pay the costs of pollution control

COMMUNITY

HISTORY

Concepts
early laws
industrialization
urbanization

Information
Laws as early as Roman times warned of using your property in such a way as not to harm your neighbor
Industrialization and urbanization have caused more production and people living closer together that increases pollution and difficulty in not harming your neighbor

Generalization
Laws must protect the people from release of pollutants

GEOGRAPHY

Concepts
climate
environment

Information
Climate is the natural temperature, rainfall, winds and growing season of a region
The environment, including the air, water, and the earth, is being polluted by people that may cause man-made alterations in the climate

Generalization
People may pollute the earth to the extent that the environment will be altered

POLITICAL SCIENCE

Concepts
laws—local, state, nation
representatives
government

Information
Laws need to be passed to control pollution at all levels
Representatives need to vote for laws that protect all the people
Government must enforce the laws

Generalization
Laws must be made and enforced that will protect all the people

SUMMARY

Vital to the social studies are the concepts and information about human actions from the social sciences. Every topic studied draws content from one or many, if not all, of the social sciences. The methods of inquiry of the social sciences also lend themselves to the social studies as ways to explore solutions to problems or investigate events that occurred in the past. Without the social sciences, the social studies would exist only as a methodology of instruction.

SELECTED REFERENCES

Beyer, B. K. (1971). *Inquiry in the social studies.* Columbus, OH: Charles E. Merrill.
Bookchin, M. (1989, August). Death of a small planet. *The Progressive,* pp. 19–23.
Brock, J. O. M. (1965). *Geography: Its scope and spirit.* Columbus, OH: Charles E. Merrill.
Living with our legacy. (1990, April 23). *U.S. News and World Report,* pp. 60–65.
Martin, R. S., & Miller, R. G. (1965). *Economics and its significance.* Columbus, OH: Charles E. Merrill.
McDonald, G. J. F. (1970, January). Caring for our planet. *Current,* p. 21.
Moncrief, L. W. (1970, October). The cultural basis for our environmental crisis. *Science,* p. 510.
Moore, V. D. (1970, February). Guidelines for the new social studies. *Instructor, 79,* 112–113.
Parker, W. C. (1988, March/April). Thinking to learn concepts. *Social Studies, 79,* 70–73.
Rose, S. (1970). The economics of environment. *Fortune,* p. 183.
Ward, P. (1971). The awkward social science: History. In I. Morrissett & W. Stevens (Eds.), *Social science in the schools: A search for rationale.* New York: Holt, Rinehart, & Winston.

LEARNING ACTIVITY

Since you may not understand the contributions of all of the social sciences, organize six groups with your classmates, with each group to act as social scientists in one of the disciplines. Select a problem to pursue such as pollution of the environment (discussed in Chapter 2), or some other choice. Each group should research and discuss how their discipline would attempt to solve the problem including the major concepts involved, methods used, and their resulting conclusions. The group should determine the best way to present their ideas to the class. They might develop a skit, present a TV panel, produce transparencies containing information, and other choices. After the groups have completed their work, each should make its presentation.

When the group presentations are completed, record in your journal your summary statement of what each of the social sciences contributes to the social studies.

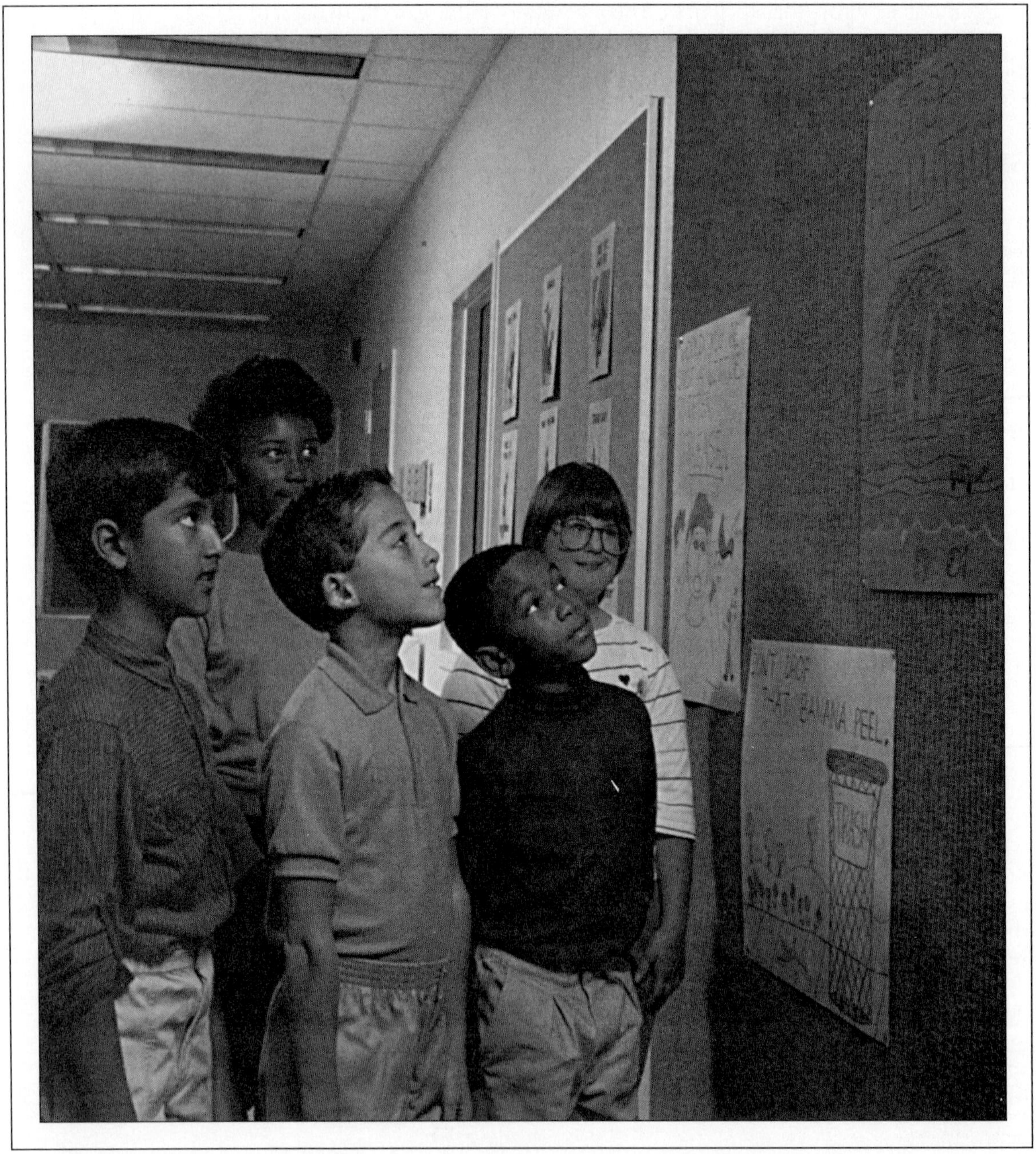
THAT BANANA PEEL.
TRASH

PART **II**

PROGRAM PLANNING AND CONTENT SELECTION

PART II begins the discussion for planning of the curriculum for social studies education. Ultimately, the teachers are the curriculum decision makers based on their conception of social studies, an assessment of the children in the classroom, local and state guidelines, and national agencies and projects. A brief history of the development of the social studies curriculum provides a perspective on why it appears as it does today.

More specific planning is demonstrated through the development of a unit. The components of a unit are discussed with examples from an integrated unit on Africa. The evaluation procedures that may be used are also illustrated.

The diversity of our nation and thus the diversity of our schools necessitates a discussion of multicultural education which essentially means consideration for the uniqueness of the individual, whether the uniqueness is a result of age, gender, race, religion, ethnic group, or disability.

Selecting the content that will be taught in the social studies is not an easy task. Numerous topics vie for attention. Current issues, global, law related, and economic education have been selected for emphasis since they remain essential to a dynamic, thought-provoking social studies curriculum.

CHAPTER 3

CURRICULUM DEVELOPMENT

How DO you as a teacher decide what and how social studies will be taught in your classroom? Much of what happens in social studies will be dependent upon your conception of social studies and how important a part of the curriculum you think it is. If you believe as Rita does that social studies should focus on knowledge of the past, then much of the content will be historical and the children will be required to remember the information. You may not feel that so much time is needed in the curriculum for social studies. However, if you believe that social studies should deal with issues that affect student lives as Hugo does, then the students will play a more active role in their learning, the social studies may be integrated with other subject areas, and you may view social studies as a vital part of the curriculum. It's important that you recognize what you believe about social studies and how you will present it in your classroom. Until this happens, social studies instruction may be nothing more than reading the textbook and answering the questions at the end of the chapter. Unless you are aware of how social studies impacts the lives of your students, you may not recognize the importance of your decisions. Once you have clarified your conception of social studies and determined the value that you place upon it, then you can begin to make some decisions about your social studies curriculum.

TEACHER DECISION MAKING

As indicated earlier and illustrated here in Figure 3.1, the first step is to verify your conception of social studies and consider your background experiences,

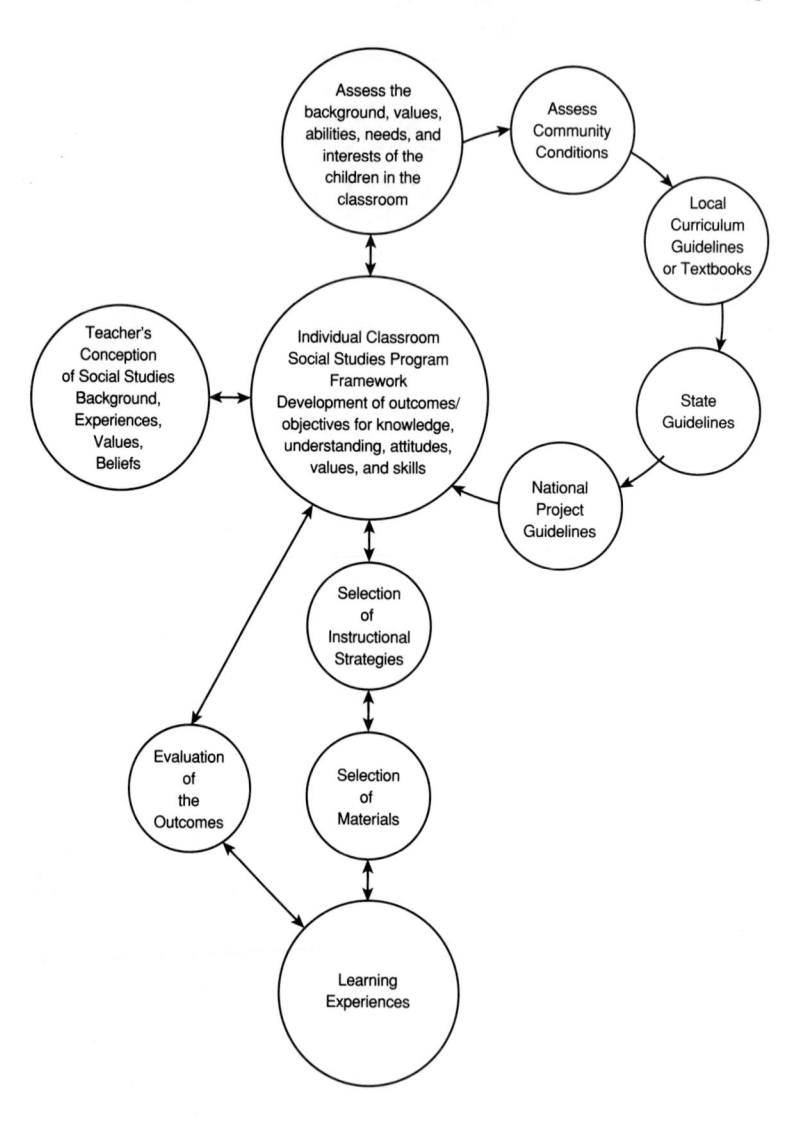

FIGURE 3.1 Decision-Making Process for Individual Classroom Social Studies Program

values, and beliefs. The next step is to consider the background, values, abilities, needs, and interests of the children in your classroom.

Assessment of the Children

Most teachers will find children in their classrooms who have characteristics similar to those described earlier. Children come to them with *different experiential backgrounds*

(Jessica has lived on the streets and in homeless shelters, Terrance has experienced a world of violence that many only hear about, Gwen has traveled quite extensively while Anthony has never been outside the neighborhood, Roya has lived in two different cultures and Carl has a narrow view of one, Ceci has been exposed to much cruelty while Gwen has experienced mostly love), *different value systems* (Carl's family believes in hard work while Robert's does too but must accept welfare; Roya, Jessica, and Ceci believe their families are most important, while Anthony looks to the neighborhood gang for support, and Terrance hopes for a better place to live for himself and his family), *different skills and abilities* (Robert has a difficult time learning his school subjects but Carl speeds through his without difficulty, Anthony is an expert with a basketball while Roya has trouble jumping rope), *and different interests* (Gwen wants to learn more about Mexico while Ceci would like to learn more about Africa), but many of them have the *same needs and aspirations:* to have a feeling of worth, to meet with success, to deal with failure, and to learn to live and work with others.

How do teachers accommodate these differences? How can teachers plan a social studies program that will be meaningful for all the children?

Home, community, and school environments play important roles in the ability and aspiration levels children achieve.

> Some students will have suffered from a lack of appropriate formal educational experiences, others from a lack of intellectual experiences in the family, and still others from a lack of educational experiences in the community. The adverse consequences of these three types of deficiencies may all manifest themselves in the same way on standard measures of academic achievement, but the realization that the sources of the deficiencies may rest with the school, the family, or the community—or all three—will sensitize us as we move to identify the size and location of the educationally disadvantaged population. (Pallas, Natriello, & McDill 1989, p. 16)

The aspiration level also is affected by the amount of motivation, interest, and support children receive from their environments, which include the home, the peer group, and the school. Obviously, social studies program planning should be influenced by these factors.

Children with apparent lower academic achievement and aspiration levels need enriching experiences to stimulate their interest in learning and increase their motivation to achieve. "Classroom studies document the fact that disadvantaged students receive less instruction in higher order skills than do their advantaged peers" (Means & Knapp 1991, p. 284). However, they need the opportunity to do problem solving in which there is more than one possible answer. Teacher expectations for them are important. Goals should not be outlined that would be unreasonable and frustrating to the children, but neither should the teacher possess the attitude that "they can't do anything."

The above average in academic achievement should be challenged by more in-depth studies of topics and extensive use of students' own initiative to complete work; the quality of their work should be expected to be higher; they should be provided with material that will interest and excite them at their ability level. Next teachers need to consider how the community may influence the social studies program.

Community Influences

Environmental factors influence the type of social studies program that is introduced into a classroom—a meaningful series of learning experiences for children in a rural area would not necessarily prove as fruitful for children in an urban community or in an affluent suburban district. The reason for this variation obviously lies in the everyday experiences of each group of children. Many of the situations confronting the children in the city, suburbs, and rural areas would differ greatly. The resources available within the communities may differ considerably. Some may have museums and libraries, while others are lacking.

The socioeconomic level of the children in each area also affects their experiential background. It should be realized that not all children from similar environments will have the same experiences. The children from an affluent suburban home may have traveled extensively, been exposed to an enriching vocabulary, and been surrounded by books, magazines, and newspapers. Urban children from a poverty area may have traveled no more than four blocks from home, or rural children may not have been outside their community, never have seen books until entering school, and received little direct communication from adults. Because they bring such different experiential backgrounds to the school situation, the children from these environments certainly should not be confronted with the same social studies experiences. Children with rich experiential backgrounds benefit from a program that builds upon their experiences and expands their horizons. They are able to handle more abstract material. In comparison, children with a paucity of experiences need a program that will provide the experiences lacking in their backgrounds. A major portion of such a program would include field trips, a wealth of visual materials (such as pictures, videos, films, filmstrips, books, and magazines), enriching cultural activities, and concrete experiences for vocabulary development. Obviously, programs for both areas would contain certain basic elements, although they would vary in their approach and content.

The ethnic and racial composition of the community is important. Implementing multicultural studies of the racial and ethnic groups within the community will enrich the program, but more importantly will instill a feeling of pride in the children for their heritage. Before introducing specific curriculum guidelines, a historical look at how social studies curricula have developed would be helpful.

Historical Perspective of the Social Studies Curriculum

Learning more about the development of social studies in the curriculum may be helpful to teachers as they make decisions about the purpose and content of their programs. A historical perspective on the process of social studies curriculum development should provide teachers with some basis for decisions. During the colonial period, the main purpose of education in America was to teach religion and morality. The ability to read the Bible was a most important skill. However, after the Revolution, there was a need to promote patriotism and a knowledge of the new nation. History and geography became important subjects. In 1784, Jedidah Morse published *Elements of Geography,* which gave the combined history and geography of each state and country it included. *An Introduction to the History of America,* a textbook by John McCulloch published in 1787, introduced American history as a separate subject. Thereafter, separate history and geography texts were published. Most of the learning was memorization of facts and dates.

Free public elementary schools were legislated in 1835. These elementary schools became important in the attempt to reunite the country after the Civil War. Civics, along with history and geography, became an important but separate subject area. A book written by McMurray, originally published in 1903, titled *Special Method in Geography* suggested a sequence of study whereby "general movement is from home and neighborhood outward first to the home state, then to the surrounding states, to the United States and to North America as a whole, later to Europe and the rest of the world" (McMurray, cited in Akenson 1987, p. 160). This conceptual framework later became known as the expanding environments curriculum or widening horizons.

The term *social studies* did not come into being until 1916 when the National Educational Association Committee report called for the inclusion of social science content in elementary and secondary schools.

> The report defined the social studies as those areas of content in which subject matter related directly to the organization and development of human society and to man as a member of social groups. The content of the social studies was to be drawn from the social sciences organized in terms of the maturity level of elementary school children, and presented for the purpose of developing intelligent, loyal American citizens. (Ragan & McAulay 1964, p. 15)

With the beginning of social studies, the idea of practicing good citizenship began also. Students were not expected to learn facts, but to consider them in making decisions. Instruction was to be organized "on the basis of concrete problems of vital importance to society and of immediate interest to pupils" (National Education Association 1916, p. 15).

With some modifications in recent years, the expanding environments or widening horizons theory of social studies curriculum structure for the elementary schools was first initiated in the state of Virginia in 1930. Paul Hanna, one of its designers, continued refinement of its structure over the years. This theory advocates that the child should first study the environment around him or her in terms of familiar, basic human activities. For example, in kindergarten or first grade the child studies the activities of the family and home. In second grade, the environment is expanded to the school and the local community. Successively, throughout the remainder of the elementary grades, the child is introduced to the community, state, nation, western hemisphere, and world. The theory contends that, initially, a child understands best the environment that is most familiar to him or her. The curriculum content centers around the human activities involved in production, communication, government, transportation, protection, creation, religion, recreation, education, and the expression of aesthetic impulses. Figure 3.2 illustrates this structure. Critics of this conceptual framework (Egan 1982) indicate that such a curriculum virtually obliterates history from the elementary school.

Many conditions in our society have been responsible for suggested alterations in the widening horizons theory. Frequently, educators view the advent of Sputnik as the impetus for radical changes in the educational programs. In the area of social studies, however, it would be unfortunate to fail to point out

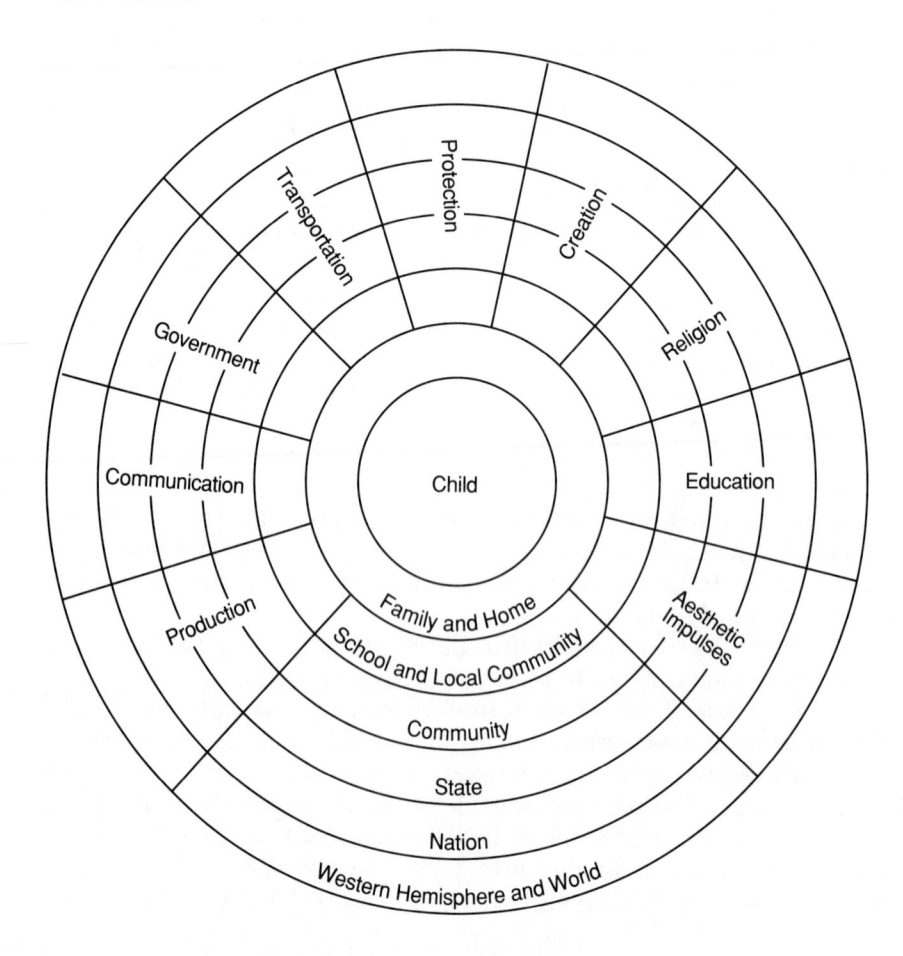

FIGURE 3.2 Widening Horizons Curriculum Design Organized Around the Content of Human Activities

conditions that initiated change prior to Sputnik. For example, the position of the United States as a world power following World War II placed greater strain on the social studies to prepare citizens to accept that tremendous responsibility. The United States could no longer isolate itself without concern for what was happening in the rest of the world. The problems in international relations between the communist and noncommunist countries during the cold war period necessitated a more thorough study of foreign ideologies. In addition, it was advocated that students needed a broader understanding of their American heritage in order to provide a basis for comparison. Equally important in the development of new educational programs was the emergence of underdeveloped nations seeking a place in the diplomatic world. Nations such as China, Egypt, and the African countries that in the past were rarely included in the social studies curriculum must now be a part of it.

Educators such as Jerrold R. Zacharias and Jerome Bruner influenced the social studies curriculum with their research and development programs, which stressed the structure of the discipline and a major change in the theory of instruction. Social studies, however, was one of the last areas to be affected by these programs.

Project Social Studies, which was initiated by the U.S. Office of Education in 1962 to encourage social scientists and educators to develop new programs, added pressure to social studies education. These new programs emphasized the inclusion and extension in elementary social studies of content from all of the social sciences. They also emphasized that the skills of the social scientists should be acquired by the students.

Federal monies that placed emphasis on educating the culturally disadvantaged resulted in the development of programs and materials for these students. A natural outcome of this emphasis on individual differences was the establishment of programs for students of exceptional ability.

More recently, pressures around the world and within our society have influenced the teaching of social studies. The realization that problems of population, food and energy resources, and pollution are global, necessitates that students acquire knowledge about them and also learn what actions they can take to effect solutions. In other words, they are citizens of the world, not just citizens of a town, state, or nation. The fall of the Communist regimes around the world has lessened the cold war against communism, but has heightened the need to better understand our democratic form of government.

The Civil Rights Movement, Women's Movement, and the recognition of the rights of the disabled (PL 94-142) and the aging necessitate that students receive a multicultural education. Multiculturalism recognizes the rights and contributions of the individual whatever the age, sex, race, religion, ethnic group, or disability. Students need to learn about cultural diversity and different value systems as well as how to resolve conflict when it arises.

The rapid urbanization of our nation has changed the living patterns of people. The close contact of people in an urbanized and suburbanized society requires the development of better human relations skills and an understanding of the problems created by the crowded cities and suburbs. Skills are needed that will help individuals to cope with problems such as economics — how to buy wisely and where to go if products are faulty; political efficacy—familiarizing oneself with the power structure and the rights of the individual related to the laws that govern; and career possibilities—discerning what jobs are available and how to prepare for them.

Technological advancements also have had their effect. Mechanization has virtually eliminated pride in craftsmanship and created a need for some replacement for that reward. Unemployment has increased, which has necessitated retraining to acquire skills needed in the job market.

Family relationships have changed. The composition of families may be nuclear, with mother, father, and children, or single parent, commune, and extended family. Male and female roles within the family have altered. Communication within the family has been assaulted by the media. Divorce is becoming more prevalent. Both parents are often working. These conditions suggest that family members may not have as much influence on one another as formerly. Do children still acquire their values from their families or do they need to pursue value issues in school?

These conditions have caused various groups to suggest changes in the social studies curriculum. Global education, career education, law related education, economic education, political socialization, environmental issues, and moral development are just some of the topics vying for a place in the curriculum.

How will teachers decide what is important? The next step in the teacher's decision-making process looks at local school guidelines or the adopted textbook.

LOCAL SCHOOL GUIDELINES AND TEXTBOOK

As teachers plan their social studies programs, they may be assisted by their school district guidelines. Some school districts develop extensive curriculum frameworks or guides that outline the rationale, goals, objectives, skills, and structure of the content to provide a framework for teachers to follow, but also to avoid extensive overlap of content. Also, this provides teachers with a blueprint for planning the social studies program for their classrooms. Local curriculum guidelines take into account the community conditions, the educational goals of the school district, and the material resources available to the teachers. Teachers need to adapt the guidelines to fit the needs and abilities of the children in their classroom. Sometimes, school districts do not develop their own guidelines, but use a textbook series as a guide.

A SAMPLE PROGRAM

A sample of a social studies curriculum that was developed by the teachers in a school after they considered the local conditions is shown in Figure 3.3.

A Sample Program • 59

FIGURE 3.3

Grade: Kindergarten		Topic: "Me"
Objectives	Content	Experiences

Knowledge:
The students will learn that:
• they are unique and special.
• they share many things in common with others.
• individuals grow from children to adults.
• things change as individuals grow older.
• things change as individuals have a space.
• things change over time.
 	
Skills:
The students will develop the ability to:
• observe characteristics of pictures and people.
• compare likenesses and differences.
• acquire a sense of time.
 	
Attitudes:
The students will:
• appreciate their own characteristics and abilities and the characteristics and abilities of others.
	I. Students:
	  a. have different physical features.
	  b. have a different sized family.
	  c. have different interests.
	  d. have their own special place in their family, school, and play group.
	
	II. Students:
	  a. are important.
	  b. have families.
	  c. have similar body parts.
	  d. have feelings.
	  e. have basic needs.
	  f. have changes in their lives.
	    1. growth.
	    2. family size.
	  g. have their own names.
		1. On the figure of a child draw all the things that are in common with everyone—hands, feet, hair, eyes, etc.
		2. Draw their family members.
		3. Cut out pictures or draw pictures of things they like to do.
		4. Trace around the child with a felt tip marker on a piece of butcher paper and have the child color it to show their own physical characteristics.
		5. Role-play the activities of different family members, guess which member it is.
		6. Examine thumbprints to see the unique aspect of each.
		7. Tell a story that makes you feel happy, angry, sad, or frightened. Contrast your feelings with others.
		8. Compare the individuals in the class.
		9. Interpret pictures showing children of different countries & ethnic backgrounds and compare differences and likenesses.

Grade 3		Topic: Communities
Objectives	Content	Experiences

Knowledge:
The students will:
• develop an understanding of the concept of community, local and global.
• understand what services a community provides.
• understand that cities and communities may be planned to
	I. Community
	  a. What is a community?
	    1. groups of people living together
	    2. services provided
	    3. protection
	    4. reasons for establishment.
	  b. Types of communities
	    1. industrial
		1. Organize the classroom into a community—decide what goods and services are needed to set up those services needed.
		2. Take a field trip to several types of communities, if possible. Perhaps a rural school and a suburban school could swap classes for a day.

continued

FIGURE 3.3 *continued*

Grade 3	Topic: Communities	
Objectives	Content	Experiences

Objectives	Content	Experiences

meet both cities' purpose and the people's basic needs and wants.
• identify factors that influence the start and growth of a city.
• understand that communities fade away as well as grow.
• understand that different types of communities develop and grow dependent upon natural resources.
• understand that the functions and uses of natural resources may change and develop as a community grows.
• identify groups of people who share common goals and interests to build communities.
• develop an understanding of the concept of group and the importance of groups in society.
• understand and generalize that traditions or customs are ways of doing things that are handed down from one generation to the next.
• identify and generalize that cultures can be made up of customs and ideas that come from different cultures.
• identify and generalize that some cities are populated by people, who themselves, or whose ancestors have come from many nations.
• understand and generalize that people often see their own way of life as being most reasonable and find it difficult to accept or understand new and different ways of life and may prevent change in a community.
• understand that people moving to new communities may need to change their living patterns to adapt to the new environment.
	2. agricultural
	3. trading
	4. recreational
	5. historical
	6. other.
	c. culture of communities
	  1. What is culture?
	  2. What are customs?
	d. groups that live in communities
	  1. How are groups formed?
	  2. How do members of groups help one another?
	  3. types of groups
	    a) racial
	    b) ethnic
	    c) migrant
	    d) refugee
	e. interdependence and interrelationship of communities—local, state, national, global
	  1. supply (goods and services)
	  2. demand (market)
	  3. how communities relate to and rely on one another
	  4. problems of communities
	f. careers
	  1. types of careers that communities provide depend on size and demand for goods and services
	g. effects and changes of technology on
	  1. agriculture
	  2. future communities
	  3. geographical features
	  4. local and global communities
	  5. natural resources
	  6. needs and wants of people
	  7. individuals, families, and cultural groups
	  8. jobs.
		3. Write to chamber of commerce for brochures about various community resources.
		4. Find stories about various types of groups found in communities.
		5. Compare and contrast different types of communities.
		6. Visit grocery store to determine where various products are made.
		7. Draw chart showing where people in children's community go for various goods and services.
		8. Make a model community from boxes. Show goods and services offered as well as residential areas.
		9. Have students identify problems of their community.
		10. Develop learning center on various careers available in communities.
		11. Invite resource people to discuss careers available in community. Types of training needed.
		12. Hold a Career Day where children dress in costume for their chosen career.
		13. Cut pictures from magazines and catalogs to make a collage about a chosen career.

continued

FIGURE 3.3 *continued*

Grade 3		Topic: Communities	
Objectives	Content		Experiences

- be aware of specific places within the local community.
- understand the concepts of supply and demand.
- understand how a community provides some goods and services (supply) while providing a market for other communities.
- understand and respect laws of the community and know who makes them.
- recognize that laws have been made to cope with changes in the environment caused by people in the environment.
- recognize that communities with dense populations require more laws to protect the people.
- recognize governmental agencies, both local and national, that have been formed to protect the environment.
- recognize that community laws are dependent on state and national laws.

The school had some specific concerns about its children and wanted to design a program that would attend to those concerns. Many of the children in the school came from lower socioeconomic homes and lacked experience, had few opportunities to work cooperatively in groups, and did not get along well with their classmates. As a result, there were frequent discipline problems. Materials that were used in their current program did not relate to the experiences of the children and there was a lack of interest. The value orientations of the children often were different from those of their teachers.

As the teachers worked to delineate the objectives for the program, it was obvious that the major focus had to be on developing good self-concepts, clarifying value positions, investigating one's feelings, acquiring the ability to work with individuals and groups, and acquiring the ability to recognize problems and solve them.

An example of the table of contents from a third grade textbook that focuses on the communities both close to the student and far away provides an outline that may guide the teacher's curriculum planning, if a local guide is not available (see Figure 3.4).

FIGURE 3.4

CONTENTS

USING YOUR TEXTBOOK	2
REVIEWING MAPS AND GLOBES	4
Using Globes	4
Using Maps	6
UNIT 1 Learning About Communities	12
CHAPTER 1 WHAT IS A COMMUNITY	14
CHAPTER 2 COMMUNITIES AND GEOGRAPHY	32
UNIT 2 Our First Communities	56
CHAPTER 3 THE INDIANS BUILD A COMMUNITY	58
CHAPTER 4 THE SPANISH BUILD A COMMUNITY	80
CHAPTER 5 THE PILGRIMS BUILD A COMMUNITY	96
UNIT 3 Types of Communities	116
CHAPTER 6 COMMUNITIES HAVE DIFFERENCES	118
CHAPTER 7 RURAL COMMUNITIES	130
CHAPTER 8 URBAN COMMUNITIES	150
CHAPTER 9 SUBURBAN COMMUNITIES	170
UNIT 4 Communities Have Histories	190
CHAPTER 10 A COMMUNITY GROWS	192
CHAPTER 11 A COMMUNITY CHANGES	210
UNIT 5 Communities Have Governments	232
CHAPTER 12 COMMUNITY GOVERNMENT	234
CHAPTER 13 OUR COUNTRY'S CAPITAL	250
SPECIAL SECTION	278
EXPLORING YOUR COMMUNITY	278

STATE REQUIREMENTS AND GUIDELINES

In addition to the local conditions and/or textbooks, teachers must be aware of state requirements and guidelines that will affect their social studies curriculum.

Responsibility for social studies curriculum development at the state level generally rests with the curriculum specialists of the state departments, often with assistance from public school personnel and university and college professors of social science and education. State departments establish broad guidelines for local districts, interpret state laws, and provide leadership for initiating change within the existing programs.

Previously, state departments issued curriculum bulletins that were followed religiously. Deviations from the established program were not encouraged, and few opportunities for creative teaching were possible. In addition, adjustments necessary to provide meaningful programs adapted to local needs were lacking. Now, however, a trend toward more flexibility in the use of these bulletins is apparent; generally, they are used as guides to instructional programs. The establishment of broad guidelines from the state departments gives the needed direction and continuity to the local programs, but permits the variations necessary for adaptation to local situations.

State requirements established by the legislature are interpreted to the local districts by the state departments, such as the requirement to study the history and geography of the state or the inclusion of consumer economics. Frequently, they are also responsible for establishing programs to implement state requirements. In states where textbooks are adopted on a statewide basis, it is the responsibility of the textbook committee of the state department to make these selections. Thus, the type of text materials to be utilized by the districts is often a state responsibility.

California Framework

California is an example of a state that has developed curriculum guidelines that radically depart from the expanding environments framework. *History— Social Science Framework for California Public Schools, Kindergarten through Grade Twelve* does not use the term social studies, but explains that it is centered in the chronological study of history. "History, placed in its geographic setting, established human activities in time and place" (California State Department 1987, p. 3). The elementary grade level topics are as follows: Kindergarten—Learning and Working Now and Long Ago; Grade 1—A Child's Place in Time and Space; Grade 2—People Who Make a Difference; Grade 3—Continuity and Change; Grade 4—California: A Changing State; Grade 5—United States History and Geography: Making a New Nation; Grade 6—World History and Geography: Ancient Civilizations.

The framework suggests a change in the way history is presented. It should be presented "as an exciting and dramatic series of events in the past that helped to shape the present" (California State Department 1987, p. 3). History should be enriched with all types of literature, including poetry, myths, biography, and fairy and historical tales.

Tennessee Framework

Tennessee is a state that has adopted a modified widening horizons framework in its state curriculum guide. The rationale for the program is stated thus:

The K–8 social studies curriculum should help students understand themselves and others in order to develop a healthy self-concept and appreciation of the contributions of others. Without that understanding, they are unable to relate effectively and develop the skills necessary to live in a democratic society.

The purpose of a curriculum framework is to outline and sequence the subject matter, facts, and principles that aid the student in developing the skills of problem solving and decision making as a citizen. The goals should help students develop an understanding of the environments in which they live, work, and play. To understand those environments, it is necessary to understand the concepts of the disciplines that explain basic human activities. The content is derived from history, geography, political science, economics, and the behavioral sciences.

The intellectual development of children requires that they learn about those experiences encountered in their immediate environment. Young children learn from those people in the home. When children enter school, their environment expands to include children from other cultures. Therefore, the structure of the curriculum organizes the environments in the order in which they are encountered. Children first learn about the home, family, and school. As their work expands, the curriculum introduces the neighborhood, community, state, nation, and world. Since children have exposure to many other cultures through personal experiences and the media, it is important that they also learn about other cultures before stereotypes are developed. Thus, the study of other cultures begins in the earliest grades (Tennessee Department of Education 1984, p. v).

NATIONAL AGENCIES AND PROJECTS

Another source for consideration by teachers in developing their social studies program is the national curriculum projects. These projects represent the areas of concern identified by scholars and educators, relating their beliefs about what should be included in the curriculum.

Project Social Studies

During the 1960s, the U.S. Office of Education funded Project Social Studies, which was intended to supply a major impetus for curriculum changes in social studies. Projects were initiated by social scientists and educators at major universities and colleges across the nation. *The Family of Man,* interdisciplinary units for grades K–12 using culture as the core concept, was developed at the University of Minnesota by Edith West. *Development of a Sequential Curriculum in Anthropology—Grades 1–7* was instituted at the University of Georgia by Wilfred Bailey and Marion Rice. *Intergroup Relations Curriculum* for grades K–6 was produced under the direction of John Gibson at the Lincoln Filene Center for Citizenship and Public Affairs, Tufts University.

One of the most extensive projects was *Man: A Course of Study* (MACOS) developed by Jerome Bruner and Peter Dow at the Educational Development Center in Cambridge, Massachusetts. It was designed as a fifth grade course with the focus on three questions: What is human about human beings? How did they get that way? How can they be made more so?

Man: A Course of Study defines the subject matter, content, and grade-level classifications normally used in describing curriculum materials and underscores the notion that "all things that are, are in all things." The core discipline of the course is anthropology; but, because man is the subject, the scope of the curriculum ranges freely between the biology of man's origins and the humanities of his own creation.

Some organizing concepts of the course are life cycle, adaptation, and natural selection, which are introduced through the study of the salmon. In the herring gull studies, the same concepts are repeated with the focus on adaptation, territoriality, parenthood, and aggression. The study of baboons includes all of the earlier concepts, but shows the unique social organization which allows the baboon to survive in its hostile environment. The highest-order concepts are introduced through a study of the Netsilik Eskimo. The examination of this microculture highlights the humanizing forces that have shaped man. The student must relate to this alien culture, and in the process of understanding the Eskimo, will understand the forces which have shaped his/her own culture and behavior patterns (*Social Education* 1972, p. 743).

Hahn (1985) reported: It appears that the "new social studies" projects of the 1960s never reached widespread use and received only slight use by 1983, especially in the elementary programs. The era of "the new social studies," at least as manifested by Project Social Studies materials, has passed (p. 221).

At the national level there are a number of agencies that are involved in curriculum development, many of which influence social studies education. For a number of years, the National Council for the Social Studies has devoted itself to the improvement of social studies education. *Social Education* and *Social Studies and the Young Learner,* the official journals of the organization, provide information representing the current thinking in social studies. Its yearbook and other publications pinpoint problem areas in social studies and supply needed guidance and material to aid in their solution.

The National Commission on Social Studies, a coalition of social studies educators and university scholars associated with history and the social sciences, presented a document in 1988 entitled *Charting a Course: Social Studies for the 21st Century* which was intended to present a vision of what social studies should become in the next century.

National Commission on Social Studies

Grades K–3

Social studies from kindergarten through grade 3 should set the tone and lay the foundation for the social studies education that follows. An important goal in these early years is to excite student interest in social studies and to capitalize on the eagerness of young children to learn. If these years of exposure to the social studies are wasted, important opportunities for acquiring social studies knowledge are lost. An effective K–3 social studies curriculum can help students gain a better understanding of themselves, as well as a view of the world within and beyond the walls of their classroom.

In these formative years it is imperative that the social studies curriculum avoid superficiality and be well defined and relevant to the needs and interests of young learners. Many social studies concepts are abstract; nevertheless, even very young students can begin to grasp these concepts if they are presented in active and engaging ways appropriate to their interests and cognitive development.

A balance should be maintained across local, national, and global information and concepts so that children can begin to recognize how details fit into a larger whole. K–3 social studies must incorporate an international perspective and provide multicultural experiences in an authentic and culturally sensitive manner. Early on, students should learn that each individual plays multiple and varied roles and that roles change as circumstances change. For example, students in the classroom should learn to make decisions as individuals and as members of a group (p. 7).

Grades 4–6

By grades 4–6, students are ready to explore human time and occupied space more systematically. A thoughtfully developed curriculum must tap students' interest in the world around them. Three social studies courses should be taught during these grades: (a) United States history, (b) world history, and (c) geography, both physical and cultural. These courses must draw much of their content from concepts of the social sciences, especially political science, economics and anthropology. The order in which these courses are taught is less important than that each course receives the equivalent of a full year's attention.

An introduction to United States history can provide students with an expanded understanding of our civic tradition and our political system. Stories about Native Americans, early European explorers and settlers, the nation's founders, later immigrants and pioneers, abolitionists, populists, suffragists, inventors, artists, business and labor leaders, and other political, economic and cultural figures will help students to understand the diversity and historical complexity of American society.

The basic documents of American government should be introduced to students at this point. In particular, students should study the Declaration of Independence, the Constitution and the Bill of Rights, and begin to learn how these documents have been interpreted and applied in practice. Individuals and groups who have struggled to actualize democratic principles and values should be a major focus. Attention must also be given to those Native American groups who have struggled to maintain alternative cultural, political, and economic systems. The history of the United States from colonial beginnings to the present should be brought into a more complete chronological and spatial focus in these years. However, the course should not be a comprehensive survey, but taught with selective emphases to be studied in depth (National Commission on Social Studies 1989, p. 10).

Bradley Commission on History in the Schools

Another group concerned with the amount of history that was being taught in the schools was the Educational Excellence Network that supported work by the Bradley Commission on History in Schools. Their report, entitled *Building a History Curriculum: Guidelines for Teaching History in Schools,* outlines the major themes and topics for the study of history.

The Commission

> declares once more that history should occupy a large and vital place in the education of the private person and the public citizen. Unlike many other peoples, Americans are not bound together by a common religion or a common ethnicity. Instead, our binding heritage is a democratic vision of liberty, equality, and justice. If Americans are to preserve that vision and bring it to daily practice, it is imperative that all citizens understand how it was shaped in the past, what events and forces either helped or obstructed it, and how it evolved down to the circumstances and political discourse of our time. (Bradley Commission 1988, pp. 1–2)

Recommendations of the Bradley Commission included making the kindergarten through sixth grade social studies curriculum history-centered and requiring at least four years of history in grades 7–12. Six vital themes were identified as follows: civilization, cultural diffusion, and innovation; human interaction with the environment; values, beliefs, political ideas, and institutions; conflict and cooperation; comparative history of major developments; patterns of social and political interaction (Bradley Commission 1988, pp. 10–11). The Commission points out: "Although the use of dates is inappropriate in the early grades, children can begin to develop a sense of time and place ("long, long ago, far away") as they are introduced to historical literature" (Bradley Commission 1988).

The Bradley Commission was much opposed to the "expanding horizons" conceptual framework for the elementary grades citing that it was "indifferent" to historical instruction and "children are bound by time and place to remain in the present and in their own personal environment" (p. 16).

Joint Committee on Geographic Education

History was not the only subject believed to be neglected in the schools, particularly in the elementary grades. There are often complaints that children no longer study geography. The Joint Committee on Geographic Education in 1984 identified five fundamental themes that should provide the basis for geographic instruction. Those themes are as follows: Location—Position on the Earth's Surface; Place—Physical and Human Characteristics; Relationships Within Places; Movement—Humans Interacting on the Earth; Regions—How They Form and Change. More detail will be given in Chapter 10.

National Council on Economic Education

The National Council on Economic Education, formerly the Joint Council, has a long history of commitment to improve economic education in the schools. Through its network of State Councils and Economic Education Centers at colleges and universities around the nation, materials and teacher inservice and preservice programs are provided. In 1964, the group initiated a project called the Development Economic Education Program (DEEP) that continues to the present time. The three major objectives of the project are "1) to build economic understandings into school curricula, 2) to improve teacher education in economics and 3) to develop and test new teaching materials at all grade levels" (n.p.).

In cooperation with the Agency for Instructional Television, three programs have been produced to introduce basic economic concepts within a context to which children can relate. *Econ and Me* is designed for younger children. Economic concepts of scarcity, opportunity cost, consumption, production, and interdependence are applied to individuals, families, and communities.

Trade Offs is intended to be used with intermediate and junior high students. There are fifteen 20-minute video programs that portray situations where children encounter economic problems that require understanding of economic concepts and reasoning processes to solve them. *Give and Take,* twelve 15-minute video programs for junior and senior high school, provides students with the opportunity to understand economic concepts and apply them to decisions they make in their personal lives.

Law Related Education (LRE)

Several national organizations have developed law related education/citizenship programs. The Center for Civic Education developed a conceptual K–12 program entitled *Law In a Free Society.* Another program, *We the People: The Citizen and the Constitution,* was initiated to celebrate the Bicentennials of the Constitution and Bill of Rights.

Street Law, a practical law course, has long been used in high schools. First initiated in Washington, D.C., schools with Georgetown University law students, it has grown to the National Institute for Citizenship Education in the Law which has continued to develop LRE materials.

Constitutional Rights Foundation, based in Los Angeles and Chicago, provides teaching materials and teacher training in LRE. The Special Committee on Youth Education for Citizenship appointed by the American Bar Association initiates programs for leaders in law related education and provides materials for teachers through *Update* and other publications. Phi Alpha Delta, a law honorary, provides support to schools for LRE through its national network of lawyers.

SUMMARY

Teachers are faced then with curriculum frameworks and materials from agencies at the local, state, and national levels that represent interpretations of what should compose social studies education. Local guides can provide specific objectives and a more detailed presentation of the program based on the needs and interests of the children and the community conditions. State guides are broad and general, indicating a framework that includes the state requirements. National programs exemplify the current thinking of educators and social scientists. They are designed to provide exacting information and guidance for teachers with the goal of affecting the development of their social studies programs.

Rita, Julie, Hugo, and Lewis will necessarily be required to view this information through their conception of social studies. How does each piece fit into their ideas of what social studies should be for the children in their classroom?

They must decide, then, how each of the guidelines will affect their individual classroom instructional programs, always considering the needs of the children. Figure 3.1 illustrated this decision-making process and the factors affecting it.

The result of this decision-making process should be the framework for a social studies program that is based on the special needs and abilities of the children in the classroom, but broadening the scope to recognize the importance of the community, local, state, and national guidelines.

Once the framework has been decided, then the instructional objectives should be developed for each of the following areas: knowledge/understanding, values, attitudes, and skills. These objectives will provide a basis for planning the learning experiences for the children. As indicated in Figure 3.1, teachers must select the instructional strategies and materials that will be employed in the learning experiences. Evaluation should be an ongoing process to determine the outcomes of those experiences.

The following chapters will discuss the different types of instructional strategies, materials, and evaluations that can be utilized within those learning experiences.

SELECTED REFERENCES

Akenson, J. E. (1987). Historical factors in the development of elementary social studies. *Theory and Research in Social Education, 15*(3), 155–169.

Bradley Commission on History in Schools. (1988). *Building a history curriculum: Guidelines for teaching history in schools.* Washington, DC: Educational Excellence Network.

California State Department. (1987). *History—Social science framework for California public schools kindergarten through twelfth grade.* Sacramento: Author.

Egan, K. (1982). Teaching history to young children. *Phi Delta Kappan, 64*(7), 439–441.

Hahn, C. (1985). The status of the social studies in the public schools of the United States: Another look. *Social Education, 49*(3) 220–223.

Means, B., & Knapp, M. S. (1991). Cognitive approaches to teaching advanced skills to educationally disadvantaged students. *Phi Delta Kappan, 73*(4), 282–289.

National Commission on Social Studies in the Schools. (1989). *Charting a course: Social studies for the 21st century.* Author.

National Education Association. (1916). *The social studies in secondary education* (Bulletin No. 28). Washington, DC: Bureau of Education.

Pallas, A. M., Natriello, G., & McDill, E. L. (1989, June–July). The changing nature of the disadvantaged population current dimensions and future trends. *The Educational Researcher,* pp. 16–22.

Pratt, R. B. (1972). Man: A course of study. *Social Education, 36*(7), 742–744.

Ragan, W. B., & McAulay, J. D. (1964). *Social studies for today's children.* New York: Appleton-Century-Crofts.

Tennessee Department of Education. (1984). *Social studies curriculum framework.* Nashville: Author.

LEARNING ACTIVITY

Secure several curriculum guides, including your own state, any local guides, and several different textbooks. Review them by asking yourself the following questions:

1. How is the guide or textbook organized?
2. What is the apparent conceptual framework of the guide or textbook?
3. How easily can the sequence of the guide or textbook be altered if necessary for classroom adaptation?

Locate any national projects that are available, such as *We the People* or *Econ and Me.* Review the materials to discover what is unique about them. What do they offer to teachers that can't be found in curriculum guides or textbooks?

After reviewing the guides, textbooks, and national projects, write in your journal discussing how you think these materials will aid you in the planning of the social studies curriculum for your classroom.

CHAPTER 4

PLANNING FOR INSTRUCTION

ORGANIZING FOR INSTRUCTION

The way in which you organize your classrooms for instruction will affect the way you plan your social studies. If for example, you have developed a whole language program, then social studies may become a vehicle for reading and writing experiences. A concern with this approach is that more emphasis may be placed upon the children's ability to read and comprehend the content of social studies whereby concepts are taught as vocabulary and not conceptually. Problem solving and the pursuit of crucial issues may not be a part of it. However, a whole language approach may be a most effective way to teach social studies when social science concepts are integrated into the reading and writing program.

Equally distressing is the practice of social studies becoming the "read aloud" of the textbook, silent reading, or outlining the content, and answering the questions at the end of the chapter. Numerous studies have pointed out how poorly children rank social studies among the subjects taught and how boring they think it is when these methods are used (Fouts 1989; Schug, Todd, & Berry 1984).

A core curriculum approach to instruction places the emphasis on the topic that is established as the "core." Generally a social studies topic, question, or problem becomes the focus or core. The question might be, "How can the environment be improved?" All other learning experiences are then integrated with that focus—whether science, math, reading, language arts, music, art, or physical education. Critics suggest that stretching the topic to include all the subjects may not make natural connections and children may tire of it.

Project learning is based on the assumption "that children will learn skills and knowledge best by applying them to solve the kinds of meaningful and complex problems found in the real world and by developing 'projects' or 'product' that they can share with others" (Olson 1993a, p. 6). Students use information from a number of subjects organized around a big idea or common principle. They also "plan and carry out a project that forces them to engage in meaningful learning experiences" (ibid.).

Developing Objectives

Too frequently objectives for instruction are stated in vague, meaningless terms. So stated, objectives are difficult to implement in the classroom and do not communicate to others what is to be accomplished by the learning experiences. Numerous educators contend, however, that objectives stated in behavioral terms do lend themselves to observation and measurement. Robert Mager (1962) defines an objective as "an intent communicated by a statement describing a proposed change in a learner—a statement of what the learner is to be like when he has successfully completed a learning experience. It is a description of a pattern of behavior (performance) we want the learner to be able to demonstrate" (p. 3).

Mager indicates that when a teacher is writing objectives, either in behavioral or performance terms, it is advisable to include the following information:

> First, identify the terminal behavior by name; we can specify the kind of behavior which will be accepted as evidence that the learner has achieved the objectives.
> Second, try to further define the desired behavior by describing the important conditions under which the behavior will be expected to occur.
> Third, specify the criteria of acceptable performance by describing how well the learner must perform to be considered acceptable. (Mager 1962, p. 12)

Each objective need not include all of this information. Initially, objectives are written in broad terms to indicate the type of subject matter to be covered. Secondarily, specific objectives are written in behavioral or performance terms to indicate the behavior expected of the individuals after they have been exposed to the subject matter. An example of a broad objective is:

> *The students will acquire knowledge of the history of Mexico to enable them to understand the customs and traditions of that country.*

This objective made more specific and stated in behavioral terms might be:

> *The students will compare and contrast three of the Christmas customs and traditions of Mexico with those of the United States; identify two of the traditions sacred to Mexican families; list at least one of the Mexican holidays that is different from those celebrated in the United States.*

On the other side of the argument are those educators who believe that behavioral objectives standardize instruction and aim at only measurable results, thus eliminating learning that is self-directed, unstructured, and unpredictable. These educators would recommend objectives that are "specified" rather than "behavioral"—specified by a teacher according to a philosophy and taking into consideration the talents and choices of the children (Gagné & Kneller 1972).

The important aspect of stating objectives is whether the teacher has communicated what is to be accomplished by the instruction. Not all of the results of social studies instruction (e.g., values, attitudes) can be measured, nor is it necessary to attempt this, but teachers will want to have some means of determining the success of their efforts.

Still others would have what children should know and be able to do stated in terms of outcomes. Benjamin Bloom used the term "learning outcomes" to describe the goals students are supposed to meet (Olson 1993b). Some suggest that those outcomes should be first delineated as "big" outcomes—those that describe what will be the results of a program or course of study. An example might be to develop students who are "1. self-directed learners, 2. collaborative workers, 3. complex thinkers, 4. quality producers, and 5. community contributors" (Redding 1992). Obviously, it will be necessary to delineate more specific outcomes for subject areas to demonstrate how the big outcomes will be achieved. Complex thinkers would need to develop as problem solvers, decision makers, and creative and critical thinkers. In a unit an outcome might be stated: "Students will demonstrate their problem-solving ability by identifying the problems faced by the Pilgrims when they landed at Plymouth." A lesson outcome would be stated: "Students will identify several solutions to the problem of limited food for the Pilgrims." Critics of outcome-based education suggest they are vague and fluffy and therefore can be satisfied by almost any level of achievement (Olson 1993b).

Objectives of the social studies are grouped into three areas: knowledge and understanding, values and attitudes, and skills. *Knowledge and understanding* are a part of the cognitive (knowing) domain; *values and attitudes* are a part of the cognitive, as well as the affective (e.g., prizing, feeling) domains; and *skills* are abilities or proficiencies.

Knowledge and Understanding

A student acquires information rather than knowledge. The information becomes the student's knowledge when it has been processed and integrated into previous knowledge. In the social studies, as in any subject, children should not be required to learn facts or information merely for their acquisition. The information they are to acquire should be selected on the basis of its capacity to further their understanding. One of the most important aspects of the social studies is the area of understanding. Obviously, facts are of little value unless they increase one's understanding of a subject or problem.

Understanding requires the individual to synthesize several pieces of information and relate them to one another to comprehend the connection between the previous knowledge and the newly acquired information. Understanding of a problem is essential before an individual can attempt to solve it. With understanding, various pieces of information can be fitted together for a possible solution. For example, it would be better to learn that Washington became president of the new nation because the people trusted the leadership he exhibited during the Revolution rather than merely to memorize the fact that he was our first president. Rather than learn the names of the states and their capitals to reel them off in rote fashion, it would be better for students to learn that state capitals are generally located near the centers of the states to better serve the peoples of those states.

Objectives developed in the area of information are selected to further an understanding. An example of such an objective would be:

> *The student will acquire information about the minority groups of the United States to better understand how much they contribute to our society.*

Measurement of an individual's achievement in the area of understanding becomes difficult unless the individual applies this synthesized knowledge to a new situation. Therefore, objectives under the heading of understanding must include this application.

An example of an objective for the area of understanding is:

> *The student will understand that the mobility of people is dependent upon a variety of individual goals, such as adventure and greater opportunity, and will identify the different goals of the groups that have been encountered.*

Attitudes and Values

Attitude is a continuing area of concern in the social studies, because it is believed that attitudes determine behavior. An *attitude* is defined as a relatively enduring organization of beliefs about an object or situation that causes an individual to respond in some manner. A belief

> within an attitude organization is conceived to have three components: a *cognitive* component, because it represents a person's knowledge, held with varying degrees of certitude, about what is true or false, good or bad, desirable or undesirable; an *affective* component, because under suitable conditions the belief is capable of arousing affect of varying intensity . . . when its validity is questioned; and a *behavioral* component, because the belief . . . must lead to some action when it is suitably activated. (Rokeach 1968, n.p.)

Therefore, the cognitive component may affect an attitude as knowledge is acquired about a particular situation. For example, viewing films of the modern cities in Africa would change the belief that Africans only live in grass huts. The affective component may be activated by confrontation with behavior that is inconsistent with the individual's belief "on how one should behave in that situation." For example, the teacher displays an interest in and appreciation for the primitive art of Africa and the children have always believed this type of art was "junky." The children will be required to reassess their attitudes toward the artwork. The atmosphere of the classroom affects the attitudes developed. If a teacher is attempting to develop an attitude regarding the importance of recognizing the worth of the individual, but does not allow each person to express an opinion nor accept the contributions of each member of the group, it is doubtful that this attitude will be successfully conveyed to the students.

Measurement of attitude is best accomplished by observing the behavior of individuals in a given situation. Undoubtedly, there will be occasions when children will display the actions they feel are expected of them, thereby making measurement difficult. And there also will be times when teachers misunderstand or misjudge the behavior of children and are unable to assess their real feelings or emotions.

Examples of objectives for the area of attitudes are:

The student appreciates that cooperative behavior is necessary to accomplish certain tasks and willingly offers to work with others.

The student values the contributions to our heritage of the many subcultures and expresses an appreciation for them.

"A value, unlike an attitude, is a standard or yardstick to guide actions, attitudes, comparisons, evaluations, and justification of self and others" (Rokeach 1968, p. 160). "A person's value system may thus be said to represent a learned organization of rules for making choices and for resolving conflicts—between two or more modes of behavior or between two or more endstates of existence" (p. 161). Values are much more difficult to change since they are generally learned early in the socialization process, at home and within the peer group.

Previously, values often were taught by the process of indoctrination, where the teachers indicated what was right or wrong based on their own value systems. However, studies have suggested that there are stages of development and that the school can best influence children's values by helping them to grow into the advanced stages of personal development. Children can be helped to clarify their own value positions through the experience of analyzing conflicting value situations and exploring their own feelings and values in different situations. An example of an objective in the valuing area would be:

The students will analyze their value positions when confronted with a problem situation by listing alternative solutions, their consequences, and value issues.

Skills

A *skill* is defined as the ability to become capable or proficient at performing a task or tasks. In stating objectives for this area, the individual's potential should be determined. Because skills are developmental, an acceptable achievement level varies according to the individual's maturation level. For example, a primary grade child cannot be expected to perform certain skills with the same proficiency as would an intermediate grade child.

Skills are developed sequentially—some must be acquired before others. For example, children must learn to read before they can acquire skill in locating information; or, they must understand spatial relationships before they can develop skill in map reading. Skills are divided into three subgroups: social, intellectual, and motor.

Social skills are concerned with the interaction of individuals within a group. Obviously, children who are unable to get along with members of their own class or who constantly display uncooperative behavior will find it difficult to understand and appreciate the necessity for establishing cooperation among other groups or nations. A teacher must first strive to develop the social skills within the classroom. Examples of such objectives would be:

The student will develop leadership ability by assuming the role of group leader.
The student will acquire skill in cooperative planning by working with a group toward the completion of a task.

Intellectual skills include skill in doing research, critical thinking, problem solving, making oral and written reports, outlining, and taking notes. The development of these skills need not be limited to the social studies; they offer an excellent opportunity for integration, especially with the language arts. For example, critical thinking can be introduced in reading and then applied in the social studies. Examples of such objectives would be:

The student will identify the problem, hypothesize several solutions, collect data to test the hypotheses, and draw conclusions.
The student will critically analyze a newspaper article to determine what is fact and what is opinion.
The student will demonstrate the use and understanding of the seven-color key of a map.

Motor skills include proficiency in manipulative activities such as construction, painting, and drawing. These skills often allow students to express their understanding of social studies information. Sample objectives would be:

The student will demonstrate understanding of the events leading up to the American Revolution through the depiction of these events in cartoon form.
The student will construct a relief map using clay.

Continued practice is essential to ensure increased proficiency of skills. Some skills which will be practiced relate only to the social studies, while other skills could be used in any of the subject areas.

Unit Planning

One of the more frequently used approaches to organizing for instruction is the *unit plan*. "Unit planning, or unit teaching, refers to the practice of organizing a set of instructional experiences around selected themes, questions, or topics" (Welton & Mallon 1992, p. 237). Thematic units or integrated units allow for learning experiences to be linked with other curriculum areas, but do not necessarily connect them to all areas. One of the most crucial aspects of developing a thematic or integrated unit is the selection of the theme or topic. Does the theme or topic provide for meaningful questions to be asked and valuable learning experiences to be developed? For example, the theme might be Africa, which would provide for many important learning experiences in several subject areas. A sample integrated unit on Africa begins on p. 79.

The basic components of a unit remain pretty much the same regardless of whether it is thematic, organized around a problem, or pursues a critical issue. The organization of a unit consists of:

1. Purposes—why the topic was chosen.
2. Objectives—what will be accomplished in the process of teaching the unit.
3. Outline of Unit—including content and how it will be integrated with other subjects.
4. Learning Experiences—including initiation, individual and cooperative experiences, integration with other subject areas, and culmination.
5. Bibliography—references for the teacher and children including materials such as videos, games, and multimedia kits.
6. Evaluation—a measure to determine the success achieved in accomplishing established objectives.

Organization is the key to unit planning—One learning experience must be related to another in order to avoid fragmentation. Planning of the unit may be done ahead of time by the teacher or it may be planned with the children. An earlier definition of a unit focused on the role of children in the planning. The *Dictionary of Education* (Good 1945) defined it thus: "an organization of learning activities, experiences, and types of learning around a central theme, problem, or purpose developed cooperatively by a group of pupils under teacher leadership" (p. 436). This definition is based on the theory that the children are motivated to learn material that they help to select and to plan in cooperation with the teacher. It also suggests that children can understand a topic more readily if they study it in the context of various subject areas.

The unit is a blueprint for broad or in-depth coverage of a topic. Topics can be covered in breadth, including as many aspects as possible, or in depth emphasizing only selected aspects. A unit may extend for several weeks or be completed in several days. Learning experiences may be planned for children to work individually, but more frequently small groups or cooperative groups are used. Unit teaching provides excellent opportunities to meet the individual needs of children. If children are shy and need the experience of working with others, the teacher can place them in a group where they won't be dominated, but where they can develop their leadership skills. Other children who have exceptional art skills can utilize those skills in painting a mural or constructing a diorama.

Overall goals for unit teaching include, but are not limited to, the following:

Acquire facts and information sufficient to develop an understanding of the topic or question under study.
Develop methods of acquiring accurate information from a variety of sources.
Understand the interrelationship of content areas.
Acquire skills in working with members of a group through cooperative planning and participation.
Learn to communicate with members of a group through a variety of means.
Understand the importance of establishing effective human relationships to achieve established goals within a group.

Developing the Unit

What Will You Teach? How Do You Decide?

As indicated in Chapter 3, the teacher will need to process certain information before making a decision. Do local or state guidelines require certain topics to be taught? Is the teacher required to use a textbook and only teach those topics? Are there needs or interests of the children that should be pursued? For example: Are there different cultural groups within the classroom or do the children have difficulty getting along with one another? Are there community, state, national, or world issues that need to be addressed, such as: How can air pollution be controlled? How are election campaigns run? How can wars be avoided? Does the school, public library, or community have sufficient resources to teach the unit or can they be acquired from other sources?

Sometimes teachers may want to develop an interest inventory to aid in determining the focus of the students' interests. It may include short answer questions, from pupil/teacher conferences or discussions, or the following type of inventory, to which the children can respond by checking the appropriate column—like, dislike, or not sure. Sample questions might be:

1. Do you like to learn about the following:
   a. People from different countries, such as Japan? India? Egypt? Kenya? Vietnam?
   b. The way in which a country is governed?
   c. Why many people in our country and the world don't have enough to eat?

d. Why countries have wars?
   e. Important leaders such as Jesse Jackson? Boris Yeltsin? Queen Elizabeth?

Components of a Unit

Purpose. Why has this particular topic or theme been chosen? The teacher needs to determine the reason why a particular topic, question, or problem will be studied. Is it related to a local, state, national, or world issue? Will it lend itself to the development of certain skills? Is it content that should be acquired? An example of the purpose for teaching a unit on Africa for the fourth grade follows: "Africa—A Land of Contrasts."

Africa is a continent that is experiencing rapid changes. Countries that for many years were ruled by European nations have gained their freedom and are struggling with the problems that face all new governments attempting to be recognized by the modern world. For too long, the ideas and impressions that children have had about Africa are those from a TV world of animals and jungles. This unit presents a view of Africa that shows its cities, industries, and problems similar to those of other countries of the world. An overview of the continent will be developed and will be followed by an in-depth study of one country—Kenya.

A crucial part of any social studies program is the development of a set of relevant objectives. Such objectives are related to purposes, understandable to all, and many can be measured by the student's behavior. For instruction to be valuable, the teacher should have a clear idea of how the instruction will affect student behavior.

Objectives for the Unit

Once the teacher has decided upon the topic, theme, problem, or question, then it is time to decide on the specific objectives that are to be achieved with the unit of study. Here is where a teacher's conception of social studies will play an important part in the decisions. If the teacher believes as Rita does, that the historical background of a country or issue is vital and that children need to learn this information, then many of the objectives for the unit will be acquisition of knowledge/understanding. However, if the teacher views social studies as reflective thinking as Julie does, then the process skills will be more important than the content. Lewis, who believes children need to acquire the concepts and method of inquiry of the social sciences, will develop objectives to meet these goals. Hugo, on the other hand, will use his conception of social studies as socio-political to select the topic for study. He will be sure that it has value issues involved and that children can actively participate in the learning experiences and put their conclusions into action.

Obviously, a teacher can formulate objectives for all of them: knowledge/understanding, attitudes/values, and skills. Knowledge/understanding objectives may be written to indicate that children will acquire information, acquire concepts, or arrive at generalizations. Examples follow:

- *Acquire information*—The students will acquire information about the physical features of Africa.
- *Acquire a concept*—The students will extend their concept of culture and how it develops.
- *Arrive at a generalization*—Geography influences the culture developed within a country and thus modifies the environment.

Attitude/value objectives are not taught directly, but it is expected that they may develop as a result of the learning experiences that students have during the unit.

- *Attitude:* The students will develop a respect for the traditions and contributions of other cultures.

   The students will learn to accept the opinions of others and understand why opinions vary.

   Skill objectives may be a major focus of the unit, particularly if the teacher is more concerned with the process of learning than the product. Some examples of skill objectives might be the following:
- *Skills:* The students will develop the ability to identify and define a problem situation.

   The students will formulate hypotheses for tentative problem solutions utilizing the information presented and previously acquired information.

   The students will develop the ability to work cooperatively with a group.

   The students will develop the skill of locating information through a variety of sources.

Content

This section gives a broad outline of what will be included in the study and how it will be integrated with other subjects. It may expand as children pursue their questions, but some sections may be deleted if they do not fit as well. However, it does provide a focus for teachers. In addition, if the theme, topic, problem, or question is something that the teachers do not have sufficient background information on which to guide the study, then they will need to research it. Also, the teachers will use the outline to search out the resources needed by the children to complete the study.

An outline follows for an integrated or thematic unit on the continent of Africa, for fourth grade with emphasis on the country of Kenya.

DAY ONE
   Initiation
   Language arts activity—Write a letter to a friend in the United States describing your life in one of the African countries. Gives the teacher an idea of students' knowledge of Africa.

Problem-solving activity—Use natural resources map to hypothesize some of the physical features and problems on the continent. Formulate questions to research.

Map activity—Use globes and relief maps of Africa, North America, and the world to discuss where Africa is located in relation to North America. Locate major landforms and rivers.

Math activity—Compute distances from hometown to Africa, lengths of rivers; estimate travel time with airplane, boat, and overland travel for different places in Africa.

Research activity—Form small groups to research the various landforms and vegetation of Africa—use a variety of books.

Land Forms	Vegetation
1. Desert	1. Rain Forest
2. Plateau	2. Savanna
3. Mountains	3. Veldt
4. Great Rift Valley	4. Oasis
5. Rivers	

Music activity—Play African music from different cultural groups while children are completing their research.

Art activity—The groups work together to develop murals of their regions to use as a backdrop for the presentation of their research reports.

Science experience—Locate the rain forest; discuss why the region receives so much rain. *Rain in a Jar*—Plant a terrarium to observe.

Reading activity—Read from Harold Courlander's *A Treasury of African Folklore*.

DAY TWO

Language arts activity—Groups present their research through oral presentations, as a panel discussion, or by means of guided tours using maps and murals.

Reading and writing activity—Introduce the concept of culture through brainstorming.

Introduce various cultural groups in Africa through video, for example, *Africa: Land and People* or filmstrips and audio cassettes such as *Africa: Beyond the Myths*. Provide books on varying reading levels about African cultures, also videos, game books and artifacts. Have children form small groups or, as individuals, have them research different cultural groups in African countries and prepare a travel brochure describing their group.

Science activity—Check terrarium; record what is happening in the jar.

Math activity—Discuss the major historical events of different groups coming to the African continent and develop a time line to represent them.

Reading activity—Introduce the country of Kenya with the reading of a folktale. Introduce concept of traditions.

Prepare for the African festival to be held the next day.

DAY THREE

Integrated activity—Stage African festival with artifacts, murals, music, food, games, dances, and travel brochures. Invite any resource persons from the community.

Writing activity—Children write a story about what their day would be like if they lived in one of the African countries.

Math activity—Children figure what their expenses would be to travel to their African country and spend a week.

DAY FOUR

Reading activity—Read and discuss the historical development of Kenya concentrating on war for independence (1952–1957). Read story "The Devil at Yalahun Bridge," which depicts the reaction of educated Africans to the British before independence.

View video of different life-styles in Kenya—village life and city life.

Math activity—Compare the area and population of Kenya and the largest cities with those within their state.

Language arts/valuing activity—Tell story about a family in Kenya and their problems with finding work. The family in Kenya lives in the small village of Nyeri outside Nairobi. The father, Patrick, was a freedom fighter, but cannot find work and the family does not have enough food to get along. Patrick is a carpenter and might find work in Nairobi, but that would mean leaving his family. It is possible that Patrick might only find a job as a shoeshine person. One of the boys, Kimani, is old enough to go to the city to find work, but he has no skills. If he goes to the city, it is doubtful he would find work except as a car park attendant and if he is lucky, maybe as a waiter. Another boy, named after the Olympian Kipchoge, is a runner and hopes to be famous too, some day, in the Olympics. He does not have time to work. The mother, Ruth, does not want the father or son to leave home. She would rather have her daughter, Grace, marry someone with money. Grace wants to marry a poor goatherder. What should the family do? Form five groups and assign the role of one family member to each group. Have them discuss possible alternatives for the family and consequences of actions. Discuss the values that are important to the family.

Art activity—Construct masks of each family member to use with role playing activity on Day Five.

Science activity—Discuss the plants and animals of Kenya.

DAY FIVE

Language arts activity—Prepare for role playing activity. Have students select person from each group to role play the family situation.

Do a second role play if there is a different view represented.

Debrief the role players—discuss how each felt in taking the role. How did they react to the family's problems? How might the Kenya family's problems be similar to problems families have in this country?

Math activity—Plan safari trip to Kenya; select places to visit and distances to be traveled each day.

Art activity—Make passports; take pictures or draw portraits.

Science activity—Determine climate in Kenya at the time of year; discuss what type of clothes should be packed.

Music activity—Listen to traditional music heard in Kenya.

Language activity—Listen to tape of Swahili language; learn to say "hello," "good-bye," "how are you."

Writing activity—Write about your trip, what you saw, things you did, people you met, foods you ate, and your most exciting experience.

The preparation of the outline and the objectives provide guidelines as the teachers plan for the learning experiences. Recognize that social studies content underlies all of the activities.

Learning Experiences. There are a variety of learning experiences that can be planned in the development of the unit. Some examples follow:

Initiation. The teacher is responsible for providing the setting for the study. The ability and experiential level of the children will serve as possible guidelines for determining the amount of information to include in the initiation. A problem-solving situation can be used for the introduction. Other initiation activities might include an arranged environment, exploratory questioning, films, stories, poetry, and folktales.

Arranged environment. Use of a number of prepared exhibits and bulletin boards creates a classroom atmosphere that lends itself to the topic for study. Bulletin boards supply two types of stimulation: (a) information about the topic, presented by charts, pictures, and newspaper clippings, or (b) the presentation of a series of searching questions to be answered during the study.

Displays would include books and magazines that present discussions of the topic at varying levels of reading difficulty. The books should contain stories as well as facts. Other displays might show selected artifacts relative to the topic. Criticism of the arranged environment points out that it lacks pupil/teacher planning and creates an artificial beginning for the pursuit of the study. Gradual development of the bulletin boards and exhibits by the children throughout the study is suggested.

Exploratory questioning. Teachers need to know the extent of their students' understanding or misunderstanding of a topic before beginning the study. Introducing a topic through a stimulating question period provides teachers with information to help them plan the direction and depth of the study. It also creates excitement about the topic. Such questioning can be incorporated with any initiation or used exclusively for the initiation. For example, when the topic is concerned with the study of Africa, the teacher might have the children react to questions such as: What do you think of when someone mentions Africa? How would your life change if you moved to Africa? What are some of the contributions that Africans have made to our heritage?

Generally, more information about individual understanding can be obtained when children are requested to write their answers; however, oral questioning stimulates more interest in the topic. Assessment of the answers in terms of general misconceptions as well as the amount of present knowledge about the topic should direct the focus of the study. Writing a letter to a friend in the United States as if you were living in Africa, included in the previous outline, is an example.

Video or filmstrip presentation. A video or filmstrip used to introduce the study can present information and/or questions. Those providing provocative information may foster immediate interest that may not be sustained.

Reading stories, poetry, or folktales. Stories related to the topic that present situations similar to those in the children's lives provide stimulation. Poetry and folktales also catch the interest of children. *Children's Books to Enrich the Social Studies* is a good source for information concerning this type of material.

Lesson Planning

Developing individual lesson plans for the various learning experiences is helpful to the teacher. A lesson to initiate the unit and provide for teacher/pupil planning might look like the following:

Goal: Introduce a unit on Africa and give students an opportunity to plan their learning experiences with the teacher.
Objectives:

To interest students in studying about Africa.
To identify some questions about Africa that students would like answered.
To develop skill in observation and interpretation.
To develop skill in hypothesizing.
To develop skill in identifying problems.

Materials: Transparency map of Africa with natural resources identified (see Figure 4.1). Overhead projector. Blackboard.

Procedure: Teacher introduces the students to the map transparency and explains the key. The following dialogue between teacher and students might occur:

TEACHER: What can you learn about Africa from the map?
SANDRA: It has many natural resources.
TOM: Not so many when you think how large Africa is.
RIKA: Yes, but some of them are so valuable like diamonds and uranium.
TEACHER: What can you tell about the physical features of the continent from the resources?
JEAN: Many of those minerals are found in mountainous regions.
BUZ: Not all. Oil is found in flat areas, also phosphate.
JIM: Yes, and I've seen copper mines on plateaus.

FIGURE 4.1 Natural Resources of Africa

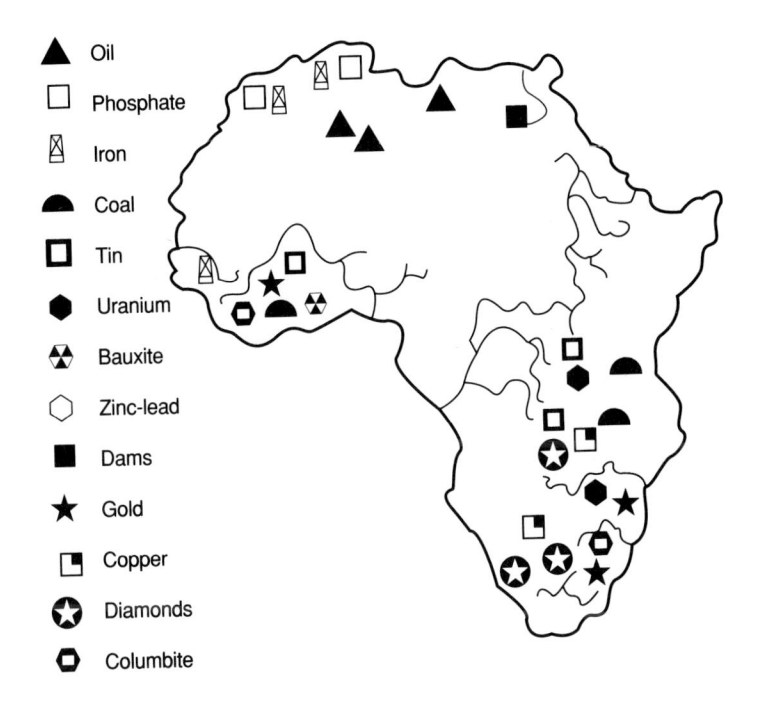

▲ Oil
☐ Phosphate
⛏ Iron
⬔ Coal
▢ Tin
⬢ Uranium
⬭ Bauxite
⬡ Zinc-lead
■ Dams
★ Gold
▣ Copper
✪ Diamonds
⬣ Columbite

TEACHER: So far we think there are mountains, plateaus, and plains. What do the rivers tell you about the land?

MYRTLE: Usually, the sources of rivers come from mountains.

TODD: Look at that large area where there aren't any rivers. That must be all desert.

TEACHER: Can you hypothesize about where people might live?

SHERMAN: It seems more would be concentrated near the resources and rivers—the eastern and southern sections.

TEACHER: Do you see any problems that might result from the distribution of resources?

JIM: Since some places don't have resources, maybe they fight over the land.

TODD: Some places may have a lot of poverty.

REED: They have so many different resources, there must be lots of industries.

TEACHER: What type of industries might they have?

KUNTO: There is coal and iron, maybe they have steel mills.

ROSS: If they have uranium, do they make nuclear power?

MARIA: No, I don't think Africa has that much technology. Those are different countries with the resources and maybe they don't trade with one another.
SCOTT: Don't some European countries control the resources in Africa?
TEACHER: You've raised a number of questions about Africa. Suppose we list them. (Writes them on blackboard)
SCOTT: What are the physical features of Africa?
REED: What industries do you find in Africa?
ANGELO: Shouldn't we find out the different countries in Africa?
TEACHER: Why do you think so?
ANGELO: To understand how the continent is divided and how the people are governed.
TEACHER: How would you state the question?
ANGELO: What are the countries in Africa and their governments?
MARIO: What is the history of the countries and how did they develop?
RON: Where are the cities? Most of the time you think of jungles and huts.
RUTH: What is the climate like and how do the people dress?
TINA: What type of music and art is there in Africa?
SCOTT: What kinds of traditions are important to the people? You know, what do they value?
TEACHER: Africa is such a large area, do you think we should try to learn about the entire continent?
SCOTT: Let's find out general information about all of Africa, then we can decide if there's an area where we might want to concentrate.
TEACHER: Is that satisfactory to everyone? We've listed a number of questions to research. Look at them carefully and decide which one you'd like to choose.
SCOTT: Can we work in small groups so several people can look for information on each topic?
TEACHER: Good idea—we should find more information when we work together on a problem and you can help one another.

Teacher will divide students into small groups to research the answers to the questions.

Evaluation: Teacher can determine if objectives were met by observing and reviewing the results of the discussion.

1. Did most of the children become interested in Africa?
2. Were they able to hypothesize using previous knowledge and information on the transparency?
3. Were they able to identify some possible problems facing the countries of Africa?
4. Did they arrive at some questions to research and learn more about the African continent?

This initiation lesson provided an opportunity for the children to become actively involved in the planning of their learning experiences. Even though the teacher had previously identified some goals, it is possible to guide the discussion toward them.

Individual and group activities that meet student needs and interests. Unit organization has the advantage of providing the opportunities to meet individual needs. Children who have special interests or skills can be guided toward tasks that fulfill these needs. Research can be conducted in areas of a study that are of particular interest to individual children. Those of exceptional ability can engage in research in greater depth and thus acquire skills beyond the normal level. Children who have talent in music, art, writing, or drama have an opportunity to use these skills.

In the previous dialogue, it's obvious that Scott is outgoing and probably possesses leadership ability. He easily can assume the responsibility for organizing a small group through which he can help other children. Maria, on the other hand, would prefer to pursue the topic of history on her own. Tom and Reed are both talented in music and art. Continuing in this manner, other group or individual activities may be organized around the interests and abilities of the other children.

Group activities contribute to the individual's development. For example, the child who has difficulty in getting along with other children and who is assigned to a group activity of real interest to him/her hopefully will acquire skills of cooperative behavior. Equally important is the opportunity for the child with leadership ability to channel this energy into worthwhile activities. Shy children who would hesitate to enter into activities and discussions in front of the whole group will often do so within small groups. Activities that encourage discussion of important aspects in the study aid the development of oral language skills.

Integrating activities. The development of an understanding of the relationship of one subject area to another is made possible through integrating activities, which help children realize that knowledge in one subject is related to other subject areas. These activities also provide meaningful practice of skills acquired in other areas. As noted in the outline of the unit, each of the subject activities was developed using the overall theme or topic.

Language arts. Skills introduced in the language arts acquire more meaning when they are applied in the content areas. Children realize a purpose for acquiring skills when they can put them to use. Unit teaching provides numerous opportunities for the use of language skills.

Methods for encouraging the development of oral language skills might include reports of individual or committee research, panel discussions or debates on facets of the study, role playing incidents to clarify understandings, and class discussions about the topics. Interviewing individuals to secure information also develops oral language skills. Listening skills, too, are sharpened during these experiences.

Outlining, note taking, and preparing written reports are skills needed for research activities. Critical reading skills are necessary to determine if the source of the information is fact or opinion. Locational skills involving the use of the table of contents, index, cross references, and appendix are necessary when seeking information during the study. Journal writing can help the students clarify their understanding of the topic under study.

Art, music, and physical education. Construction activities, such as building a model African village or a salt and flour relief map, add considerable understanding to a study and correlate learning experiences. Painting or drawing murals provides opportunity for interpreting events. Making artifacts from various cultures—for example, making groundnut (peanut butter) stew when studying an African country—makes a study more realistic.

Frequently, topics provide opportunity for integration with music—for example, constructing drums when studying an African culture or listening to the music of the country. Learning the dances native to a country helps develop an understanding of its people. Children enjoy learning the games that are played in the countries under study.

Math and science. Math and science lessons may or may not be as easy to integrate into a topic under study. Measurement of distances, computing costs of travel, or comparing area and population of a country with our own are examples of math activities that might be planned.

Science lessons could include the study of plants and animals found in a region or the climatic conditions and how they affect the people. Science experiments, such as creating a rain forest in a jar, can provide effectively integrated lessons when studying Africa.

Lesson plan for an integrating activity:

Reading and writing
OBJECTIVES:
  Students will formulate their concept of culture.
  Students will acquire information about some of the cultural groups in Africa through observation of videos or filmstrips.
  Students will acquire skill in researching a topic using a variety of resources.
  Students will use their writing skills to develop a tourist brochure explaining their cultural group of Africa.
MATERIALS:
  Blackboard, video *Africa: Land and People,* filmstrip *Africa: Beyond the Myths,* books on varying reading levels discussing different cultural groups, game books, music tapes, artifacts, and construction paper to prepare a travel brochure, pens, pastels or crayons.
PROCEDURE:
  Teacher introduces the concept of culture by asking the following questions: (See Figure 4.2.)

FIGURE 4.2

Questions	Possible responses
What do you think of when you hear the term *culture*? Record responses on board.	people music clothes art customs religion food beliefs holidays houses language civilized buildings man-made
If you were to place those things that are similar in a group, what would you put together? Why do you group them that way?	beliefs art civilized religion music man-made customs clothes people language food holidays houses buildings

What would you call each of these groups? What would you label them?
  Why there is culture:
    civilized
    man-made
    people
  Things that cultures make:
    art
    music
    clothes
    food
    houses
    holidays
	Ideas that develop in a culture:
	  beliefs
	  religion
	  customs
	  language
	  holidays

If you were trying to tell someone what culture is, what would you tell them?	Culture is how a certain group of people live, the way they believe, dress, what they eat, their clothes, their music and art. All things they have in their lives.
Why do people who live in different places develop different cultures?	It depends on the weather, how hot or cold it is, what grows on their land, what kind of resources they have, if other cultures joined them, what they do with their resources.
What are some cultures you know about?	Our own. Mexican. Japanese. Chinese. Thailand.

continued

FIGURE 4.2

Questions	Possible responses
What might happen if different cultures didn't believe in the same things like religion or how to use the land, but lived in the same country?	They might have trouble. Wars. Try to take over the land. Try to change people's beliefs.
What would you conclude about culture?	Culture makes you what you are. Sometimes different cultures don't get along.

"We're going to view a video of some of the cultural groups of Africa." After video is shown, children decide which of the cultural groups they want to research. Small groups are formed to research their group and develop the travel brochure. Children should be reminded that they should read the material about the cultural group and then write the brochure in their own words.

EVALUATION:

Teacher determines whether students understand the concept of culture by their responses to the questions.

The reading and writing objectives will be evaluated by the completion of the travel brochure and its contents.

Culminating activities. Culminating activities draw together the learning experiences of the unit. These activities should emphasize the main points, identify the interrelated ideas, and provide a composite view of the topic. As a result of these activities, children should be able to formulate generalizations that can be applied to new situations. Examples of culminating experiences follow:

Committee reports. The completed research of the committees can be presented in a variety of ways—TV or radio productions; talks illustrated with prepared charts, bulletin boards, and realia; or a movie roll that includes information from every cooperative group, writing a Big Book about the country or preparing travel brochures.

Tours. The study of a country provides the opportunity for planning a guided tour to emphasize the important historic, recreational, and geographic points of interest. Illustrative materials such as maps, murals, and pictures supply background.

Dramatizations. The production of drama requires interpretation of the information secured and ensures better understanding of the topic. Children portraying the characters and illustrating the points of interest will understand better and retain longer the information acquired.

Videos, films, and filmstrips. Audiovisual aids such as video, films, and filmstrips can be used effectively for culminating activities when they review information previously investigated.

Bibliography

An extensive bibliography listing the materials available for the teacher and the children should be included in the unit. Resource books, videos, films, tapes, records, pictures, community resources, and suggested field trips should be included for reference.

Sample Bibliography for African Study

Aardema, V. (1991). *Traveling to Tonda: A tale of the Nkundo of Zaire.* New York: Knopf.
Campbell, E. (1991). *The place of lions.* Tanzania: Harcourt Brace Jovanovich.
Chiasson, J. (1987). *African journey.* New York: Bradbury Press.
Dee, R. (1991). *Tower to heaven.* New York: Holt.
Gordon, S. (1987). *Waiting for the rain: A novel of South Africa.* New York: Orchard Books.
Isadora, R. (1991). *At the crossroads.* New York: Greenwillow Books.
Mollel, T. M. (1990). *The orphan boy.* New York: Clarion Books.
Nicol, A. (1965). The Devil at Yalahun Bridge. In *Two African tales.* Cambridge University Press.
Pitkanen, M. A. (1991). *The children of Egypt.* Minneapolis: Carolrhoda.
Schermbrucker, R. (1991). *Charlie's house.* New York: Viking.
Stanley, D. (1994). *Shaka, king of the Zulus.* New York: Mulberry Books.
Steptoe, J. (1987). *Mufaro's beautiful daughters. An African tale.* New York: Lothrop, Lee & Shepard Books.
Weir, B., & Weir, W. (1991). *Panther dream: A story of the African rainforest.* New York: Hyperion Books for Children.
Williams, K. (1993). *Galimoto.* New York: Lothrop, Lee & Shepard.
Williams, K. (1991). *When Africa was home.* New York: Orchard.

Evaluation

The methods of evaluation to be utilized during and at the completion of the unit must be planned. These evaluations are attempts to determine whether the objectives of the unit were successfully achieved. Evaluations must be made in terms of the success with which individual and group performances meet the objectives as indicated in Figure 4.3. Continuous evaluation throughout the unit guides its direction. Teachers should be evaluating their teaching procedures and their effectiveness in guiding the activities of the children. An assessment of the kinds and uses of materials is also important.

Different types of evaluation will be used, depending upon the objective that is to be achieved. For example, with an objective that indicates certain behaviors should develop, observation is the most useful way to determine if they are occurring. The checklist with a description of the behaviors is helpful for the teacher.

A checklist for observation of small group work might have the following criteria:

1. Are the leaders effective?
2. Are groups sharing material?

FIGURE 4.3 Process of Evaluation

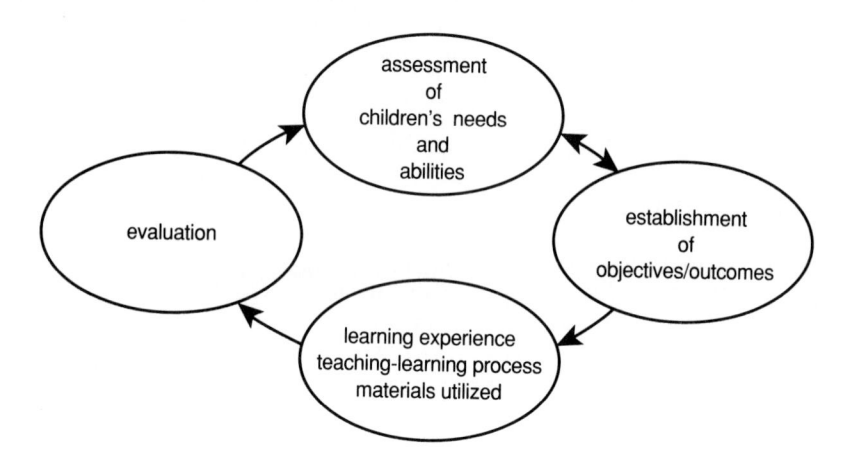

```
              assessment
              of
              children's needs
              and
              abilities
    ↗                              ↘
evaluation              establishment
                        of
                        objectives/outcomes
    ↖                              ↙
              learning experience
              teaching-learning process
              materials utilized
```

3. Is each person doing his/her share of the work?
4. Are there any interpersonal problems?
5. Are the children having any difficulty locating information?
6. What, if any, are the problems?
7. Do all children participate in the decision making?

Observation. During a class discussion, teachers use observation techniques. As they conduct a discussion, teachers observe the expressions on the children's faces. Are they interested? Which children are always ready with the answers? Are there shy children who never enter the discussion? Do the children appear to understand? Would another method of instruction be more effective? Are the materials effective? Does the child understand what he/she values? Does he/she act upon his/her values? Is the child a visual learner? Do some children need more concrete experiences? Because it is often difficult to remember the answers to these questions for each child, teachers find it necessary to develop a record for reference. The most common method used is a checklist of the objectives of the learning experience on which the teacher records each child's success or failure in achieving the objectives. Figure 4.4 presents a sample checklist.

Another checklist method involves keeping a separate sheet for each child, as shown in Figure 4.5. Use of the checklist facilitates observation and makes it more systematic. The checklist provides the teacher with definite behaviors to observe and a valuable record for use in reporting the children's progress.

A checklist for use when children are making oral presentations might have these criteria.

1. Did each child speak so all could hear?
2. Did each child make eye contact with the audience?

FIGURE 4.4

	Willing to Share	Listens to Others	Possesses Creative	Completes work on	Expresses Opinion	Identifies Value
1. Kay	U	U	O	O	O	O
2. Bill	O	S	S	U	U	U
3. Rita	S	S	S	S	S	O
4. Gay	O	O	O	O	O	S

O Outstanding
S Satisfactory
U Unsatisfactory

3. Were the children listening to one another?
4. Was the information presented so that it was easily understood?

Rating scales. Rating scales are more effective when the teacher is attempting to pinpoint a child's performance on a scale ranging from excellent to poor. Also, scores from rating scales are more easily translated into letter grades if these are required by the school's evaluation system. Figure 4.6 is a sample rating scale that a teacher might use during an observation period.

FIGURE 4.5

Another method of recording on a checklist involves keeping a separate sheet for each child, as shown in the following example.

Name __Gay__   Grade __5__

Map Skills		Social Skills	
Ability to interpret color key	✓	Gets along well with others	
Locates places readily		Accepts responsibility	✓
Ability to compute distances	✓	Shares materials	✓
		Supports value beliefs	

Objective: The child participates effectively in small group activities.

FIGURE 4.6

Objective: The child participates effectively in committee activities

	Excellent 5	Good 4	Average 3	Fair 2	Poor 1
1. Contributes ideas to group goal.					
2. Does share of the work.					
3. Listens to the opinions of others.					
4. Works well with all types of children.					
5. Locates information.					

Anecdotal records. Some teachers prefer to make specific notations about children's behavior. With this procedure, they record statements about how each child reacts to learning situations or responds to statements from peers and the teacher. An example:

Stewart was quite disturbed by Kim's reference to colored people. He corrected her, but also showed hostility toward her during game time.
Rita improves daily in her ability to understand the valuing process. She quickly identified the value issues in today's role playing.
Truman is constantly verbalizing his answers during work time.

This type of record is particularly helpful when teachers are reporting pupil progress to parents through conferences or letters.

Conferences. The opportunity to converse with a child on a one-to-one basis is often a revealing form of evaluation. Attitudes, understandings, needs, abilities, and interests may be assessed by this method. Certain guidelines should be followed while conducting an individual conference.

1. Identify the goal of the conference—for example, direct the conference toward learning about the child's attitude toward people of another culture.

2. Prepare questions and discuss them during the conference—for example, "If you were to take a trip anywhere in the world, where would you go? Why?"
3. Establish good rapport with the child as soon as possible—discuss some personal event, a game, an interest.
4. Listen carefully to what the child has to say and make notations about the child's answers after the completion of the conference.
5. Leave the conference with a word of encouragement to the child and a definite plan of action.

The children should be prepared for the conferences and have their own goals and questions in mind. Before the conference, they might ask themselves: Are there questions I want to ask? Do I understand what we are studying? Does the teacher have suggestions for the improvement of my work? Do I have any projects or research I want to complete? If children have a thorough understanding of the purpose of the conference, it will be more profitable for them and their teacher.

Individual conferences can also be used for oral testing. The child who has difficulty with reading or who has a mental block about tests can have the test administered in a conference situation. Also, diagnostic instruments can be administered.

Individual conferences are open to criticism, especially if the class is large, because of their time-consuming nature. However, five or ten minutes spent with an individual child is well worth the time in terms of the results. In addition to obtaining the intended evaluation, the teacher will also get to know the child and may be able to spot possible problem areas. Ten minutes in an individual conference could help solve a problem for a child that might otherwise go unnoticed. In the conference, the teacher also has the opportunity to guide the child toward self-evaluation with questions such as, Are you satisfied with your work? Do you think you could do better? What do you see as your problems? The number of individual conferences held will depend upon their success, their intended purpose, the children's reactions, and the teacher's schedule. The other children can complete individual work or group work while conferences are being conducted.

Group discussion. The total class or small groups can evaluate a mutual experience. This type of session permits children to compare their group's performance with the performances of others and to assess their role in the total group process. In this situation, children should learn the role of constructive criticism. The following example of a group discussion after the presentation of an oral report by a committee of sixth graders illustrates these values.

TEACHER: As we look at the guidelines for presenting an oral report, how well do you think Kim's group followed them?
JERRY: I didn't think the report was very good.
SANDY: Me, neither.

TEACHER: What is our first rule in evaluating someone else's work?
JERRY: Look for something that was well done and comment on that.
TEACHER: Yes, and if we criticize their work, what should we include?
SANDY: We should tell what was wrong and how it might be improved.
TEACHER: Right; shall we try again?
JUAN: The group used pictures to illustrate their talk, which made it easier to understand.
KATHY: Yes, and the artwork was so beautiful.
MURPHY: Some of the members of the group did not speak out so we all could hear and that spoiled their report.
SID: If they had moved out in front of the table, it would have been easier to hear them.

In this example, the teacher quickly turned what might have been a useless evaluation session into positive constructive criticism.

In another group session, the children might evaluate the behavior and performance of the group on a field trip and the value of the trip. The teacher would ask for comments on general behavior and request that children refrain from pinpointing individual actions that might embarrass the children involved. In assessing the value of the field trip, the children compare what they learned with the goals that were previously established for the trip.

Group discussions can be conducted daily to evaluate topics such as groups working together, the effectiveness of materials utilized, or the children's understanding of a video, an outside speaker, or a reading. Such discussion aids teachers in determining the effectiveness of a particular teaching technique. Through discussion and comparison of the work completed by individuals and groups, these sessions also lead the child toward introspection and evaluation of his/her own behavior and achievement.

Child self-evaluation. One of the goals of instruction in any subject area is that of self-evaluation. The children who can look at their progress objectively and discuss their strengths and weaknesses have achieved a valuable goal. Checklists based on the objectives of social studies are helpful, for they allow children to record their achievement. The process of asking questions about their activities aids children in self-evaluation. Examples of items for such checklists are:

1. Do I try to do my best work?
2. Do I look carefully at all sides of an issue?
3. Do I enjoy working with others?
4. Do I listen carefully to what others have to say?
5. Do I respect others who are different from me?

Another method of self-evaluation involves keeping a record of a series of experiences, for example, in a journal or log. As the children record descriptions of the activities, they should be encouraged to discuss their role and the degree to which they achieved the goal they had established. Children, too, need to realize that there are limitations to their abilities and that they should not set unrealistic goals for themselves.

Teacher-made tests. Another form of assessment or evaluation may be a teacher-made test. The type of test teachers devise depends upon: (a) what they are attempting to evaluate and (b) their method of instruction. For example, the teacher who has presented purely factual information would not give an essay test that evaluates understanding. It is advantageous for teachers to prepare their own tests, for they can then base the test questions on the things they deem most valuable for evaluation.

Essay tests can present problem-solving situations, determine understanding, and assess attitudes. The reliability of scoring an essay test is questioned, however, and the time required to score such tests is considered a disadvantage.

Objective tests can test a wider variety of topics and they are more easily scored, but they require more time in planning and writing than essay tests. The Educational Testing Service suggests the following steps in preparing an objective test:

Step 1. List the major topics covered in your particular teaching unit. This list should not exceed five.
Step 2. Indicate the number of items you want to devote to each topic.
Step 3. List under each topic the things you want students to know about, understand, or be able to do.
Step 4. Collect materials on which to base items (textual material—typed or read by teacher, pictorial material, music, or specimens to be examined).
Step 5. Begin writing of the items for your test.
Step 6. Submit the items for review by another individual.
Step 7. Rewrite or replace defective items.
Step 8. Arrange the items into a test. May be arranged from easy to hard or by common subject matter.
Step 9. Prepare directions for the test.
Step 10. Prepare an answer key.

Different test elements that can be included are: (a) completion, (b) alternative response, (c) multiple choice, (d) matching, and (e) rearrangement.

SUMMARY

Not all teachers will plan units, but it does provide for broad or in-depth coverage of a topic. A unit aids in the efficient organization of learning experiences, but more importantly it provides opportunities for integration with other subject areas. Learning is not fragmented into different subject areas for short periods of time.

Some teachers will use the unit organization provided by their textbooks. Others will plan individual lessons to be taught separately. This may be necessary if a particular issue arises and needs only the limited time of one or two lessons.

SELECTED REFERENCES

Fouts, J. T. (1989). Classroom environments and student views of social studies: A replication study. *Theory and Research in Social Education,* n.p.

Gagné, R. M., & Kneller, G. F. (1972). Behavioral objectives? Yes or no? *Educational Leadership, 29*(5), 394–400.

Good, C. V. (1945). *Dictionary of education.* New York: McGraw-Hill.

Greig, M. E. (1963). *How people live in Africa.* Chicago: Benefic Press.

Mager, R. F. (1962). *Preparing instructional objectives.* Palo Alto, CA: Fearon.

Olson, L. (1993a, February 17). Progressive-era concept now breaks mold: NASDC schools explore "Project Learning." *Education Week,* p. 6.

Olson, L. (1993b, December). Who's afraid of O.B.E.? *Education Week,* pp. 25–27.

Redding, N. (1992). Assessing big outcomes. *Educational Leadership, 49*(8), 49–53.

Rokeach, M. (1968). *Beliefs, attitudes and values.* San Francisco: Jossey-Bass.

Schug, M. C., Todd, R. J., & Berry, R. (1984). Why kids don't like social studies. *Social Education, 48*(5), 382–387.

Welton, D. A., & Mallon, J. T. (1992). *Children and their world.* Boston: Houghton Mifflin.

LEARNING ACTIVITY

Writing goals, objectives, and outcomes for instruction is not too difficult after you have decided on the topic and what you think is most important for you to achieve in your instruction—information and understanding, values and attitudes, or skills.

Select a topic, problem, or project for an appropriate grade level and develop objectives/outcomes for each of the three areas. When you are finished compare them with those written by a classmate. Did you write them in behavioral terms or specified? Did you understand the difference between objective and outcome?

Write in your journal your reaction to organizing for instruction and writing objectives/outcomes. How do you want to approach the planning process? As an integrated unit? Whole language? A project approach?

AN ALTERNATE LEARNING ACTIVITY

Talking to parents about your social studies program and why you think social studies is important for their children is a vital part of a teacher's role. Place yourself in the situation described below and prepare your presentation.

Complete the learning activity making your choices from the options in parentheses.

As a beginning teacher, you have accepted a position in a/n (rural, urban, suburban) district and have been assigned to a school in a/n (low, middle, upper-middle) socioeconomic area. You are teaching grade ___. One of your first responsibilities will be a presentation to the parents of the children in your classroom during "Parents Night." During previous years, emphasis has been placed on describing the reading and math programs. This year the principal has indicated that the emphasis will be on social studies. In the presentation, you are to discuss the definition, purpose, and objectives of social studies. You may discuss some specific topics you would teach to illustrate the points in your presentation if you so choose.

In preparation for your presentation, read several different authors' opinions about social studies. Interview at least three (each) parents, teachers, and students from the type and socioeconomic level of school that you have chosen. Ask them the following questions:

1. How do you define social studies?
2. What does social studies contribute to a child's education?
3. How do you rank social studies with the other subjects in the curriculum?

After you have completed the reading and interviews, prepare a ten-minute presentation for the parents, using language that they will understand.

Record in your journal some of the things you want to think about before you discuss your social studies program with parents.

CHAPTER 5

MULTICULTURAL EDUCATION

AS DESCRIBED in Chapter 1, as a teacher you will find much diversity in your classroom whether it is cultural, economic, racial, ethnic, or a disability. The diversity will make your classroom an interesting and exciting environment in which to teach. The social studies provides an ideal subject within which to study that diversity. However, it will mean that the content you choose, the materials you select, and the teaching strategies you use should lend themselves to that diversity. One of the ways in which the diversity has been recognized is through multicultural education. Different people have different ideas about what multicultural education is and/or should be. Dependent upon those ideas, different approaches to multicultural education have been developed. This book views multicultural education as an attitude—a way of looking at the uniqueness of an individual regardless of the race, culture, sex, disability, or economic status and recognizing each individual's contribution to the world, providing learning experiences that will help all children to be the most that they can be.

Multicultural education is often defined as meaning the "many cultures" that make up our society. But how do we define culture? Lampe (1988) points out that we often confuse race, ethnicity, and culture. Race refers to the physical characteristics of people

> such as color of skin, eyes, hair, form of nose, head, hair, or lips and is not limited *to a nationality or culture.* Members of different races often share the same culture, and no common culture is found among all members of any racial group. It could not be otherwise because race is based on nature while culture is based on nurture. (emphasis added) (p. 116)

Different groups in Africa belong to the same race, but have developed different cultures.

Ethnicity differs from race in that it refers "to an important dimension of an individual's self-image which is based on ancestry, race, religion, or nationality" (Gordon, cited in Lampe 1988, p. 116). "An ethnic group is defined as a group that exhibits each of these characteristics: A shared common history and tradition, a shared sense of peoplehood, and a common way of life or subculture" (Lampe 1988, p. 116). As Banks (1989) relates, teaching about Mexicans in Mexico is not the same as teaching about Chicanos in East Los Angeles.

"One way of looking at culture is to consider it as a set of hidden recurring patterns of behavior and thought; hidden because each person learns to behave appropriately in a given culture. It thus becomes difficult to explain why persons do what they do and how they learned those behaviors" (Cushner & Trifonovich 1989, p. 319). Triandis (cited in Cushner & Trifonovich 1989) differentiates between objective and subjective components of culture. Objective components include those that are visible, such as food, dress, and holidays, while subjective components are less tangible, "such as attitudes, values, norms of behavior, and the roles people assume" (p. 318). As Cushner and Trifonovich point out, it is at the subjective level that most misunderstanding and communication problems exist.

If teachers only present the food, dress, or holidays of a particular culture, are they then only looking at the surface or objective level and not really helping students to understand why a culture has those customs or traditions? When children are socialized ("Socialization is the process by which individuals learn what is required to be successful members of a group" [Cushner & Trifonovich 1989, p. 319]) into a culture and then enter school only to find that the school socialization requires a different set of behaviors, how do the children reconcile these differences, or can they? Are they able to understand that there are different ways that people view the world and react to that view? "Learning a culture is similar to learning a language. Few people receive formal instruction on how to be an appropriate member of a particular cultural group. Rather they learn by observing others, by trial, error, and continuous reinforcement. In other words, culture and language are learned affectively, not cognitively" (Cushner & Trifonovich 1989, p. 319).

What of multicultural education? Is it best learned cognitively or affectively? Should children learn about all cultures or learn about culture as a system and what that system includes regardless of the culture? Do individuals belong to more than one culture? It seems important to realize that some groups that ordinarily aren't recognized as a culture have actually developed a culture unique to their disability, such as those who are physically or mentally handicapped or are blind or deaf. What about children who may be labeled educationally disadvantaged or underprivileged? Are they without a culture or is the culture merely unique to their situation?

Multicultural education in this book is defined with the belief that all cultures, hence all children, should be considered when planning instruction, whether they are racially, ethnically, socioeconomically, physically, mentally, or sexually stereotyped.

Statistics suggest that by the year 2000, 36 percent of school-age children will be minority and some of these minorities are from countries that are different from earlier immigration groups (1820–1945). These countries in rank order are: Mexico, the Philippines, Korea, China/Taiwan, India, Cuba, the Dominican Republic, Jamaica, Canada, Vietnam, and Iran (Hodgkinson 1993). Twenty-three percent of our children live in poverty and most of these live in the inner cities and the rural areas. Whether children are members of minority groups, living in poverty, physically or mentally disabled, or affected by sexism, recognition of these conditions and some provisions in the curriculum and teaching strategies are imperative.

Fillmore (1993) argues:

> . . . that multicultural education must begin in kindergarten and be continuously reinforced throughout the school years. What children must learn are some fundamental attitudes and values concerning life in a multicultural multilingual society. They must be taught, early in life, that they live in a world where people come from many different places and backgrounds, but they are more alike than they are different. They need to recognize that differences in looks, likes, beliefs, and behavior are neither good nor bad—they are just differences. They have to learn that differences are what make people interesting, and while it might be a whole lot easier to be with people who are exactly the same as we are, it can be a whole lot more interesting to be with people who are different. Most of all, they need to discover that in order to succeed socially in a multicultural world, they have to accept and respect differences in others, rather than reject and abhor them. In short, they must be educated to think and live as citizens of a multicultural world. (p. 12)

Goals for multicultural education have been identified by many individuals, but Banks (cited in Bullard 1991) may have expressed them best:

- to "transform the school so that male and female students, exceptional students, as well as students from diverse cultural, social, racial and ethnic groups will experience an equal opportunity to learn in school"
- to "help all students develop more positive attitudes toward different cultural, racial, ethnic and religious groups"
- to "empower students from victimized groups by teaching them decision-making and social skills"
- to help students develop cross cultural dependency and view themselves from the perspectives of different groups. (p. 5)

Banks (1989) further states that "helping students to acquire the competencies and commitments to participate in effective civic action to create equitable national societies is the most important goal for multicultural education in the twenty-first century" (p. 4).

CULTURAL, RACIAL, ETHNIC, AND RELIGIOUS GROUPS

Why do some children use disparaging terms like "nigger" or "slant eyes" to describe a person from a race different from their own? Why do some children make fun of customs or dress that differ from theirs? Why do some children avoid playing with or selecting certain children for teams because they belong to a different religious group than they do? Why do some children view Native Americans as savages wearing feather headbands and using tomahawks or all Africans as living in huts in the jungle? Why do these things happen?

One reason may be that textbooks and classroom activities reinforce myths and stereotypes by presenting inaccurate information, providing insufficient information that builds the context of a culture, presenting only one perspective of the culture and using loaded words, not dealing with controversial or complex issues that confront the culture, as well as selecting visuals that do not effectively represent the culture (Cortes & Fleming 1986).

Another reason is the failure to confront the issues of hatred, prejudice, and ethnocentrism in the classroom. Subtle and not so subtle examples of these issues occur in classrooms every day whether they are exhibited toward racial, cultural, ethnic, religious, or even disabled groups. "Ethnocentrism refers to the tendency to (1) react to another culture only from the viewer's culture and (2) to regard one's own culture as superior. Prejudice, on the other hand, refers to judgments about other socio-cultural groups before one knows the facts—in other words a preconceived opinion" (Martin 1985, p. 606).

In addition to rectifying the above problems, one of the important goals of multicultural education must be to develop positive self-concepts of minority children, as well as teaching them to appreciate the heritages of their groups. A number of changes in content and teaching strategies will be necessary to accomplish these goals.

As mentioned earlier, children need to understand the differences between race, ethnicity, and culture. In addition, they need to understand the terms of nationality and religion as they refer to groups. Sociology and anthropology provide us "with a framework to comprehend, in a systematic manner differences and similarities among the plethora of world communities" (Freedman 1984, p. 201). Understanding certain cultural components, such as norms, values, mores, folkways, customs, and traditions as a part of a cultural system that any culture possesses, may well help children to better understand other cultures as well as their own. Martin (cited in Freedman 1984) "found that, under certain teaching conditions, when a culture is portrayed as a behavioral pattern rather than as a series of isolated events, negativism toward that culture is substantially diminished" (p. 201). It is important for children to realize that many of the customs and traditions that they experience within their own culture have counterparts in other cultures, even though they appear different.

Not all cultural groups can be studied because there are too many. Banks (cited in Willis 1992) believes that students should be taught "about concepts—such as immigration, intercultural interactions and racism—using various groups and their experiences as the vehicle to explore them" (p. 2). Ladson-Billings (cited in Willis 1992) agrees that teachers should focus on key ideas not single groups. "To explore issues of language, for example, teachers might have their students study French Canadians or consider why Americans from Mexico and Puerto Rico tend to retain their native language (many travel back and forth from their homelands). A unit on migration could deal with the Irish, Native Americans, and Chinese" (p. 2).

Research on the reduction of prejudice has reported that

- Facts alone are not sufficient to reduce prejudices.
- Social class prejudice may be stronger than racial or religious prejudices.
- Persons with high self-acceptance tend to have a low degree of prejudice.
- The cognitive, affective and behavioral components of prejudice are not necessarily related.
- Films and other media tend to improve attitudes between groups.
- Social contacts between groups may reduce prejudice. (Pate, cited in Martin 1985, p. 606)

Teaching strategies that have been suggested to reduce prejudice include critical thinking and cooperative learning. Walsh (1988) indicates that we should teach children to ask questions; go beyond superficial to substance; take positions on issues, explain and defend those positions; be aware of multiple perspectives on issues and knowing all sides of an issue; and assess information carefully and fairly. An example might be to look at the westward movement from the perspective of the European American and that of the Native American tribes. With these abilities, children should be encouraged to avoid making judgments before having all the necessary information, thus reducing prejudice.

Research reports that students who work "in a cooperative learning environment have more positive race relations, greater self-esteem, greater concern for others, more positive attitudes toward school and teachers, higher levels of reasoning, increased perspective taking, more on-task behavior, and higher achievement than other learning environments yield" (Conrad 1988, p. 284). In cooperative learning situations, children are not competing but rather are helping one another to achieve a task. By working together children recognize differences within the group, but learn to appreciate and respect those differences and the capabilities of their group members.

Reducing ethnocentrism in the classroom can be accomplished through learning experiences that give children an opportunity to discuss how stereotypes are formed, how they feel about certain cultural groups, learning about the positive contributions of cultural groups, and considering the wide variety of behaviors that are exhibited within any culture (Freedman 1984; Martin 1985). Some examples of these learning experiences follow.

Learning Experiences

1. Children divide into groups of six or eight and sit in a circle. They should remove all rings or bracelets. One student is blindfolded while another in the group comes forward to allow that student to explore his or her hands. They should note the texture, size, nails, fingers, and similar features. Then remove the blindfold and have the student go around the circle exploring the hands of those in the group until he or she identifies those explored. Repeat until all have had a chance to participate.

Call the class back together and discuss the following questions:

- Were there obvious differences among the hands?
- Were you surprised when you found out whose hands they were?
- How did you feel about touching or being touched?
- How did others react when you touched them?
- Why do we react in different ways (racial, cultural, social, familial, and sexual customs)?
- Can the diversity of responses to touching result in misunderstanding between people (Pasternak 1977)?

2. The teacher initiates a discussion about culture as follows:

- What is culture? Tradition?
- Are people born knowing how to act in ways acceptable to their culture? Why or why not?
- What do people learn from others in their culture?

Have students divide into groups of four to six. Using materials describing various cultures, list the traits that reflect these cultures, such as languages, foods, clothes, customs, arts, ideas, and the way people act. Have the students make lists of the cultural traits and their meanings within their groups. Record them on posters or the blackboard. Discuss the similarities and differences listed and the significance of various traits (Grant 1977).

3. The inquiry process can be used to explore stereotypes. As mentioned later in Chapter 8, the discrepant data technique is used whereby pictures or slides are shown to reinforce the stereotype, such as Mexicans riding burros, wearing straw hats and serapes, and eating tacos. Students develop a generalization about Mexicans. Then discrepant data is introduced showing the modern cities, industrial plants, and Mexicans involved in a variety of occupations. This then broadens the students' concept of the Mexican culture and the generalization would then be restructured.

4. Have students develop a collage of a Native American tribe (or any other group). Examine the collages for possible stereotypes. Show pictures of contemporary Native Americans teaching, practicing law, or at work in other professions. Ask students if they would recognize Native Americans on TV, in the movies, or anywhere in society without buckskins and feathers. What does this tell us?

5. To help students understand conflict and to resolve it when it arises, first start with a discussion of conflicts they face within themselves. Should I buy a new bike or save my birthday money? Do I hit my sister when she bothers me or try to discuss the matter with her?

After children have identified some conflicts, talk about how they resolve them. How do they make their decisions?

Then discuss conflicts that arise on the playground or in the classroom. How can these be resolved?

Investigate conflicts that occur in the community or society.

Try to determine what causes these conflicts. Is it cultural beliefs and customs? If people understand their differences, can conflicts be resolved?

Curriculum Development

Controversies abound when attempting to make decisions about how to formulate curricula for multicultural education. How do you include all cultures, and should you? Will the focus be Eurocentric (European in outlook and content) as it has been in the past or should it be Afrocentric emphasizing the contributions of Africa and black Americans?

Since the population of the United States has become increasingly diverse, most people agree that children should be provided "with a fuller, more balanced truth about their own history and culture than they have had up to now" (Viadero 1990, p. 11). How this should be accomplished is the question. Critics of the Afrocentric approach state that it is not presenting a pluralistic view of our nation, but rather a particularistic view that encourages children "to seek their primary identity in the cultures and homelands of their ancestors" and "neglect the bonds of mutuality that exist among people of different groups" (Ravitch 1990, p. 18). Asanti (cited in Viadero 1990) contends that the current curriculum reinforces racial insensitivity among whites and leaves black children feeling inferior and disconnected from their studies. He further states that African-American children have lost their identification and as a result are not rooted in historical values.

Banks (1989) identifies four approaches to teaching multicultural content. The one most frequently used, since it is the easiest, is the Contributions Approach that adds ethnic heroes to the curriculum. This does not change the mainstream curriculum and students "do not attain a comprehensive view of the role of ethnic and cultural groups in the U.S. society" (p. 4).

The Additive Approach also does not change the basic structure of the curriculum but adds content, concepts, themes, and perspectives usually through the addition of a book, unit, or course. This approach "can be the first phase in a more radical curriculum reform effort designed to restructure the total curriculum" (p. 4) that occurs in the Transformation Approach. "This approach changes the basic assumptions of the curriculum and enables students to view concepts, issues, themes, and problems from several ethnic perspectives and points of view" (p. 4). Baptiste and Baptiste (1977) use slavery as an example, indicating that it has typically been introduced with the Civil War and linked with Afro-Americans. They suggest that

> Historically, numerous groups of people at one time or another have been slaves or enslavers. Ancient history or modern times offer starting points for this concept. The multicultural process is reflected in an exploration of the slavery concept which involves the use of many groups of people as both slaves and enslavers. A more valid conception of the term can be realized when students are given the opportunity to study slavery from a comparative perspective, which uses the underlying economic structure, religious beliefs, cultural values, and geographic environments. (pp. 110–111)

Using all the elements of the Transformation Approach, but adding "components that require students to make decisions and to take actions related to the concept, issue or problem" (Banks 1989, p. 5) is identified as the Social Action Approach. Teachers may use any of these approaches over time and gradually increase the amount of ethnic content in their curriculum.

Teachers will not be able to learn everything about every culture that may be present in their classrooms, but they should try to learn the essentials to know how to interpret their students' behavior (Boardley-Suber, cited in Willis 1992). When teachers encounter an unexpected behavior, they should try to determine whether it is a reflection of the child's culture. They can learn about the children's culture from the students, their families, from school counselors and teachers of English as a Second Language (ESL). Talking to the students can help teachers learn much about their culture. Students can also write histories about their experiences and where they have lived (Willis 1992).

Teaching Strategies

Banks (cited in Willis 1992) relates "To help diverse students achieve, teachers should use 'a variety of teaching styles that are consistent within various cultural and ethnic groups'" (p. 7). Some do not agree that certain groups should be labeled with a particular learning style since not all members of that group may learn best that way. However, there are some generalizations that can be made. African-American students respond better to collaborative hands-on approaches, while Hispanics learn best when they have a personal relationship with the teacher and can interact with peers as do Native Americans (Willis 1992). Thus, it is important for teachers to use a variety of visual, oral, and tactile strategies.

Numerous teaching strategies have been suggested to increase the amount of ethnic content in the curriculum. One that shows great promise is the Anthroliterary Approach. It was originally developed by anthropologists "to study cultures inaccessible to direct observation" and "uses the oral or written literature of a cultural group to gain insight into its way of life" (Goodman & Melcher 1984, p. 200).

"Traditional folklore is a valuable resource for educating children about other people's cultural heritage, since it is a primary source of cultural knowledge. That is, folktales were often used to teach children about their own heritage, values, and customs" (p. 200). The example that is used is the study of the Ashanti people of West Africa through the *Ananseem* "folktales about Kwaku Anasi, a spider who acts like a human being in a human setting" (p. 203).

Teaching students about Native Americans through myths, legends, and folktales is advocated by Musser and Freeman (1989) to eliminate the stereotypes that are often present in the learning experiences in elementary schools. Frequent use of tepees, feathers in hair, and making tomahawks lead children to believe all Native Americans were the same. In addition, they are frequently depicted in books and the media as "savage," "warlike," and "hostile" (Musser & Freeman 1989, p. 5). Using the folklore of Native Americans provides them with an awareness of their beliefs, values, and history.

Recent children's fiction and nonfiction books can add much to the understanding of different cultural groups. Many of these books give a personal view of the lives of the people as they face problems possibly unique to their culture (Garcia, Hadaway, & Beal 1988; Roney 1986).

Whatever the source of the ethnic content, its inclusion in the curriculum is vital to enrich the lives of our children to make them aware of the multicultural nature of our society and its development.

PHYSICALLY AND MENTALLY DISABLED GROUPS

Just as with any other group, when physically and mentally disabled children are mainstreamed into the classroom, teachers must adapt instructional procedures and content so all children can participate.

A prerequisite to concern about instructional procedures and content is a sensitizing to the needs of the disabled. These children may come to the classroom with very low self-esteem in addition to their disabilities. They may not have learned the necessary interpersonal skills to get along with their peers. Most of these children have been faced with negative and hostile attitudes toward them from people they have encountered.

In exploring differences and disabilities in each child in the classroom, understanding and appreciation can be achieved. To understand the disability and its effect on the person is important. Children can relate the unobserved heart murmur as well as the observable confinement to a wheelchair and the effects of these disabilities on each child. Exploring the strengths of each child is equally important.

When children who are not disabled have the opportunity to work and share with disabled children, encounters outside the school setting then become more meaningful, eliminating the stereotypes previously learned.

Disabled children can benefit when participating in the mainstream of society by increasing their self-esteem and by making a contribution.

Children should learn about the contributions of the many famous disabled people such as Thomas Edison, Franklin Roosevelt, Helen Keller, and others. Also, disabled adults in the community can come into the classroom to discuss the problems they face in society and how they have coped with them.

Children can make posters for "Hire the Disabled" week. This gives them an opportunity to relate the contributions that the disabled persons make to society.

Adaptations in instructional strategies and content will vary depending upon the type of disability. Children who are mentally disabled will need instructional materials to match their level of ability. Different instructional approaches will be necessary to meet the learning styles for auditory, visual, and physical learners. Many opportunities for the children to meet with success will be needed. Teachers should capitalize on their strengths, such as artistic or mathematical ability. Topics chosen for study should be of interest to the children. Children with visual and auditory disabilities will require more effective use of materials. Concrete experiences are a necessity for the visually disabled. An opportunity to explore the faces of classmates to know them better and feel more comfortable with them is an example. A map with raised features increases their understanding of the concept of mountain or valley. When pictures are used, a more detailed description of them will be necessary.

Taping information for the auditorily impaired is a necessity. Classmates can do the taping. Children in the classroom can learn a few phrases in manual communication to help the children feel more comfortable. Another possibility is a project whereby a group of children or the class designs a new form of communication, such as picture drawing or knot tying.

Children working in pairs can draw on the strengths of each and compensate for a disability whatever it might be. Also, older children coming into the classroom can provide individual or small group assistance. Sometimes, children prefer help from older children rather than their peers.

GENDER STEREOTYPING

There have been practices within the schools which develop or reinforce gender stereotyping. For example, textbooks and materials have frequently depicted women in the home or as nurses, clerks, or secretaries. Men have been stereotyped as strong and nonemotional, working in leadership roles. Often, women who have made contributions in history have not been included in the text materials.

Many times children are assigned tasks that are gender stereotyped—the boys do jobs that require strength while the girls water the plants. In addition, games or physical education classes may be segregated so that girls and boys are not permitted to participate in the same type of games. Toys or play centers may segregate children when girls are encouraged to go to the doll and homemaking areas while boys investigate the math and science centers. Forming separate lines for leaving and entering the classroom reinforces segregation.

Additional gender stereotypes may occur in the school faculty and administration. Women may stay in the classroom and not take on the administrative role, while men may be pressured to be administrators.

Some positive steps that can be taken include the following:

1. Select textbooks and materials that depict males and females in traditional and nontraditional roles.
2. Provide career education that presents the full range of options available to males and females.
3. Study the contributions of men and women equally, both in historical and contemporary times.
4. Provide role playing situations where both sexes can explore all types of feelings and emotions.
5. Have children analyze advertising and TV programs for gender stereotyping.

LIVING IN POVERTY AND HOMELESSNESS

Another factor that needs to be considered in multicultural education is that some children come from lower socioeconomic cultural backgrounds. These children are often labeled as educationally disadvantaged. One in four children lives in poverty (Kennedy, Jung, & Orland, cited in Cushner & Trifonovich 1989) and an estimated half million are homeless (Linehan 1992). How do these conditions affect their schooling? How can teachers make social studies meaningful for these children?

There are several conditions that most of these children experience that will adversely affect their school life. Frequent moves cause these children to have no sense of roots, personal space, or possessions (Linehan 1992). Many come from minority groups. It is estimated that 46.2 percent of black children and 38.7 percent of Hispanic children live in poverty, while 16.1 percent come from white families. Another factor is the number of children who come from non-English-speaking homes (Pallas, Natriello, & McDill 1989).

Children who are homeless or live in poverty often see life as temporary, are restless, leave projects half finished, cling to any possessions, are easily frustrated, and have poor/short attention spans (Linehan 1992). In addition to constant moving, these children change schools frequently, which further complicates their lives because they see no continuity or structure to it. They have difficulty making friends and are fearful that if they do make friends, they will soon leave the school.

Many of these children live in overcrowded living conditions, whether in a homeless shelter or an apartment with extended family members. Most do not have space or privacy to do their homework, and also may be tired due to lack of sleep. They may have limited parental attention and excessive inappropriate stimuli such as shouting, crying, and loud radio or TV playing. The children's parents often lack formal education and social know-how, are unemployed or in low-paying unskilled jobs, and move frequently; these same conditions often are perpetuated in their children. Discipline in the home is frequently of a physical nature—authoritative, inconsistent, and immediate—to alleviate a present situation as soon as possible. Patriarchal authority reigns in the home with the frequent exception of the black family, which may be dominated by the mother.

Children are given responsibilities early—for example, the care of younger children or particular household chores. This results in less concern for the self and more for the group. Early independence gives way to peer domination, which replaces the family as a socializing agent and source of values (Passow, Goldberg, Tannenbaum 1967). Frequent illness and lack of proper food, health, and dental care decrease the learning efficiency of the children.

Of equal and possibly greater importance are some of the positives of the culture of the educationally disadvantaged. These might include an interest in vocational education; parents' and children's respect for education in spite of their dislike for school, where they sense a resentment toward them; hidden verbal talent; freedom from self-blame and parental overprotection; lack of sibling rivalry; and informality, humor, and enjoyment of music, games, and sports. These positives may provide a basis upon which teachers can build a more adequate educational program.

Initially, experiences offered these children should be vital and motivational. They should build upon the children's present backgrounds. First, the children should be reintroduced to their immediate environment and helped to understand it. Then, their horizons should be expanded to a wider environment. Have the children ever been on a bus, gone to the supermarket, visited a museum, baked cookies, had someone really listen while they talked, or experienced approval upon completion of a task?

Some claim that enriching experiences are not enough. They claim that the educationally disadvantaged do not have enough time to participate in the same experiences as privileged children. Therefore, selection and exclusion of experiences is necessary to provide those activities which will produce a faster-than-normal rate of progress. Their discussion primarily is aimed at the preschool program; however, it certainly should be considered when planning programs at any level (Means & Knapp 1991).

Educational deprivation is synonymous with language deprivation. It is apparent that the educationally disadvantaged child has mastered a language "that is adequate for maintaining social relationships and for meeting his social and material needs, but he does not learn how to use language for obtaining and transmitting information, for monitoring his own behavior, and for carrying on verbal reasoning" (Bereiter & Engelmann n.d., p. 42). The disadvantaged child cannot use language to "explain, to describe, to instruct, to inquire, to hypothesize, to analyze, to compare, to deduce, and to test" (p. 31). If such language deprivation has not been corrected by the time the child enters the formal school, it certainly should affect the approach used for teaching social studies. The focus should be on complex meaningful problems that extend basic skills instruction in the context of more global problems, and make connections with students' out-of-school experience and culture (Means & Knapp 1991).

Another condition that further makes life and school difficult for some children is the lack of enriching experiences and even basic resources. Most are uncomfortable since they do not have clothes that are like the other children's since often they receive hand-me-downs. Many of these children do not receive proper nutrition nor necessary health and dental care. Families are frequently unable to provide learning experiences, such as trips to museums, books to read and the time to read to their children, or provide opportunities to participate in activities such as sports, dance, art, or music instruction.

As a result of these conditions, children often come to school with underdeveloped language skills, poor self-concepts, a lack of social skills, and possessing a cultural background that differs from most of the children in their classroom. Teachers need to make some adjustments in their classrooms and the content of social studies to accommodate these children.

One of the first things that teachers need to do is to investigate their own feelings and beliefs about the situations that these children come from. As a teacher, can you accept them as you would any other child in your classroom even if they may be unclean, tired, frequently not interested in learning, and often without background experiences that prepare them to understand social studies concepts and motivate them to learn about historical events and others' cultures? If so—and it is crucial that you do accept them and appreciate their potential as any other child—then it is important to make adaptations in your teaching strategies, and not necessarily the content, but how you link the content to the lives of these children. It is important for children to realize how whatever is studied is connected to them.

Role of the Child in the Classroom

Teachers need to explain the role expected of the children in the learning situation. This explanation frequently has not been reinforced by the home environment. The children first must be motivated to learn. By showing they expect the children to be successful, teachers assist them in building good self-concepts. As the children gain confidence, they become less dependent on teachers. As they become involved in learning activities, their interest increases. Hopefully, they will then understand their role as learners.

In the beginning, the environment should be more structured in order that the children may learn the advantages of organized behavior. Freedom of decision and choice can be permitted as the children learn self-discipline.

Classroom Conditions

More than any other single factor, the importance of providing an interesting and stimulating classroom cannot be overemphasized. Children need to feel that the classroom is a place where they are safe, where they will learn and be respected as individuals, not rejected because they have had different experiences. Examples of some items that should be included in the environment are small animals, such as rabbits, snakes, and birds, or a plant. Such items present the children with an opportunity to learn to care and be responsible for living things, which are often not a part of their world. Equally important is the experience of sharing the responsibility for the upkeep of the classroom. Children need to know that a certain space belongs to them, whether a desk or a cubby, something that others do not have permission to invade. Pictures of people and places within the community should be used to help children to identify school with the outside world. Books, books, and more books are needed at varying levels of difficulty and should contain stories of experiences relating to and expanding upon the child's experiences. Vast amounts of concrete materials and visual aids are necessary. These classroom conditions are important for all children, but vital for the educationally disadvantaged.

Role of the Teacher

The presence of teachers who can be trusted is crucial to the success of these children in school. Teachers must understand and be sincerely interested in the children. They must be cognizant of the most effective teaching techniques for these children. Also, they must be willing to accept them as they are and help them to learn as much as possible.

Teachers with middle-class backgrounds will need to learn about the cultures of these children and how to work cooperatively with the parents to achieve the best results. The teachers are an important link between the home and the school. They should never discredit the values, beliefs, and customs of these children, yet should offer them an awareness of another way of life. Many homeless children do not want their classmates to know they are living in a shelter. Their privacy should be respected. Parents are interested in the practical value of schooling for their children, and they should be made to feel welcome and involved in school activities. However, some homeless and parents who live in poverty feel they are not welcome at school or don't have the clothes, or aren't articulate enough to talk with the teachers, and will not come. Therefore, "new strategies should be developed to reintegrate the school and the families and communities in which students live" (Comer, cited in Pallas et al. 1989, n.p.). Some of these parents cannot read or help their children with their homework and are ashamed to ask for help. Homework, if assigned, should be something the students can do and should reinforce class work.

A tremendous responsibility is placed on the teacher, since motivation for learning is often lacking. Generally, such motivation can be created by a responsive teacher using carefully selected materials, methods, and topics. However, teachers and schools "must become more aware of and involved in the family and community contexts of their students, both to understand the problems these contexts present for the education of students and to learn to draw on the strengths of families and communities to enhance the education of students" (Pallas et al. 1989, p. 21).

Selection of Content

There are certain factors inherent in the social studies that are more problematic than in other subject areas. Content in social studies requires more reading than almost any other subject. Most topics are removed from realities of life chronologically and spatially. And many of the values, attitudes, and behaviors are contrary to those of the homeless and economically disadvantaged children as well as cultural and ethnic groups. Also, the materials available portray experiences that are often remote from the lives of the children. An awareness of these factors will permit teachers to compensate for them. Considering the learning experiences as well as the problems inherent in the social studies, what should be included in the content of the social studies program?

The goal of such a program for educationally disadvantaged children is to learn the same basic concepts of social studies as any elementary schoolchild; however, adaptation will be necessary to relate the content to their everyday lives. The following model serves as a basis for planning programs.

The model does not provide an exhaustive list of the content to be included in the social studies, nor are the grade lines intended to be restrictive. It attempts to show a pattern of relationships between the concerns of the immediate environment and the removed environment. This model stresses the necessity of beginning with the here and now and expanding to that which is distant and past.

Immediate Environment   *Removed Environment*

Kindergarten–Grade 1

Immediate Environment	Removed Environment
Home, family, and school—Discussion centers on the type of family relationships that occur in the environment of the child. An example might be the presence of additional adults in the home, such as aunts, uncles, grandmothers, or the absence of a father. No attempt should be made to place emphasis on	Select a culture that has a similar family relationship—for example, have Mexican-Americans study about Mexico.

the typical mother-father-child relationship. Discussing children without homes should be done with great care. To develop the self-concept, stress should be placed on individuals and their roles.

Local community—Stress available libraries, museums, parks, recreation areas, and community services.

Important people—Discuss leaders in the community and nation but, most important, select leaders from the children's culture, such as Martin Luther King, Jr., for African-American children.

Grade 2

Democratic processes—Discuss the problems of minority groups, using those apparent within the classroom, for example, the failure to choose a favorite game of a small group or the presence of more girls than boys in the classroom.

Group minority problems in national relationship.

National heritage—Stress contributions from their particular cultures, such as music, art, science, politics, and so on.

Symbols such as a flag, holidays, freedom.

Economic concepts—Work in the family, neighborhood, school.

Other areas of the nation with similar problems.

Study problems of lack of money, resources, unemployment.

Environmental problems—Pollution of the neighborhood playground, streams, and air.

Worldwide pollution problems.

Grade 3

Historical—Choose a local memorial, monument, or early settlement of the area.

Early pioneers, Native Americans, people who came from lands specific to the group's ancestry.

Relationship of urban and rural areas—Children in rural areas learn about their contributions to cities in terms of food, labor, and purchases; children in the city learn of their contributions to the country.

Cities or rural areas beyond local environment.

Communication—Within the classroom use methods beyond spoken language, for example, facial expressions, actions.

Systems including different languages relating to their cultural background.

Transportation—Stress modes used in their community and the problems presented.

Link to previous study of cities and their available modes of transportation.

Grade 4

Geographic concepts of locale—Study climate, rainfall, and terrain.

Similar geographic conditions in other areas of the world. Contrasting geographic conditions existing in close proximity to the local environment and in other parts of the world.

Social, economic, and political problems of the community. How values affect decisions that are made.

National and world problems of a similar nature.

Grade 5

Governmental processes—Begin with class organization, school, and community.

State and national government and relation to early development and birth of the nation. Contrasting governments.

Local racial or nationality problems.

Discuss the Civil War, Spanish-Cuban-American War, etc., to help the children understand the possible origins of the problems.

Grade 6

Family background of children in classroom. Neighboring community's ancestral background. Community projects—Neighborhood improvement, visiting home for elderly, vocational opportunities.

Nations of children's ancestors. United Nations.

Special Instructional Considerations

Adaptation of the content is important, but it is not sufficient to allow these learners to receive maximum benefit from the instruction. Other necessary considerations involve organizational patterns, teaching methods, activities, and materials.

Organizational Patterns

The organization of the class affects subject areas other than the social studies, and it is an important consideration. Team teaching has been used successfully with minority, less advantaged, and underachieving children. A faculty team comprised of several teachers provides more individualized instruction, increased motivation for learning, different teaching styles, and flexibility in scheduling (Pavan 1992). Children need the opportunity provided by the team to identify with many adults. Discipline is maintained more readily and neophyte teachers are more effectively introduced to working with children in a team-teaching situation.

Organization based on nongraded continuous progress is beneficial because it removes the failure complex and emphasizes individualization of instruction. Children are grouped by ages; they begin working at their respective levels and move ahead as rapidly as possible (Pavan 1992). Interest grouping across class or grade lines, specifically in social studies, provides increased motivation because children are encouraged to select their own group based on their interest in a topic. Cooperative learning groups, organized according to specific skills or friendship groups, add to both the interest and the flexibility of the program. Children can learn to work more effectively with others and move freely from group to group. Assign "buddies" to new children to help them adjust to school (Linehan 1992).

Teaching Methods

This chapter previously stated that educationally disadvantaged children have difficulty with abstract reasoning and need more concrete experiences to facilitate learning. Teachers must adapt teaching methods to avoid pursuing abstractions without providing concrete examples. However, it is important for teachers to move from the concrete to the abstract. "Classroom studies document the fact that disadvantaged students receive less instruction in higher-order skills than do their more advantaged peers" (Oakes, cited in Means & Knapp 1991, p. 283). As a result, "disadvantaged students receive less exposure to problem-solving tasks in which there is more than one possible answer and in which they have to structure problems for themselves" (Anyon, cited in Means & Knapp 1991, p. 283). However, the teachers should use open-ended questioning to motivate thinking and remove the block of the "one right answer" syndrome. Repetitive use of this method is necessary because first experiences may be discouraging. An example of the type of open-ended inquiry that should be used with the children to help them understand their problems is portrayed in the following dialogue. There has been an argument between two children in the group. The teacher pursues the causes of the argument with the children:

T: What was the fight about?
P: About Tanya and him shooting each other.

T: Why do you suppose he pulled the chair out from under Tanya?
P: Because Tanya was hitting him.
T: Why was she hitting him?
P: Because he was bothering her. She was bothering me.
T: Why was she bothering you?
P: Because I didn't let her use my Footsie [a toy attached to the foot for jumping].
T: So what seems to be the trouble between the two of them? What was the problem?
P: That Michael . . .
T: What really was the problem?
P: He could of told on her.
T: Now stop and think about it. What really was the trouble? What do you think the real problem was?
P: That I didn't let her use my Footsie.
T: In other words, she wanted something that you had. So what really was the problem then? What do you think it was? Yes, he wouldn't share with her. Can you think of what might have been a different way to behave?
P: Everything would have been all right—if he hadn't pulled the chair from under her.
T: You think that if they had shared, everything would have been all right. Tanya and Michael, will you show us how it would have been if you had shared? Show us what would have happened if you could have shared.

[The children role play the sharing process.]

T: All right, what makes the difference here?
P: He shared with her so no fight would start.
T: Why do you suppose people behave the way they do? Who do you suppose . . .
P: Because they don't want to get in trouble.
T: Stop and think a moment, Tanya, why is it that people don't want to share? Or why is it that they behave the way they do?
P: Because they don't like the other people. Sometimes they are spoiled.
T: What do you mean by spoiled?
P: They always want their way.
T: Anyone else?
P: They aren't bothering other people. But Tanya asked Michael for a Footsie and then they ask someone else and they say no. Like if they ask someone and they say yes, they are a nice guy.

The main difficulty for the children in this discussion was the ability to concentrate for any length of time and to stick to the line of questioning.

However, they have sophisticated insight into their own and others' behavior. The repeated use of this same approach will lead to improved concentration on the part of the children, and they will be better able to follow the questioning. In this activity, the children were participating in inquiry; they identified a problem (group behavior problem), tested out their ideas and arrived at some generalizations (they think most want people to mind their own business). By beginning the inquiry process with a problem that is a part of their daily experiences, the teacher is able to motivate more active participation on the part of the children in the class. Everyone has had the experience of being in an argument and can contribute to the discussion. This activity then leads to the presentation of a problem that is abstract or out of the immediate environment, such as a community problem: Why can't people agree on a location for the new school? Why don't we have a playground in our neighborhood? Why is there pollution in our city or local community?

It should be remembered that in addition to enabling children to acquire inquiry skills and higher-order thinking skills, this activity is contributing to the alleviation of aforementioned factors that define the educationally disadvantaged. The children are improving verbal skills and their own self-images through successful participation, and are learning the social skills of give and take in a discussion.

Also to be recognized is the fact that the teacher is modeling a thinking process that the children should begin to develop through repeated exposure. As a result, the children begin to ask their own questions.

It is important to relate the activities of school to the children's outside world. Therefore, current affairs and controversial issues must be a part of the instruction. Children soon realize that what they are learning aids them in solving their daily problems and provides an understanding of the problems of others. They soon realize that history is happening right now and that there is a relationship between the past and current events.

A variety of approaches to solving the same problem should be used. As in the problem identified in the previous dialogue, at another time, the teacher might divide the children into small groups and have them discuss how to solve the problem. When the small groups report back their solutions, the children can see that there may be several ways to solve the problem with the same end result. By giving children open-ended questions to which there is no single right answer, they can invent strategies to solve the problems (Means & Knapp 1991). An example might be: How can we encourage the people in our neighborhood to keep it clean? or How can we keep the drug dealers away from our school and neighborhood?

Another teaching strategy that is suggested is the use of dialogue as the central medium rather than transmission (Means & Knapp 1991). In transmission, the teacher gives the information to the children; in dialogue, both children and teacher influence the nature of the exchange. Both contribute and learn from one another.

Activities

Role playing is regarded as a most effective technique to use with the educationally disadvantaged (Shaftel & Shaftel 1968). It permits children to work out a situation physically, or be active participants in an incident.

An increasing number of experiences should be provided for the use of oral language. Verbalization in discussions, role playing, reporting, and dramatizations are all vital methods to be used. Talking first in small groups will increase the child's confidence in meeting a larger group situation. By reading information and stories to the children, the teacher facilitates learning for the disadvantaged reader and increases listening skills. However, care should be exercised in making certain children understand the vocabulary and concepts of what is being read. Concrete materials should be used to illustrate the reading.

It is important to get the children out into the community to become acquainted with the conditions and problems that exist. For example, the students could do a local traffic survey, inspect housing conditions, make a photo scrapbook of the community, interview local public officials and community members about community problems, or tackle some local clean-up problem, or help some elderly members of the community.

Simulations, or simulation games, as they are frequently called, present a possible opportunity for more active involvement in learning. A simulation, through authentic materials—whether videos, tapes, graphic prints, or printed material—is intended to recreate a situation as close as possible to real life. The players take roles of the individuals in the simulation. A problem with several alternatives (with no one correct alternative) is presented for the players to solve through the simulation. Teachers can produce their own simulation games inexpensively and thus build them around the problem areas that are most relevant to their particular classrooms. Games and simulations are purported to be motivating and competitive and should help in the development of decision-making skills.

Situations in which children may express their feelings and emotions must be provided. Honest appraisal of feelings such as hate, love, trust, and distrust should be included. These experiences help children understand themselves and others. Experiences in which each child meets with repeated success are vital to the educationally disadvantaged. Praise and encouragement should be built-in factors of every experience.

SUMMARY

The aim of multicultural education is to provide an environment in which children of either sex and of any racial, economic, ethnic, or disabled group can grow intellectually, develop good self-concepts, and participate in meaningful human relationships. Teachers will need to assess materials, teaching strategies, physical environments, and curriculum to determine that particular mix which will be needed by the children in each classroom.

SELECTED REFERENCES

Banks, J. A. (1989). Education for survival in a multicultural world. *Social Studies and the Young Learner, 1*(4), 3–5.

Baptiste, H. R., & Baptiste, M. (1977). Developing multicultural learning activities. In C. A. Grant, *Multicultural education commitments, issues and applications* (pp. 110–111). Washington, DC: Association for Supervision & Curriculum Development.

Bereiter, C., & Engelmann, S. (1963). *Teaching disadvantaged children in the preschool*. Englewood Cliffs, NJ: Prentice-Hall.

Bullard, S. (1992). Sorting through the multicultural rhetoric. *Educational Leadership, 49*(4), 4–7.

Conrad, B. D. (1988). Cooperative learning and prejudice reduction. *Social Education, 52*(4), 283–286.

Cortes, C. E., & Fleming, D. B. (1986). Changing global perspectives in textbooks. *Social Education, 50*(5), 376–378.

Cushner, K., & Trifonovich, G. (1989). Understanding misunderstanding: Barriers to dealing with diversity. *Social Education, 53*(5), 318–322.

Fillmore, L. W. (1993). Educating citizens for a multicultural 21st century. *Multicultural Education, 1*(1), 10–12, 37.

Freedman, P. I. (1984, September/October). Multiethnic/multicultural education: Establishing the foundations. *The Social Studies, 75*, 200–203.

Garcia, J., Hadaway, N. L., & Beal, G. (1988, November/December). Cultural pluralism in recent nonfiction tradebooks for children. *The Social Studies, 79*, 252–255.

Goodman, J., & Melcher, K. (1984, December). Culture at a distance: An anthroliterary approach to cross-cultural education. *Journal of Reading, 28*, 200–207.

Grant, C. A. (Ed.). (1977). *Multicultural education: Commitments, issues and applications*. Washington, DC: Association for Supervision & Curriculum Development.

Hodgkinson, H. (1993). American education: The good, the bad, and the task. *Phi Delta Kappan, 74*(8), 619–623.

Lampe, P. E. (1988, May/June). The problematic nature of interracial and interethnic communication. *The Social Studies, 79*, 116–120.

Linehan, M. F. (1992). Children who are homeless: Educational strategies for school personnel. *Phi Delta Kappan, 74*(1), 61–66.

Martin, D. S. (1985). Ethnocentrism revisited: Another look at a persistent problem. *Social Education, 49*(6), 604–606.

Means, B., & Knapp, M. S. (1991). Cognitive approaches to teaching advanced skills to educationally disadvantaged students. *Phi Delta Kappan, 73*(4), 282–289.

Musser, L. S., & Freeman, E. B. (1989). Teach young students about Native Americans. *The Social Studies, 80*, 5–9.

Pallas, A. M., Natriello, G., & McDill, E. L. (1989, June/July). The changing nature of the disadvantaged population: Current dimensions and future trends. *Educational Researcher*, pp. 16–22.

Passow, H., Goldberg, M., & Tannenbaum, A. J. (1967). *Education of the disadvantaged*. New York: Holt, Rinehart, & Winston.

Pasternak, M. G. (1977). *Helping kids learn multicultural concepts*. Nashville, TN: Nashville Consortium Teachers Corps.

Pavan, B. N. (1992). The benefits of nongraded schools. *Educational Leadership, 50*(2), 22–25.

Ravitch, D. (1990). Diversity and democracy. *American Educator, 14*(1), 16–20, 46–48.

Riessman, F. (1963, April). The culturally deprived: A new view. *School Life, 45,* 113.

Roney, R. C. (1986). Multiethnicity in children's fiction. *Social Education, 50*(6), 464–466, 468, 470.

Shaftel, F. R., & Shaftel, G. (1968). *Role playing for social values: Decision making in the social studies.* Englewood Cliffs, NJ: Prentice-Hall.

Viadero, D. (1990, November 28). Battle over multicultural education rages with new intensity. *Education Week,* pp. 1–11, 13.

Walsh, D. (1988). Critical thinking to reduce prejudice. *Social Education, 52*(4), 280–282.

Willis, S. (1992, September). Multicultural teaching: Meeting the challenges that arise in practice. *ASCD Curriculum Update,* pp. 1–8.

LEARNING ACTIVITY

Think about your experiences with cultural, ethnic, racial, disabled, and socioeconomic groups. What types of experiences have you had? Have you ever experienced prejudice? Have you ever been a minority in a situation? Have you interacted with groups from a different cultural, racial, or ethnic background than your own? How did you react? What is your experience with disabled groups? Have you ever experienced poverty or interacted with people who came from different socioeconomic backgrounds? Have you ever met any homeless children? Have you ever been in classrooms where you observed discrimination against a religious, ethnic, racial, or socioeconomic group? Write in your journal your thoughts about these experiences. Discuss some experiences you think you need and some questions you may have about working in classrooms with great diversity. If you feel comfortable, share your thoughts with your classmates. Find out how they are feeling and what readings or experiences you might plan together.

CHAPTER 6

SELECTED CONTENT FOR EMPHASIS: CURRENT ISSUES, GLOBAL, LAW RELATED, AND ECONOMIC EDUCATION

CURRENT EVENTS, whether they happen in their community, their state, or their nation may have an impact on children's lives. Children often do not have enough information to understand why these events have occurred, how they will affect their lives, and what if anything they can and should do about them. Teaching children about these events prepares them to participate in their world, not just exist. It helps them to learn how to control events in their lives, not let events control them.

As events occur in communities, the nation, and the world, it becomes necessary to emphasize certain content in social studies. Our children need information and skills to understand and cope with these issues facing them. The fall of Communism in Russia and the Eastern European countries; the ethnic and racial strife in countries around the world; hunger and wars depriving people of safe and comfortable lives; pollution robbing people of a healthy environment; and the depletion of natural resources threatening future existence—all force us as teachers to help children identify, understand, and deal with these problems. As a nation, the United States can never exist in isolation. The political, economic, cultural, and social relationships in the world make us an integral part of that world and necessitate that we learn how to live and participate in that world. Developing a global perspective that recognizes that we are a human family—and, if the problems of the world are to be solved, they must be solved with that family cooperating—is an important concept for children to grasp.

Concern that children be law-abiding citizens suggests that it is important for them to understand laws, our legal system, and how they fit into it. The research indicates that law-related education programs have become a part of social studies curricula more frequently than other content projects (Hahn 1985). The rise of crime and violence in our nation provides another impetus. If law related education programs can serve as a preventive measure against juvenile delinquency (Johnson 1984), then there is no question but that it should be included.

Economic news that reports the closing of businesses, the loss of jobs, and sometimes even cuts in school programs is not easy for children to understand. Why doesn't my mother or father have a job when the other kids' parents do? Why do things I want cost so much? Why can't I have the same things as my friends have? Why is our country in debt? Why do people buy products from other countries? These and other economic questions are asked by children every day. How can they understand the answers if they do not have knowledge of our economic system and how it works?

These arguments as well as other factors justify the need to emphasize the teaching of current events, global education, law-related education, and economic education. The major argument is to enlighten children and give them a better opportunity to become participating citizens in our democratic society.

CURRENT ISSUES

Numerous purposes can be listed for teaching elementary school children about the daily events that happen around them; however, none is so pressing as the need for helping children become knowledgeable citizens—interested and active participants in the affairs of their world. Perpetuation of our democratic way of living requires the attainment of this goal.

Another vital purpose involves the development of children's awareness concerning the social and political problems that exist in our country. The discrimination against racial and minority groups that causes serious difficulties within many cities and towns, the extreme poverty that deprives people of a decent living, the differences of opinion in our political parties concerning important issues, and the environmental concerns are only examples of the many problems that we face. The early attitudes that children develop about these problems and their ability to attempt to solve them are important outcomes of instruction in this area.

Our rapidly changing world affects each child's life. Failure to understand the reasons for and the effects of change is frustrating. Through the study of current issues, hopefully the child becomes aware of, understands, and can make informed opinions and decisions about changes in the world.

Not all change is positive. Children need to learn how to think about or reflect on changes to determine whether they are positive or not. For example, is the military coup of a country's government best for the people or does the building of a freeway through a heavily populated residential area cause more upheaval compared to the benefits of rerouting traffic?

Events that occur in other parts of the world often affect our nation. When Iraq invaded Kuwait, the United States along with United Nations forces became involved in the Persian Gulf War to stop the aggression. Many children were affected when relatives were sent to the Gulf in the armed forces. It is difficult for children to understand the complicated relationships that create these situations. Why does the United States go to war to help another nation?

Also important for children to understand is the power wielded by their own and other nations. Where does that power come from and how do we use it? How will the actions of their nation affect their futures?

Research and discussion of the events that happen in their daily lives permit children to relate school to the outside world. They realize that what they learn in school aids them in solving their own daily problems and provides them with an understanding of the problems of others. Children soon begin to see that history is also what is happening right now and that there is a relationship between past history and current events.

The goal of studying current issues is to help children acquire the habit of reading newspapers, listening to news reports, and discussing these events with others. Hopefully this habit will be retained throughout adult life to help them make the decisions citizens are required to make. The children will find it difficult to understand completely many of the items they hear or read about, e.g., inflation, abortion, ethnic cleansing, and it is important to discuss and clarify these items. The children can also increase their skills in critical reading by looking at all sides of an issue and evaluating the sources of information. Oral language through reporting and discussion can be developed. Recognizing propaganda techniques, recognizing important news events, and summarizing news reports can also be improved.

Goals/Anticipated Outcomes

A major goal/outcome for teaching current issues is to develop knowledgeable active citizens of the community, nation, and world. Citizens who are knowledgeable of what is happening around them and are willing to participate in whatever action needs to be taken.

Another important goal/outcome is to develop an awareness of the tremendous social, economic, political, and environmental problems of our nation and world. To develop a caring and concerned attitude toward these problems is vital.

Change will occur and a goal/outcome for children is to understand the nature of change and how some changes are positive while others may be negative.

When studying current issues, a goal/outcome should be to develop an awareness of the relationship between school learning and the events in the children's daily lives.

An additional goal/outcome will be the children's increased proficiency in decision making and problem solving by using skills of critical reading, thinking, evaluating, summarizing, oral language, and vocabulary.

When to Start

As soon as children come to school, they should be introduced to current issues within their understanding. As an introduction, teachers can start with reports of events in the children's lives. The first idea to be learned is that events make news. The next step is to learn what news is important. Many teachers start the day with the development of a class newspaper containing items about the children's lives. After the children understand what a newspaper should contain, items are included from other rooms in the school, the community, the nation, and the world. Here is an example of what such a newspaper might contain:

Today is October 24, 19__. The weather is warm and sunny.
Sharon Gray's house burned last night. It is located at 24 Locust Street.
Shadyside School will hold an Ice Cream Social. It will be Wednesday at 8:00 in the evening.
The Riverside Community Park will build a swimming pool. Boys and girls can learn to swim.
Learner Creek is polluted. Plans are being made to help clean it.
National elections will be held next month. Our parents will elect a president of the United States.

A variation of this activity might be for small groups of children to prepare their own newspaper or draw pictures of current events and discuss them with the class; or teachers can clip pictures from newspapers and magazines and discuss them with the children, who can then develop captions that demonstrate their understanding of the events in the pictures.

To provide children with a thorough understanding of important events occurring locally, nationally, or worldwide, the teacher should plan problem-solving situations or units of study. Examples of such events might be: a natural catastrophe such as a flood, tornado, or hurricane; political campaigns; space events; wars and confrontations; and events that relate to past or current topics of study.

An example of a problem-solving situation from a natural catastrophe might be: How do local, state, and national governments help people during and after a flood? Another problem might surface during a political campaign: How can you determine the true facts when the candidates give conflicting information?

Continuation throughout the elementary school grades of these and other activities concerning current events will foster favorable attitudes toward and natural concern about world affairs. Enthusiasm and interest displayed by the teacher are vital factors in the success of these activities. The more teachers are personally involved in the current issues, the more likely they will engage children in them (Passe 1988).

Learning Experiences

Some suggestions for learning experiences are:

1. Bulletin Boards—A bulletin board should be reserved for displaying news items or pictures relating to current issues. An important point to remember is the necessity for the frequent change of its contents. Captions on the board such as "How Will Today's News Affect You?" or "Where Are Things Happening?" help stimulate interest.

Division of the board into areas for local, state, national, and international items helps children differentiate the news events. Have children place their news item in the proper category. The use of a world map on the board enables children to locate the area of the news event and helps them develop map skills. A thread of yarn attached to the location of the event and leading to the written report helps the children associate the place with the event. Responsibility for the bulletin board can be assigned to committees of children or can be a joint obligation of the teacher and the children.

2. News Reporting—A variety of organizational patterns can be used to assign children the responsibility of reporting the news. For example, one child might be assigned the responsibility for the news of one day or one week, or committees of children could be assigned the responsibility for a certain period of time. Tape recordings of these reports provide some variety. Children could be cub reporters and assigned a "beat," e.g., the mayor. They keep track of the mayor for a period of time and categorize the mayor's actions on a data retrieval chart in order to draw some conclusions about the mayor.

The establishment of a mock radio or TV station within the classroom supplies greater reality for the news-reporting situation. Special broadcasts or programs can be planned when outstanding events take place. Some classrooms may wish to conduct a daily morning news broadcast with reporters assigned specific areas of the news. Intermediate grade children may provide the news program for the entire school over the public address system. Included in these programs may be school news of interest to all.

Items for children to remember when reporting the news should include:

- Do I understand what is happening in the news event?
- Can I discuss it with the other children?
- Do I know enough about it to answer most of the questions the children might ask?
- Are there any words that I'll need help in pronouncing?
- Is the event of interest to most children, or will it add knowledge to a topic we are studying?

3. Class Newspaper—The organization of the class into a newspaper staff to publish and distribute a school newspaper provides realistic experience for news reporting. Reporters can be assigned to secure news of the different classes, the school office, and special events. Additional reporters can use

outside sources to obtain significant local and national news. Many language skills, as well as social skills, are developed by interviewing people and writing news reports.

The entire school can be organized to prepare the newspaper if an individual class doesn't want to take on the total responsibility. Generally, one of the intermediate grades handles the organization of the paper, and reporters are selected from the other classes.

A field trip to a local newspaper provides background information and increased interest in newspaper publication. If a field trip is not possible, a resource person from the newspaper could visit the classroom.

4. Role Playing, Discussion, and Debates—Role playing can be used to advantage with news events. It requires that children have a thorough understanding of the event before they attempt to act out the situation for others. They do not have specific lines to learn but rather discuss it in their own words. Dramatizing a summit meeting or the speech of a famous person helps children realize what the event was like. In a dramatization, it is necessary to write out a script with different characters portrayed.

Discussions can be organized in many ways. The whole class might research a specific topic and attempt to present different points of view, or a news program might be watched on TV—either at school or at home—and discussed. When differences of opinion occur within the group, a debate provides a valuable experience. Both sides can present their views and the children in the class can decide which side presents the best argument. Before the debate takes place, ground rules must be established for time limits on speaking, the use of notes, and the manner of answering the opposition.

5. Reading Newspapers—The presence of copies of a daily newspaper in the classroom or library provides excellent stimulation for developing the habit of reading newspapers. It is also advisable to secure several popular news magazines to complete the resources. Even primary grade children can benefit from the pictures presented.

Mere reading of news materials without learning to recognize biased presentations and propaganda techniques is useless. Providing children with news materials that relate differing points of view helps them to understand how the same news events can be reported quite differently, depending on the viewpoint of the reporter. Propaganda techniques such as the use of emotionalized words; vague, general statements; name calling; or the bandwagon, testimonial, or plain-folks treatments are examples that elementary school children can recognize.

Emotionalized words are those that stir very strong feelings within us whenever we read them. "Loved ones," "mother," "home," "our rights," and "our duties" are examples of words used to blind us with emotion, and thus distract us from the main point of the article. An example of their use might be "Vote for Joe Doakes, he'll protect your home and loved ones." We are so concerned about our home and loved ones that we are willing to vote for Joe Doakes without first determining if he has the proper qualifications. Newspapers and magazines also use emotionalized words to excite people about reading certain articles. We frequently see headlines such as "Mother Loses Home," "Rights Are Blocked," or "Children Beaten."

Children often use the *bandwagon technique* to secure permission for something they wish to do—it is the "everyone's-doing-it, why-can't-I," trick. It is the idea of following the crowd or doing it because others are to attain a goal.

The *testimonial* is frequently used in advertising. If a famous personality uses a product, then the product must be good for everyone. In politics, too, a candidate supported by a person who is well known gains additional support from the public.

The *plain-folks technique* is used by politicians. They appear to dress, act, and think like the people from whom they are seeking votes. An example of this is the politician who visits the farm, milks the cows, pitches hay, or drives the tractor to convince the people that he is really one of them. Actually, he may never have done these things before.

Name calling is used by various individuals and groups to label someone favorably or unfavorably. Many people automatically stop listening to or reading about someone who has been labeled a name that is unsavory to them. Names such as "communist," "liar," and "traitor" influence people against the individual so labeled. "Good guy," "patriot," and "democrat" are names that may influence a person favorably.

Vague, general statements about a topic confuse individuals. Failure to include any proof about a claim makes it difficult to determine its accuracy. "Many politicians are crooked" is an example of a vague, general statement.

Children should be able to identify and give examples of the different propaganda techniques, and they should relate this understanding to the material they encounter in newspapers, magazines, on television, and in person. Here are some sample statements:

- *Plain folks.* Sam Arthur, a man of the people, one who came from humble beginnings, is the man for you.
- *Name calling.* Joe Doakes is a communist and should not be permitted to run for office.
- *Testimonial.* Mr. President endorses candidate John Smith for governor. You'll want to vote for him.
- *Emotionalized words.* She is a protector of our rights.
- *Bandwagon.* Millions of people use Granny's Glue and so should you.
- *Vague, general statement.* Everyone agrees that new sidewalks are needed in Jonesville.

Examples of activities that provide children with the opportunity to recognize these propaganda techniques follow:

Have children read newspapers, magazines, and ads to find examples.
Listen to some popular newscaster on radio or TV as he or she makes statements such as those listed above.

Suggest that children listen to TV at home and bring to class examples of these statements.

As the children become more sophisticated, they can identify how people use voice inflections and facial expressions to convey the same messages. They may listen and/or watch candidates during political campaigns.

Develop campaign slogans or develop advertisements for products. As children develop slogans for political candidates or ads for their favorite products they can use examples of these techniques.

Controversial Issues: Social, Economic, Political, and Environmental

For a variety of reasons, many teachers step lightly when controversial issues arise in the news or in the classroom. Fear of losing jobs, prejudices, lack of knowledge of the issue, school policy, community feelings, or a lack of concern are all possible causes for a teacher's timidity in this area. Controversial issues—from racial problems to the population explosion—are found in almost every newspaper or newscast. How can they be avoided? Should they be avoided?

Certain controversial issues should be discussed in the elementary school, for children need the opportunity to study all sides of an issue and to make their own decisions. Teachers should use discretion when selecting issues for study. Several criteria should be applied:

1. Are the children mature enough to understand the issue thoroughly?
2. Do the children have sufficient background experiences to appraise the issue critically?
3. Will the study of the issue help attain the goals of the school and the community?
4. Is the issue of social, political, economic, or environmental significance?
5. Does the policy of the school permit the study of such an issue?
6. Will the children become better-informed, thoughtful citizens as a result of the study?

The manner in which a teacher approaches the study of controversial issues is of vital importance. Teachers who have a chip on their shoulder about an issue, or those who are prejudiced, opinionated, or possess an extreme point of view and teach only one side of an issue would be wise to ask someone to assist them with the study. They might team with another teacher who holds another point of view or bring in a carefully selected outside person. Teachers who feel they cannot discuss an issue without showing their prejudice do the children a disservice in attempting the study. One of the main purposes in having children research issues is to develop in them the habit of approaching any issue with an open mind, securing the facts on all sides, and then making a decision when necessary. A prejudiced teacher who permits that prejudice to show defeats this purpose.

Most controversial issues can be so charged with emotion that it is difficult for the teacher to ask children to assess all sides of an issue unemotionally. An example might be prayer in the school. A teacher may not always be successful in this task, but should encourage students to attempt to control their emotions and view issues objectively. Simple issues, such as resolving the fair treatment of others in the classroom, may be the starting point for understanding differences of opinion.

Social Issues

The teacher must decide whether the social issue will require an extensive study or can be handled in several class discussions with individual and group research. This decision will depend upon the children's expressed interest in the issue and the issue's relation to the previously stated criteria for selection. The approach to a social issue requires objectivity on the part of the teacher and the supplying of materials that present all sides of the issue.

Suppose some type of confrontation among groups in the community took place in your town last night. Today, depending upon the person reporting the event, it is being given labels such as "racial," "vandalism," "a demonstration against injustice," or "an attempt to overthrow the law." The children arrive in school very excited about the event and eager to discuss it. What do you do? How do you approach it? Obviously, you can't ignore the issue because it is a part of the children's world. Rather than permit the children to tell what they have heard about the event, the teacher might suggest that they list a series of questions for which they will be required to secure answers.

1. How did the confrontation start?
2. Where did it start? or, Why did it start?
3. Is it known who was responsible for starting it?
4. How much damage was done? or, What were the outcomes?
5. Why did the confrontation begin?
6. Will it happen again?
7. What can be done to prevent it from happening again?

Answers to these questions should be found by listening to news reports (in school when possible) presented by many stations, reading papers, and talking to several people who were in the area, if this can be arranged. All children should record the answers they secure, give the sources, and then compare them the next day in school. If it is determined that the event was caused by some deep-seated community problem, a thorough study of the issue should be undertaken by children in the intermediate grades, if school policy permits. Young children should pursue the topic to the depth of their understanding and ability to secure information. Children should interview citizens of the community, assess their feelings about the problem, find out what laws govern the problem, and determine whether the laws are being enforced. The teacher should provide the opportunity for children to discuss possible solutions to the problem. Children should learn that the true facts involved in this type of situation are often difficult to find. They should assess the validity of the information they secure by checking the source, and determining if the source is reliable. Other examples of social issues that could be researched and discussed are abortion, population control, capital punishment, drug abuse, and school busing.

Economic Issues

Most communities are faced with economic problems similar to those faced by the nation—welfare programs, high prices, unemployment, strikes, and so on. To study a local issue first may prove beneficial before attempting to understand a national problem because some of the children's families may be affected by the local problem. If this is true, care should be exercised to avoid embarrassment for these children.

Within any community, there is an area where people in lower socioeconomic levels are living. Depending on the community, conditions will vary, from run-down tenements along garbage-lined streets to neat, small dwellings. People here have few modern conveniences; many live on welfare or have low-paying jobs from which they do not earn sufficient money to care for their families. Frequently, this means that children do not receive adequate medical and dental care, do not have clothes for school, and do not have recreation opportunities, such as playgrounds, pools, or any type of camping or vacation experiences. Some communities provide these services for lower-income families while others do not. How should teachers approach these issues—or should they? It is extremely difficult for children to understand why these conditions should continue to exist, especially if they live within them, and equally as difficult to comprehend, if they live in affluent areas. Why do some people live in large, beautiful homes, able to take care of all their own needs, while others live in crowded, run-down areas and need welfare programs to care for their families?

Older children in upper elementary classes should tackle such issues. Questions similar to the following should be pursued:

1. Are there sufficient jobs available in the community?
2. If not, why not?
3. Do the unemployed have the training or skills for the available jobs?
4. If not, why not?
5. Does the community provide the same services for the poor areas as for the affluent—garbage collection, playgrounds, pools, recreation programs, schools, vocational training?
6. Can volunteers provide medical and dental care?
7. Are there any solutions available? What are they?

Much of this information will have to be secured from public officials through interviews or letters as well as through public documents in the library and courthouse. Any follow-up action that can be taken should be done, such as writing letters to public officials discussing the findings or any solutions the children might have concluded. If it is a solution the children can accomplish, such as cleaning up a park or helping to paint houses, then these should be attempted.

Homeless people have increased in numbers in many communities. Children may need to visit shelters, interview people, prepare games and toys for homeless children to understand their plight and the reasons they are homeless. If any homeless children are present in the class, the issue must be approached with considerable sensitivity.

Political Issues

During the preelection period there are political issues that should be pursued. For example: There are two candidates running for office and it appears from the newspapers and TV ads that one candidate is using smear tactics to try to win the election. The children should attempt to investigate the charges by either attending speeches made by the candidates and asking questions, or by inviting the candidates to the classroom. It may not be possible to determine whether the charges are true or false by these activities, but the children will better understand the candidates and their positions. If additional investigation is warranted, the children may interview residents in the community to learn their feelings about the candidates, or utilize any records such as previous issues of the newspapers which might contain information about the candidates' charges.

Another political issue might be "How does the local school board election affect our school?" Children determine what each candidate thinks should be done to improve the school or how each believes the funds should be raised and spent.

Environmental Issues

In our nation, historically, the people have not been concerned about preserving the environment or our natural resources. When the country was founded, it was believed that there were unlimited resources for humans to use in any way they wished. Trees and sod were destroyed to clear land for farming without any concern for their replacement or what ecological imbalance this might create. Disposal of wastes was not a problem as long as one did not contaminate another person's water supply. As the population increased and the industrial revolution advanced, pollution became a critical problem; but unfortunately, the cultural habits of the people had been established. Those who have worked hard for an improved standard of living do not want to give up the goods and services they have earned, even though the increased production of these goods and services increases pollution. Also, historically we have believed that the people should make decisions about pollution control and protection of natural resources. Often lawmakers do not pass strict control laws if these would cause financial burdens to certain interest groups;

or, local voters won't support a bond issue for improved sanitation if it will increase their taxes. Another difficulty in fighting pollution is the importance that is placed upon technology. Many believe that technology can accomplish anything including saving our environment, or producing synthetic resources when the natural resources are depleted. How can these cultural habits be changed? Obviously, it is crucial that young children develop an awareness of the gravity of the issue.

The issue is not only a national one, for humankind has advanced technologically to the extent that its activities affect the rest of the world. There are no local problems any more that can be left to local economic or political convenience. "We have not reached a point in human affairs at which the ecological requirements for sustaining the world community take precedence over . . . the more transient value systems and vested interests of any local society" (McHale 1971, p. 29). But how does humankind solve these tremendous problems? What solutions does it seek? "The next fifty years may be the most crucial in all man's history. . . . The knowledge with which we might make the correct decisions is barely adequate—yet our gross ecological errors may reverberate for many generations" (McHale 1971, p. 39).

Environmental issues may appear to be more difficult to approach since many are global, but are they different from others in terms of the number of different views that are held, solutions advanced, and positions represented? Possibly they are different in that the individual does not really know how grave the situation has become. Will we be without air to breathe, water to drink, and food to eat? Are our energy sources in danger of depletion? Many danger signs point in this direction, and thus it is of utmost importance that children learn about the environmental issues if they are to survive. The intent is not to make the children fearful, but rather aware of the seriousness of the problem.

How does the teacher present these issues? There are a number of approaches that might be used, but it is crucial that children be confronted with an actual situation, since reading about it or watching films will not bring about the same level of awareness.

One first grade class filled their aquarium with water and threw litter into it. They observed what happened to the water and the debris in a very short time. With the cooperation of the custodian, you could permit each child in the class to throw one piece of paper on the floor each day and leave it until the end of the week, so they will realize how rapidly they can pollute their room with litter.

Another type of activity that is a confrontation situation is to shut off the drinking fountains for a day and not permit the children to have any water. This type of activity should be done only after a letter has been sent home informing the parents of the purpose of the activity. You may want to extend this activity to the elimination of lunch for a day to emphasize what it would be like to go without food. Be sure none of the children have medical problems that would prevent them from participating. After the environmental issues have been brought to the awareness level of the children, it is important that they apply their problem-solving and decision-making skills to these issues.

The teacher may want to approach the issue from the viewpoint of one of the social science disciplines as was done in Chapter 2. Suppose the children start with the economist, since many people claim that pollution control would cost too much, either in terms of money or jobs, if it were strictly enforced. There are numerous newspaper and magazine articles that express the views of the economist on pollution. Children can discover that the economist expresses the view that pollution can be reduced by producing fewer goods or a different variety of goods, by recycling more of what has been produced, and by changing the form of wastes or their manner of disposal. Here, the decision-making skills of the children can be increased. How do you decide which goods you would be willing to go without or have in limited amounts? Do you cut down production of goods and face unemployment? Is this the best solution?

Changing the form of wastes or their disposal seems to be a more possible solution. The economist looks at the amount of money to be spent to control wastes and the amount of value that would be received as a result of it. For example, the disposal of solid wastes—garbage—is one that plagues every large city. Each person in the United States throws away a great deal of garbage each day. What can be done with it? There are areas, such as one outside Chicago, where garbage is used in landfill projects to provide recreational areas. This landfill area has been constructed with alternating layers of clay and garbage to become a ski and toboggan slope. The economist determines whether the cost of hauling garbage to the location will be less than the profits gained from the recreation area. The cost of this eventually will be paid by the people who use the recreation facilities. Also, property values around the area will increase once the landfill has been completed. The main problem is moving the garbage from areas of concentrated population, where there is limited use of landfill techniques, to areas where the garbage can be used. The economist will question—does it pay? In most cases, the answer would be yes.

However the teacher chooses to approach environmental issues, it is important that young children develop an awareness of the problems. Any vital social studies program must include the study of current issues. If they are omitted, the children will be growing up outside the mainstream of society.

Resources

Engle, S. H. (1989). Proposals for a typical issue-centered curriculum. *Social Studies, 80,* 187–191.
Evans, R. W. (1989). A dream unrealized: A brief look at the history of issue-centered approaches. *Social Studies, 80,* 178–184.
Hahn, C. (1985). The status of social studies in the public schools of the United States: Another look. *Social Education, 49*(3), 220–223.
Isham, M. M., & Mehaffy, G. L. (1985). Issues in social studies education: Experimentation in the social studies. *Social Education, 49,* 571–574.
Johnson, G. (1984). *Effects of law-related education sustained at sixteen-month followup.*

Boulder, CO: Center for Action Research. (ERIC Document Reproduction Service No. ED 252–458)

McHale, J. (1971). Global ecology: Toward the planetary society. In F. Carvell & M. Tadlock (Eds.), *It's not too late* (pp. 1–40). Beverly Hills: Glencoe Press.

Meadows, D. H. et al. (1972). *The limits of growth.* New York: Universe Books.

Passe, J. (1988). The role of internal factors in the teaching of current events. *Theory and Research in Social Education, 16*(1), 83–89.

Totten, S. (1989). Using oral histories to address social issues in the social studies classroom. *Social Education, 53*(2), 114–116, 125.

Ward, B., & Dubois, R. (1972). *Only one earth.* New York: W. W. Norton.

GLOBAL EDUCATION

"Global education involves learning about those problems and issues that cut across national boundaries, and about the interconnectedness of systems—ecological, cultural, economic, political, and technological. Global education involves perspective taking—seeing things through the eyes and minds of others—and it means the realization that while individuals and groups may view life differently, they also have common needs and wants" (Tye 1990, p. 163).

This definition of global education supports a rationale for its inclusion in the school curriculum. Problems and issues are no longer confined within national boundaries, the increasing interdependence among nations, and the need to recognize that all peoples have many more things in common than they have differences warrants its inclusion. Anderson (1980) further suggests that among other factors the American society has become globalized and therefore we have no choice but to globalize our educational system.

Goals/Anticipated Outcomes

Global living will require a change in education for the young. That education must provide not only the understanding and skills to live effectively in a global society today, but also the ability to cope with the realities of the future and appreciate those of the past.

How do teachers determine what children need to experience to become responsible citizens in an interdependent world? What skills are necessary to confront the perplexing problems of the human community? What should the objectives be?

A major goal/outcome is for children to develop the ability to perceive the world as an interdependent human community made up of cultures that have more similarities than differences. In addition, children must recognize that an individual's perception of the world is that person's own, shaped by his or her experiences, and is not necessarily a perception shared by others.

A second goal/outcome is for children to realize that the interdependent human community faces problems of overpopulation of the planet, pollution of the air and water, food shortages, energy and resource depletion, health, education, conflict, poverty, deprivation of human rights, as well as coping with an urbanized and technologically advanced society.

A third goal/outcome for global living is to develop within children a willingness to recognize the inevitability and benefits of diversity among peoples and cultures and the constantly changing status of the world. This recognition of diversity and change requires a human being with knowledge about and appreciation for the world's cultures and an understanding of the causes and effects of change.

With this knowledge and appreciation the fourth goal/outcome, human relations skills, can develop. These skills enable the children to relate and interact with people from diverse groups within their culture and diverse cultures of the world.

A fifth goal/outcome for children is to develop the ability to apply skills of inquiry and analysis to information about the world, and to assess the information critically and review it from a global perspective.

A sixth and overarching goal/outcome of children's education is to evolve a philosophy and value system that takes account of the realities of world living. Examination of values such as cooperation, justice, responsibility, standard of living, and peaceful resolution of conflict would be appropriate. The acquisition of decision-making skills which are then applied to that philosophy and value system is necessary.

The seventh and crucial goal/outcome is to help the children develop good self-concepts and the self-realization of their worth as individuals in the human community. When this has been accomplished, it is possible for them to relate more effectively to other members of that humanity.

Realistically, the above goals/outcomes are most difficult to achieve, but, optimistically, one must pursue them. In such an attempt one must continually assess the components of the school. What are the attitudes, skills, and abilities of the teachers? What are the attitudes, skills, and abilities of the children? What materials or resources are available in the school and community? What is the feeling of the community?

The approach should not be piecemeal, adding studies of world cultures or problems to the existing curriculum, but rather it should be a continuous development of a world perspective that permeates all aspects of the curriculum.

Children need to learn to function effectively in their own community, but also to view that community as just one of many within the world community.

Individuals who see global education as a threat to the continuation of a national identity will become concerned that children might be developing an ambiguity about their own country in an attempt to understand other countries' cultures and their values. Therefore, it should be emphasized that a culture develops as a result of a number of different factors and that, while each way of life may be best for that group or culture, it may not necessarily be best for everyone else in the world. Also, it should be noted that children really begin to understand their own culture and country when they learn about others.

Learning Experiences

One of the first experiences that children need would be some way to conceptualize the size and population of their country/region in relation to the other regions. This helps them to recognize the fact that they belong to one large human community. The Population Reference Bureau (1987) has a simulation entitled *Food for Thought* that gives the teacher several suggestions of ways to help children understand these relationships.

One activity provides information necessary to chart out the relative size of the major landforms and using the members of the class to simulate the relative population distribution of the world. Below are drawn the size and population information (Population Reference Bureau 1987).

3[a]	North America	2[b]	5	Europe	3
1. 16% of land, 5% of pop.			1. 4% of land, 10% of pop.		
2. 3/4 pop. is urban			2. 3/4 pop. is urban		
3. 1/4 land is agricultural			3. 1/2 land is agricultural		
10′ × 8′[c]			5′ × 4′		
4	Latin America	2	29	Asia	17
1. 15% of land, 8% of pop.			1. 21% of land, 50% of pop.		
2. 2/3 of pop. is urban			2. 1/3 of pop. is urban		
3. 1/3 of land is agricultural			3. 2/5 of land is agricultural		
10′ × 7.5′			10′ × 10′		
3	Commonwealth of Ind. States	2	6	Africa	4
1. 17% of land, 6% of pop.			1. 22% of land, 12% of pop.		
2. 2/3 of pop. is urban			2. 1/3 of pop. is urban		
3. 1/4 of land is agricultural			3. 1/3 of land is agricultural		
10′ × 8.3′			10′ × 11′		

There are several ways to use the space and population information. The teacher can mark off the land areas in the classroom and have children stand in the space. The urban areas may have the children placed very close to one another. Does everyone have the same amount of space? What happens when the areas are crowded?

Another activity uses a loaf of bread to simulate the amount of protein consumption for each of these regions. North America received 1/12 of the bread even though it has only 5 percent of the population. Latin America receives 1/12; Commonwealth of Independent States, 1/12; Africa, 1/12; Europe, 2/12; and Asia, 6/12. How do the people divide up the bread? Will there be fights over it? Will some people move to other areas that have more bread to share?

Other activities show the per capita GNP by region and the amount of energy consumption. The simulation also gives further information about the birth and death rates, the annual rate of growth of the population, infant mortality, and the years of life expectancy for each region. Contact the Population

Reference Bureau, Inc., 777 14th St., N.W., Suite 800, Washington, DC 20005 to secure the complete booklet.

In addition to understanding the land and population distribution, children need to recognize the diversity of cultures that make up our world, but along with diversity they need to recognize the similarities of people and the constantly changing status of the world. Other suggestions for learning activities are:

1. For young children, demonstrate the concept of diversity in the classroom by discussing that because children have different parents, they each look different, but because they are all human beings they have much in common. Discuss the commonalities. All have feet, legs, arms, etc.
2. To help younger children develop a global perspective, teachers can use the book *Bread, Bread, Bread* by Ann Morris that shows pictures of people around the world making, eating, and sharing bread.
3. Discuss geographic diversity and how it affects homes, clothing, food, and employment. Primary schoolchildren can learn about places where it is warm (tropical), others that are cold (arctic) the year round, and also places that have four seasons. Look at pictures of these places. What are the houses like in the warm places? How are they different where it is cold? What kind of clothes do they wear in both places? How are they different? How are they alike? What type of food grows in the warm places? Is it different in the cold places? What type of work can people do in warm places? Cold places? What happens in places where they have four different types of weather during the year?
4. Locate children's books that demonstrate how change occurs, such as *The Little House* (Burton 1942) and discuss how change occurs within each family and community. Another book for older children, *In Two Worlds: A Yupik Eskimo Family* by Aylette Jenness and Alice Rivers, shows through pictures change and new patterns of life in a small Alaskan community on the coast of the Bering Sea.
5. Develop case studies of individuals in different culture groups. Older children can interview people in their community who belong to different cultures that have immigrated to this country. Another approach is to use children's books like *The Chalk Doll* by Charlotte Pomerantz, in which a mother shares with her daughter stories of her childhood in Jamaica.
6. Visit schools that are ethnically or culturally different from the children's and invite students for a return visit.
7. Invite a family newly arrived from another country into the classroom to demonstrate aspects of their culture.
8. Trace the change of the local community through pictures and discussion with senior citizens.
9. There are two simulations that help children understand cultural differences, *Rafa Rafa* for younger children and *Bafa Bafa* for middle-grade

students. Groups of children learn new cultures and try to understand and communicate with one another during the simulations.

10. Children need information in order to understand and deal with global problems. Use of newspapers, news magazines, television programs, and other news services should contribute information and help them understand the global situations. Pinpointing where events occur by placing pictures and news articles on a large world map helps children develop spatial relationships of where they are and where the events are happening.

11. Develop the idea that decisions of individuals often affect other nations of the world (for example, oil pricing, sugar pricing, coffee pricing). To illustrate, if people stop buying so much gas, sugar, or coffee because the prices are too high, then countries from which we buy the goods will be affected. After information of world events has been acquired from news magazines, TV, and newspapers, have children develop role play decision making of world problems (Panama Canal, nuclear freeze, Israeli–Arab Middle East conflict, South African constitution). What might happen since the United States no longer controls the Panama Canal? How will the different groups in Africa react to a new constitution?

12. Actively participating with people from other countries can occur through a number of projects. For example, obtain Pen Pals. Find a teacher and class in another country to exchange letters and artifacts. Exchange programs may include artwork, scrapbooks, and other items of each country (Art for World Friendship, Friendly Acres, Media, Pennsylvania). There are several programs where children can actually adopt children in other countries who need special help. An example of such an agency is the Christian Children's Fund, Box 511, Richmond, VA 23204. The agency will send a picture and information about the child and provide for the exchange of letters.

13. The cafeteria may provide a setting to demonstrate to children what it might be like to live in a part of the world where there is not enough for everyone to eat. The teacher and two-thirds of the class may go without a morning snack and watch the other one-third eat theirs. A follow-up discussion should indicate some significant results.

    Sensitivity to the problem of hunger and food distribution might be developed—particularly in the upper elementary grades—by planning and preparing meals that correspond to the diet of undernourished people, both in terms of the portion and the balance of basic food groups. An average suburban child who sits down to a small portion of rice would gain more in empathy and sensitivity than he or she would lose in nutrition. Children with medical problems would not participate in either activity.

14. How do we help children understand their ethnocentric bias? One way is for them to see discrepancies between their own perception of a situation and that of others. Although there is little material available at the elementary level (*Rafa Rafa* is one example), teachers can get copies of

history books printed in the United Kingdom, Canada, and other English-speaking areas of the world, and read to the class those portions describing historical periods of interaction between these nations and the United States—for example, the Revolutionary War and the War of 1812. Such readings should be followed by accounts of how and why these historical accounts may differ significantly.

Another project would be to send for newspapers from English-speaking countries around the world and have the children compare the coverage of the same topics in those papers and in their local paper. Ethnocentrism can be observed not only in the way the "news" is dealt with, but also in the selection and relative space given to various news stories.

Still another way to develop an awareness of ethnocentric bias is by examining the language used in describing our relations with other peoples and cultures—past and present. Why was it a "massacre" when the Native Americans killed white men, but a "battle" when Native Americans were slaughtered?

Also, a primary teacher could point out the left-to-right pattern we use in reading and writing and call attention to the variety of ways people in other cultures read and write—both right-to-left and vertically. An example of the development of an awareness of one child to his or her own ethnocentric view is illustrated by this response to a lesson: "They write backwards, don't they" but "I bet they think we write backwards."

15. Helping children to understand the interdependent nature of our world can be accomplished at any grade level. Have children identify the places where products came from that they used from the time they awoke until they arrived at school. Example: The alarm clock was made in Japan; the TV assembled in Mexico; their shirt came from Thailand, jeans or skirt from Panama, and shoes from Korea. They put their books in a bookbag made in China and rode to school in a car built in Japan. The class can work in pairs and mark Xs on world maps to show where their products came from. A discussion of how and why these products came from all over the world helps children clarify the concepts of interdependence.

Atmosphere of the Classroom

The attitude of the teacher and the atmosphere that is established in the classroom are vital to the development of global education. A teacher who displays anything but complete acceptance of every child in the class, regardless of race, religion, or national origin, would most probably fail in an attempt to teach the children to accept those from other cultures.

A classroom where there is an attitude of mutual respect for and sensitivity toward the feelings of others provides the proper atmosphere for developing empathy for peoples of different cultures. Such an attitude does not just happen—activities must be planned to aid its growth. Children have a natural tendency to be concerned about themselves and their own problems, but they need to discover the pleasure that comes from assisting others. A classroom partner plan for helping one another with schoolwork; committee assignments that continually change members after tasks are completed; and assisting in the school library, kitchen, or office are examples of activities within the school that help children develop the ability to empathize with others. Projects initiated in the community, such as cleaning up a local lot for a playground, collecting toys or clothes for underprivileged children, singing or performing at a home for the elderly, and participating in fund-raising drives are identified as representative of the type of activity needed. It is doubtful that children will be able to develop empathy for people of another culture with whom they have no contact if they have little feeling for those with whom they associate daily.

How children view themselves and their world will determine the future of that world. To develop a global perspective, children, in addition to learning about who they are, must learn about the billions of people beyond the borders of their country and how everyone contributes to the human community.

Resources

Burton, V. L. (1942). *The little house.* Boston: Houghton Mifflin.

Cortes, C., & Fleming, D. B. (1986). Changing global perspectives in textbooks. *Social Education, 50*(5), 340–344.

Hahn, C. (1984). Promise and paradox: Challenges to global citizenship. *Social Education, 48*(4), 240.

Jenness, A., & Rivers, A. (1989). *In two worlds: A Yupik Eskimo family.* Boston: Houghton Mifflin.

Kniep, W. M. (1989). Social studies within a global education. *Social Education, 53*(6), 399–403.

Morris, A. (1989). *Bread, Bread, Bread.* Lothrop.

Nelson, J. L. (1990). Nuclear proliferation as a global values issue. *Social education, 54,* 169–170.

Peters, R. (1985). Helping students perceive the global community. *Contemporary Education, 56,* 90–91.

Pomerantz, C. (1989). *The chalk doll.* Lippincott.

Population Reference Bureau. (1987). *Food for thought.* (Available from Author, 777 14th St., N.W., Suite 800, Washington, DC 20005)

Skeel, D. J. (1981). Global education. In J. Allen (Ed.), *Education in the 80's: Social studies* (p. 78). Washington, DC: National Education Association.

Thornburg, K. (1983). Global issues in the elementary school. *Social Education, 47*(2), 138–141.

Tye, K. A. (Ed.). (1990). *Global education: From thought to action.* Yearbook of the Association for Supervision and Curriculum Development. Alexandria, VA.

LAW RELATED EDUCATION

Law-related education is intended to help children become better-informed and effective citizens. Its unique contribution to social studies is its knowledge of laws and the legal system. Children begin with concrete experiences with rules. Why do we have rules? Who makes the rules? What happens if you don't follow the rules? What is the difference between a rule and a law? What is the basis for our laws? Who enforces the laws? How can laws be changed? These are some of the questions that children ask about rules and laws. Law related education attempts to answer them.

Goals/Anticipated Outcomes

Goals/outcomes for law-related education are based on the uniqueness of the content. Children should understand the basis for laws and how and why laws are made. Helping children to understand that the laws are meant to protect them and keep them safe is an important concept of law related education.

Hopefully an attitude of respect for authority will develop. An understanding of why it is necessary to have someone in authority to be sure that order is maintained and people are protected should help children recognize the importance of people in positions of authority.

An important goal/outcome of law related education is for children to understand how one can affect the laws and the legal system. Children should recognize that laws can be changed and that people can influence their elected representatives to make those changes.

Children may not have any contact with the police unless they get into trouble. Therefore, it is important for them to understand how laws are enforced and what happens when someone breaks a law.

Understanding that the responsibility of the courts and corrective system is to determine the guilt or innocence and punishment of a person who has been charged with breaking a law is an important goal/outcome. The corrective system also supervises that punishment.

Children need to be aware of not only their rights, but also their responsibilities under the law. Being aware that you have a right to a lawyer if charged with breaking the law is important, but also recognizing that you have the responsibility to abide by the laws is an equally important awareness.

Law related education provides opportunities for children to develop their abilities to make judgments, to communicate, to cooperate, and to use information from a variety of sources. Other skills that are developed include critical thinking, decision making, valuing, and problem solving. These goals/outcomes lend themselves to children being active participants in the learning process.

Some of the above understandings and skills can be acquired in the context of other subject matter, but law related education provides some unique opportunities. For example, placing yourself in the role of a judge and/or jury member that requires you to make a judgment about guilt or innocence and/or determine the punishment that one should receive for the crime committed not only helps you better understand the courts and corrective system, but also develops your ability to make judgments and decisions.

Learning Experiences

Classroom Rules and Constitutions

As mentioned earlier, one of the first aspects of law related education (LRE) that children encounter is rules. They begin with rules at home and then they encounter rules at day care or school. Teachers often use the necessity for rules in the classroom as the basis for a learning experience. A third grade teacher began on the first day of school by asking the children what type of classroom they would like to have. She then asked them what rules they needed in order to ensure that their classroom would remain as they wanted it to be. The teacher encouraged the children to state the rules in a positive manner. Here are some of the rules they suggested:

We will respect each other's property.
We will listen when other people are talking.
We will not run or throw things in the classroom.
We will be sure that only three people are on the reading rug at one time.
We will pick up the key when we need to leave the room so only one person will be out at a time.
We will not throw berries on the playground.

At the middle of the year, the teacher asked the children to assess the rules to determine if any were no longer needed or if additional ones were needed. The children decided that they had developed responsible behavior on the reading rug and that rule was no longer needed. Also, the one indicating that berries should not be thrown on the playground could be eliminated since there were no longer any berries available. It is easy to identify the objectives for LRE that are being achieved by this rule-making and assessing experience.

Younger children can assist with the rules for their classrooms as well, but may need more guidance from the teacher to understand what rules might be needed. Older children may want to draft a classroom constitution as they study the history of our country and learn about our governmental institutions. Dulaney, DeMasi, Lendsey, and Stein (1980) suggest the following steps in creating a classroom constitution:

Step 1: Organize a discussion centering on classroom rules.
- What is the purpose of having a rule?

- How are rules made?
- Who must follow rules?
- What happens if a rule is broken?
- How can rules be changed?

Step 2: Children identify the rules that are already part of the classroom.

Step 3: Children identify rules they feel should be a part of the classroom.

Step 4: Children with teacher's guidance develop criteria for a "good rule" and examine each rule using the criteria.
Some things to think about include the following:
- Is the rule fair to all class members?
- Is the rule necessary to maintain the order of the classroom?
- Is the rule important to create a better place to live and learn?

Step 5: Children and teacher vote to decide whether to accept or reject the rules for the constitution.

Step 6: Children and teacher decide how they will change rules when necessary. (Will a simple majority be enough?)

Step 7: Children should discuss their rights and responsibilities under their constitution. All should sign the constitution with an understanding that their signature means they will obey the rules. Establish guidelines for procedures if rules are broken. The establishment of a classroom court may be the result.

Step 8: Children in fourth and fifth grades studying about the state or U.S. Constitution may want to compare them with their classroom constitution.

Why We Have Laws

Naylor (1977) uses a value clarification learning experience to help children understand why we have laws. Children are asked to place the reasons for laws on a continuum—from most important to least important.

Why Do We Have Laws?

____ ____ ____ ____ ____ ____ ____ ____ ____

Most Important Reason   Least Important Reason

- A. To tell us what we can and cannot do.
- B. To help us settle disagreements peacefully.
- C. To protect us from other people.
- D. To make sure that we do what we say we will do.
- E. To assure us that all people will be treated fairly.
- F. To punish us when we do wrong.

The letter for each reason should be placed on one of the lines along the continuum. After completing the continuum as individuals, the children should discuss why they placed the reasons where they did and also to give examples of laws that we have for each of the reasons.

Mock Trials

Using a mock trial is one of the best-known and most popular teaching strategies in law related education. For young children, the fairy tales such as "Goldilocks and the Three Bears" or "Jack and the Beanstalk" can be used as cases for mock trials. Should Goldilocks be charged with breaking and entering or trespassing? What about damaging property and eating the porridge?

In "Jack and the Beanstalk" there can be a charge of stealing or destroying property. The younger children can role play the defendant, witnesses, and jury, but you may want the lawyer and judge portrayed by visiting lawyers or take the children to a local courtroom with a lawyer and judge.

Gallagher (1989) suggests that a *pro se* court or small claims court is appropriate for elementary students to model "because complex courtroom procedures and rules of evidence are kept to a minimum" (p. 5). The class is divided into groups of three with each person choosing the role of judge, plaintiff, and defendant. Each person should eventually have the opportunity to play the role of judge. Each group should be given a case. Suggest that the plaintiff and defendant try to settle their case out of court. If this does not occur, then set up the *pro se* court. Have judges leave the room and then explain that everyone must rise when the judges return to the room. Use the statement "All rise. *Pro se* court is in session." Have plaintiffs and defendants present their cases to the judges. Try to place the groups far enough apart so they won't be distracted by one another. After hearing the arguments, the judges make a decision. Judges should give the reasons for their decisions. Those who settled "out of court" should present their cases and ask the judge what he or she would have decided before they explain how they resolved them.

Present a new case and have students rotate their roles. Follow same procedure until everyone has had a chance to be judge.

After everyone has finished, bring the class back together and discuss the following questions:

Which was the most important role to play?
How well did the participants play their roles? Were they realistic?
How did people feel when they had resolved their differences without a judge, as opposed to submitting the dispute to the court? (Gallagher 1989, p. 6)

Cases can be developed from situations that have happened in the community or hypothetical ones can be prepared. An example might be:

Mrs. Ross's dog went into Mr. Rodriquez's garden and ruined the vegetables he was growing. He claims that the vegetables would be worth $75 when they are grown even though he only paid $5 for the seeds. Should Mrs. Ross pay $75 or $5?

Published Materials

Published materials provide the opportunities for many learning experiences within LRE. *Juvenile Responsibility and Law* (Riekes, Jenkins, & Russell 1990), one of the Law in Action series, includes 19 lessons that first helps children understand the meaning of responsibility and how it relates to citizenship and the laws. Other lessons discuss the differences between juvenile and adult courts and place the children in the roles of the members of the juvenile court system. In one lesson, the children are placed in the role of the judge where they must decide among several dispositional alternatives in resolving the juvenile cases that are before them. As a result of these lessons they learn about the courts and corrective system.

A program designed for the fifth grade to help children understand the basis for our laws and our Constitution and Bill of Rights is the *We the People* (Center for Civic Education 1991) program. The book contains 22 lessons organized around five unit themes: What were the Founders' basic ideas about government? How was our Constitution written? How did the framers organize our government? How does the Constitution protect your basic rights? and What are the responsibilities of citizens? The lessons include opportunities for the students to be actively involved, practice cooperative learning, and become problem solvers.

These materials are considered a practical law approach that explains the specifics of laws, the legal system, and the Constitution. Another approach is conceptual, as demonstrated in the book, *Law in a Free Society: Authority* (Center for Civil Education 1993). For example, in the kindergarten–first grade book children are asked to identify the difference between authority and power in situations they encounter every day. Pictures depict the playground supervisor who has authority to tell children what to do while the "bully" is exerting power over the children because of their size. Other concrete pictures help them differentiate between those who have power with authority and those who have power without authority. In a conceptual approach, it is believed that children will be able to apply the concept of authority to the new situations they encounter. Other concepts in the program include justice, privacy, and responsibility.

Classroom and School Environment

When children enter school they are faced with the problem of understanding what their role will be. What are their rights and responsibilities? How will they relate to other people—their teacher, the other children, the principal? How do they react when the teacher explains that what they are doing is not acceptable behavior in school? How do they figure out what they are supposed to do?

The general "climate" of the classroom and the school plays a vital part in helping them accept the school's authority. In discussing the elementary child, Dreeban (1968) contends that "the emotions aroused in schooling derive from events in which the pupils' sense of self respect is either supported or threatened. . . . This influences the pupils in deciding whether or not they will find their early experiences at school enjoyable enough to act according to the standards governing school activities" (p. 39).

The way in which the school is governed will influence children's understanding of rules and authority. What type of atmosphere is created? Do teachers cooperate with one another? How do teachers use their authority? How does the principal exert authority? Do the rules create a pleasant atmosphere? Children may learn much more about authority, rules, fairness, and respect for people and property from the environment of the school than the learning experiences if adults don't recognize how much children learn from the models of behavior to which they are exposed.

Resources

Anderson, C. (1980). Promoting responsible citizenship through law related education. *Social Education, 44*(7), 383.

Arends, R. I., & Thomas, P. (1987). Getting law related education into the curriculum so that it stays: Messages from research and some guidelines for action. *International Journal of Social Education, 2*(2), 19–36.

Center for Civic Education. (1991). *We the people: Level I*. Calabassas, CA: Author.

Center for Civil Education. (1993). *Law in a free society: Authority*. Calabassas, CA: Author.

Dreeban, H. (1968). *On what is learned in school*. Reading, MA: Addison-Wesley.

Dulaney, B., DeMasi, J., Lendsey, J., & Stein, L. E. (1980). Learning experiences for elementary law related education. *Social Education, 44*(77), 391.

Fischer, B., Fischer, L., & Bang-Jensen, V. (1980). Governance in elementary schools: An exploration in law related education. In L. C. Falkenstein & C. C. Anderson (Eds.), *Daring to dream: Law and humanities for elementary schools* (p. 135). Chicago: ABA Special Committee on Youth Education for Citizenship.

Gallagher, A. F. (1987). How law related education fits into the curriculum. *International Journal of Social Studies, 2*(2), 37–44.

Gallagher, A. F. (1989, Winter). Access to justice. *Update on Law Related Education*, pp. 5–8.

Hunter, R. M. (1987). Law related educational practice and delinquency theory. *International Journal of Social Education, 2*(2), 52–64.

Naylor, D. T. (1977). Law studies in the schools: A compendium of instructional strategies. *Social Education, 41*(2), 176–177.

Riekes, L., Jenkins, S., & Russell, A. (1990). *Juvenile responsibility and the law* (3rd ed.). St Paul, MN: West Publishing.

ECONOMIC EDUCATION

"Young children 'spontaneously' develop notions about their own economic worlds of work, exchange, production, and consumption, aside from any formal process aimed at having them learn or master these concepts" (Vygosky, cited in Armento 1986, p. 85). Armento states, "Concept learning is an important outcome of economics programs in elementary schools, for it is fundamental to acquiring and building problem solving and decision making skills. Although it is not the only kind of economic learning young children undertake, it is clearly an important one because a considerable amount of young children's formal and informal learning time is engaged in processing experiences and reorganizing ideas of the economic world" (p. 93). She further suggests that economic content in the early years should relate to events in children's lives as they examine buying, selling, and trading transactions; the process of making goods and services; and the origin of materials and products in their everyday lives.

Very early in life children are faced with a fundamental concept of economics—scarcity. Whether it is a real scarcity, not having things they need, or a perceived scarcity, not having something they want, children must learn to understand it. They must recognize the difference between wants and needs, and make decisions about how they will use their resources. Children are consumers and it is important for them to recognize that economic decisions determine what is produced, but also how goods and services will be distributed—who gets what. Concrete experiences with events that occur in their daily lives help children develop their ability to make wise economic decisions.

Goals/Anticipated Outcomes

Goals/outcomes for economic education begin with understanding the concept of scarcity and how people make decisions about how to use limited resources to satisfy unlimited wants. Scarcity is a key concept for children to acquire since it is the basis for decision making.

Another set of concepts that should be acquired are needs, wants, consumer, producer, goods, services, specialization, division of labor, and the relationships among them. These concepts form the foundation for understanding our economic system.

The goal/outcome of understanding the concept of work (labor) and how it provides resources (money) to satisfy needs and wants is important so that children understand why resources may be limited.

Understanding the difference between public and private ownership helps children recognize why some businesses, such as utility companies, are owned by the public while others, such as a restaurant, are owned by private individuals.

When governments determine public policy (how tax money will be spent), children need to recognize how that policy affects individual economic decision making. If the government cuts spending for defense, it may mean fewer workers will remain in defense-related jobs. When people are out of a job, they have fewer resources and therefore make different decisions.

An important goal/outcome is for children to recognize that when they make economic decisions there are opportunity costs. If they have five dollars and want to go to a movie and also see a basketball game, but don't have enough money for both, one of the choices will be an opportunity cost.

Children need to understand that individuals, communities, and nations are interdependent in meeting their needs and wants. Individuals work in the community and pay taxes to both their local and national governments. Both governments provide services for the individuals.

One of the skills that should be a goal/outcome of economic education is the ability to make economic decisions. How do I use my resources?

Since children are able to develop an understanding of our private enterprise economic system through concrete experiences, it may be more difficult to understand a controlled economy, such as a dictatorship or communism, that is more abstract. However, they should be made aware that there are other types of economic systems.

Learning Experiences

Scarcity

One of the first economic concepts that children need to understand is that of scarcity. Children need to realize that resources are not available to provide all the goods and services that they want. Every day children make choices about how they will use their resources, from decisions about what they will spend their lunch money on to how they will use their energy to complete their school tasks.

One of the best ways to introduce the concept of scarcity is to relate it to a situation in the classroom. The class has decided that they would like to go to the science museum, but they do not have enough money to pay the admission fee for everyone. What is scarce? Money. How can they earn enough so everyone can go?

Another situation presents itself when most of the children want to paint during free time, but there are not enough paint sets and easels. Why are they scarce?

Needs and Wants

Children need to identify the difference between needs and wants to help them make decisions and also understand why adults in their life make certain decisions regarding how they use their resources. The teacher may help them to differentiate by asking children first to group the following on which a family might spend their money: sweater, vegetables, rent, video, shoes, bread, milk, coat, bicycle, TV, house, meat, shirt, skates, apartment. What things are alike? Children would probably group them as follows:

vegetables	sweater	rent	video
bread	shoes	house	TV
milk	coat	apartment	bicycle
meat	shirt		skates

What would we label (call) each group?

| things to eat | things to wear | places to live | things to do |

Which groups do we need to live?
Which groups could we get along without?

Children could then use magazines to cut out pictures of needs and wants. Place the headings of needs and wants on the bulletin board and have them indicate which column their picture fits in.

Economic concepts should be introduced within the context of the social studies topics that are usually taught (Skeel 1988). Here is an example of a lesson that might be taught while studying the family from *Small Size Economics: Lessons for the Primary Grades* (Skeel 1988).

Concepts: Needs and wants
Teaching Strategy: Role playing
Curriculum Context: Family
Instructional Outcomes: Children will be able to explain how families provide for needs and wants. Children will be able to role play a decision-making situation in which they decide what to buy.
Materials: Sample check, $100 in play money, ads for children's shoes from a newspaper or catalog, sweater, raincoat, and fishing equipment.
Teaching Procedure: Read the following story to the children.

Marci lives with her parents in an apartment in the city. Her father is a policeman. Her mother is a teacher in the same school where Marci goes to kindergarten.

Marci likes to go places with her parents. One place she likes to go is the grocery store. But her parents always tell her that they can't go to the grocery store until one of them has received a check from work.

Show the children a sample check. Talk about how people are paid with a check for their work. Checks can be cashed for money. Show coins and pieces of paper money. Explain how people use money to buy the things they need and want. Then go on with the story.

Marci knows that sometimes after they go to buy groceries, her parents have money left. Then they can buy other things.

Marci tells her mother that she needs a new pair of shoes. But she also says that she would like the red sweater she saw in the window of the store around the corner. Marci already has several sweaters and doesn't need the red one. Marci's mother needs a raincoat so that she won't get wet when Marci and she walk to school. Her father explains that he would like to get some new fishing equipment. Marci's parents have $100 left after they pay for the groceries. Marci's shoes cost $30. The sweater costs $20. The raincoat costs $70. And the fishing equipment costs $50.

Select children to play the roles of Marci, mother, father, and clerks at the different stores selling shoes, sweater, raincoats, and fishing equipment.

Give the $100 in play money to mother, father, and Marci. Give each store clerk an appropriate ad with prices. Have Marci and her parents go to each of the store clerks to ask how much each item will cost. Let Marci and her parents decide what to buy with the money, and then discuss their decision with the whole class after the role play.

What did they decide to buy? The possible answers include shoes and raincoat; sweater and raincoat; shoes, sweater, and fishing equipment.

Why couldn't they buy everything? They did not have enough money.

How did they decide what to buy? They bought only the things they needed, or they bought a combination of things they needed and things they wanted.

Evaluation: Give the children a new situation. This time Marci's parents have $75 left after buying groceries. Marci's mother wants some flower pots for the apartment. The flower pots cost $75. Marci's father wants to get the television set fixed, and that also costs $75. Marci wants to spend the whole day at the amusement park with her parents. That will cost $75.

Have the children draw a picture of what they would do with the money. Then ask the children to explain their choices. You can also develop an experience chart with their choices.

Consumers and Producers

Children can readily identify occasions when they are a producer or a consumer. By describing the activities that children participate in from the time they awake until they arrive at school can be used as an opportunity to differentiate between a producer and consumer.

In addition to identifying when they are a producer or consumer, the children can also identify the difference between goods and services. The underlined items are designated with a "c" for consumer or "p" for producer, and "g" for good and "s" for service.

Amy's *clock radio* (c/g) awoke her, indicating it was time to get up and get ready for school. She quickly got out of *bed* (c/g), washed her face with *water* (c/s), brushed her teeth with that new minty *toothpaste* (c/g), dressed in her favorite *blouse* (c/g), *skirt* (c/g), and pink *tennis shoes* (c/g). She rushed downstairs to join her family at breakfast. She always *squeezed* (p/g) the fresh orange juice for everyone. After eating the *cereal* (c/g) and *toast* (c/g), it was her responsibility to *take out the garbage* (p/s). She jumped on the *bus* (c/s) and arrived at school where a *policeman* (c/s) was directing traffic. She gave her *teacher* (c/s) a smile at the door and slid into her seat just as the bell was about to ring.

An interesting way to have older children sort out the difference between goods and services is to collect business cards (Lenning 1990). Children then place the cards in their appropriate group, dependent upon what the person provides. Children can also decide what occupation they will choose and design their own business cards. *More Than Money: An Activities Approach to Economics* (Lenning 1990) for grades K–3 offers numerous other ideas for presenting economic concepts to young children.

Economics America: National Council on Economic Education (1993) has produced a *Master Curriculum Guide in Economics: Teaching Strategies, K–2* that includes lessons built on the "unique world in which young children live."

The Teacher Resource Manual contains step-by-step lesson plans and reductions of the student pages for quick reference. It provides a summary of the economic content of the lessons, a list of materials needed, and suggestions for integrating economic concepts with other subject areas.

Barter and Money

An interesting way to introduce children to the money system is to initiate a barter simulation. The simulation requires the purchase of inexpensive items (enough to have one for each child), such as gum, candy, toy planes and cars, water pistols, and kites. The items should have different appeal for different children. After giving each child an item, indicate that you will give them a two-minute trading session in which they can trade their item with anyone who will trade with them.

After stopping the trading, ask children the following questions:

Who was able to trade?
Why did you trade?
Why did someone trade with you?
Were there some things you wanted but couldn't get others to trade with you?

Give the children another two-minute trading session. After the session ask some of the same questions, but also include the following:

What is barter?
What are the problems with using barter?
What have we done to solve the problems of using barter?
How does the use of a money system help?

Division of Labor and Specialization

Within the classroom, there are several ways to introduce the concept of specialization. The teacher can establish a company to produce a product such as a kite, party favor, or placemat, being sure that there are several different jobs required to complete the product. Children are interviewed individually to determine their skills and which job they should *specialize* in. Several children may be chosen to work alone and complete all job requirements. Establish an assembly line and put them to work. After completion of the products by the assembly line and the individual workers, discuss what happens in each process. Is the product produced by the assembly line of the same quality as that produced by individual workers? If not, why not? Who can produce the most products? What happens when a worker specializes?

The teacher can also use the tasks that need to be done in the classroom as an example of specialization and division of labor. Rudy is the best person to take care of the plants, while Ruth is better at organizing the art materials.

Another frequently used simulation is the development of a community in the classroom where each child takes on the role of an occupation needed or represented in their community. Once again there can be businesses that produce goods and services for the community.

As mentioned in Chapter 3, the National Council on Economics Education has developed three video programs for introducing the basic economic concepts and to develop economic decision-making skills. These programs are *Econ and Me* for younger children, *Trade Offs* for middle grades, and *Give and Take* for middle and high school.

SUMMARY

Elementary children are often faced with scarcity and the necessity for making economic decisions. It is crucial for them to recognize that they may not have sufficient resources for all of their needs and wants and, therefore, they must make choices. As a result of their choices, there will be opportunity costs. Economic decision making will continue throughout their lives while the decisions will become numerous and probably more difficult to make.

Resources

Armento, B. J. (1986). Learning about the economic world. In V. A. Atwood (Ed.), *Elementary school social studies: Research as a guide to practice* (pp. 85–101). Washington, DC: National Council for the Social Studies, Bulletin No. 79.

Econ and me. (1990). Bloomington, IN: Agency for Instructional Television.

Give and take. (1983). Bloomington, IN: Agency for Instructional Television.

Joint Council on Economic Education. (1978). *Part II: Strategies for teaching economics: Intermediate level (grades 4–6).*

Katzman, C., & King, J. (1978). *Economy size: From barter to business with ideas, activities, and poems.* Santa Monica, CA: Goodyear.

Lenning, L. R. (1990). *More than money: An activities approach to economics.* Glenview, IL: Scott, Foresman. (Goodyear Book)

National Council on Economic Education. (1993). *Master curriculum guide in economics: Teaching strategies, K–2.* New York: Author.

Schug, M. C. (1983). Elementary teachers' views on economic issues. *Theory and Research in Social Education, 2*(1), 55–64.

Skeel, D. J. (1988). *Small size economics lessons for the primary grades.* Glenview, IL: Scott, Foresman. (Goodyear Book)

SUMMARY

While events erupt around them, children try to make sense of what is happening. They need help to understand why the events occurred and how they will affect their lives.

As our world faces immense problems, cooperation among nations is vital. The earlier children recognize how interdependent the world has become, the more they are apt to appreciate the diverse cultures of the world and be willing to work with others to solve the problems.

Law related education makes children more aware of their rights and responsibilities under the law. It gives them opportunities to be active participants in their learning. It may prevent them from breaking the laws.

Whether children are deciding to buy a toy, or save their money, or are doing odd jobs to earn money to buy a bicycle, they are involved in economic activities. Repeatedly their lives are affected by their own as well as others' economic decisions.

LEARNING ACTIVITY

As you reflect on the previous chapter, envision yourself in your classroom (you select the grade and type of school—rural, suburban, inner city). Think about current issues that are controversial. What issue(s) would you discuss with your children? Why? How would you approach the issue(s)? What materials would you need to explore it properly? Is it an issue that you should discuss with your administrator? Should the parents be made aware of the study?

Consider the world today and think about your children—some may one day live in several different countries, interact with cultures from all over the world, and face problems whose solutions depend upon nations cooperating. How will you help children be prepared for these experiences? How can you help them become aware of their role in the world community?

Children experience rules and laws every day. Many times they do not understand why such rules are in place or they are totally unaware of the laws that govern their actions. Failure to help them understand why they have the rules they do and how laws affect them may cause them to be less likely to abide by them. Think about how you plan to manage your classroom. How can you help children understand why rules are important in the classroom? How can you help them be more self-disciplined? How might this help their behavior outside of the classroom? How might they react to laws if they understand why and how they are made, as well as the consequences of breaking laws? Consider some law related education activities you can plan.

How would you feel about starting a business in your classroom, such as making bookmarks or recipe books? How about developing a small community with all the necessary goods and services provided? Think how much more easily children would understand the meaning of scarcity, resources, and economic decision making. You could integrate the other subject areas, including math, language arts, art, and reading. Maybe others as well.

Write your thoughts about the above situations in your journal. Think about how they would affect your social studies program.

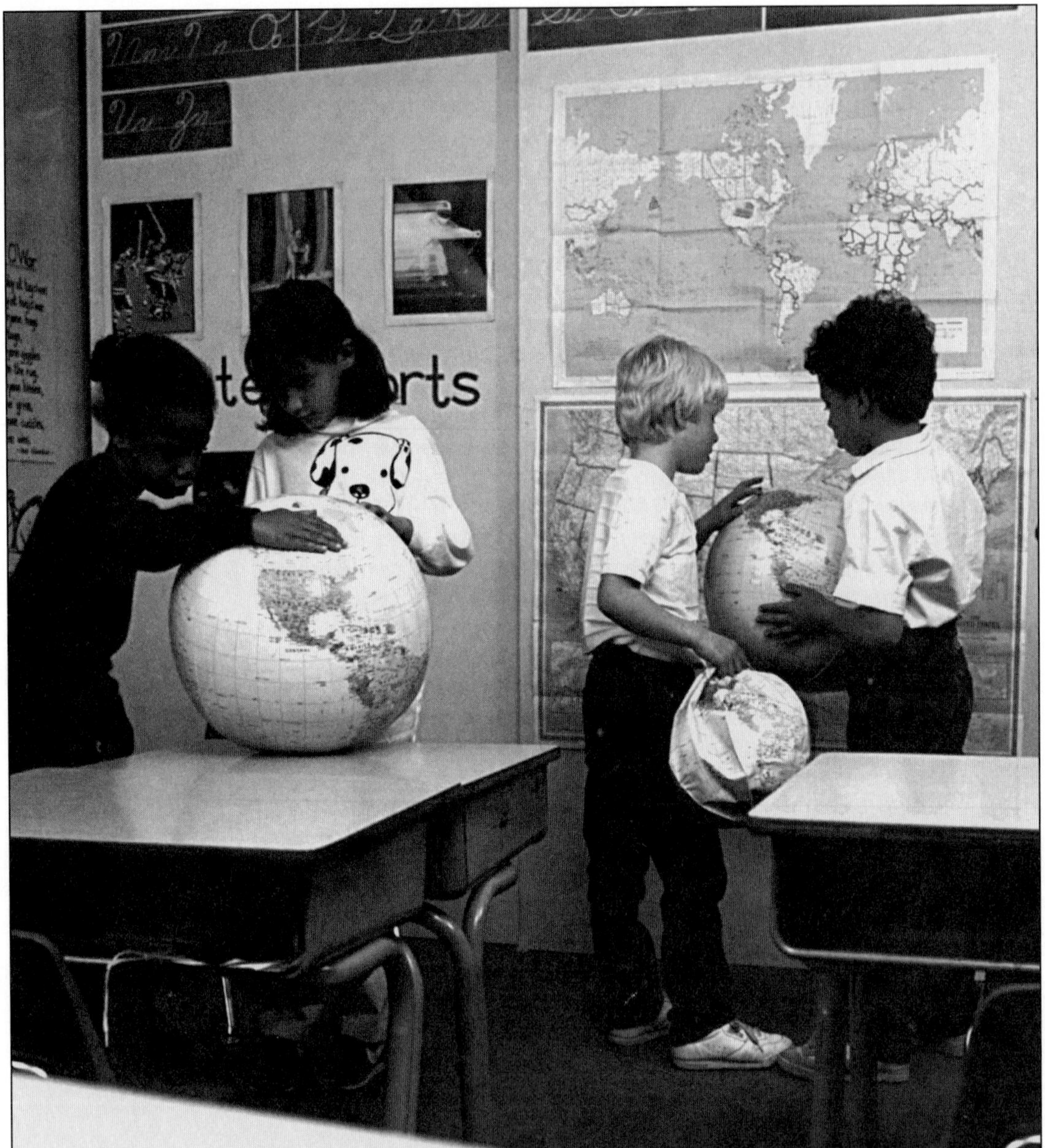

PART III
TEACHING STRATEGIES

ALTHOUGH TEXTBOOKS and state and local curriculum guides may be provided for teachers, they ultimately must design a social studies program to meet the needs of the children in their classrooms. What teaching strategies will they use? How should children learn social science concepts? Should children learn to solve problems through inquiry? What strategies should be used in valuing/moral reasoning? How should map and globe skills be taught?

This section discusses the following teaching strategies: (a) concept development, (b) problem solving through inquiry, (c) skills for valuing/moral reasoning, and (d) map and globe skills.

CHAPTER 7

TEACHING CONCEPTS

CONCEPTS ARE the building blocks of a social studies program. What is a concept? As defined in Chapter 2, "A concept is something conceived in the mind—a thought, an idea, or a notion" (Moore 1970, pp. 112–113). Another definition adds, "a concept is a mental image of something. The 'something' may be anything—a concrete object, a type of behavior, an abstract idea" (Beyer 1971, p. 111). Beyer continues, the "mental image of any given concept will vary according to the background or experience of whoever is conceptualizing" (p. 126). "No one can give the learner his concepts; thus students must construct them out of their own experiences" (Thomas 1972, p. 115).

Parker (1988) identifies "concepts—ideas about what something is—are the basic units of the social studies curriculum" and further "a concept is an idea that exists through its examples" (p. 71). As students encounter examples of concepts through their learning experiences, they extend the process of concept formation. In concept formation, students construct the concepts while thinking about examples of concepts from their own experiences or experiences that are provided by the teacher.

As related earlier in Chapter 2, concepts are stated in a number of forms: concrete such as "mountain" or abstract like "democracy." Some are so broad that they are difficult to conceptualize and must be broken down in order to be understood, for example, "culture." Within culture, other concepts are subsumed, such as customs, traditions, beliefs, institutions, etc. Other concepts may be so narrow they identify only one category, such as "lakes."

Single words like "work" are concepts as are phrases, such as "division of labor."

The content of social studies is derived from the concepts of each of the social science disciplines. How does the acquisition of these concepts help us? Concepts allow us to organize new information as we encounter it. We place that new information into a category or group, thus making it more meaningful to us and allowing us to recognize relationships within data. For example, if we have formed a concept of "shelter" as meaning a place where people are protected from rain, snow, or cold like a house, when we encounter a tent, we also place that in the category of shelter. Another experience might extend our meaning of shelter to include protection from animals, as when a child runs into the house to get away from an angry dog. We then hook that meaning of the concept into our category for shelter.

Concepts have attributes that allow us to form our ideas about their meaning. Attributes describe the concept, such as shelter provides protection. The protection that is provided may be different in different locations and the shelter may take different forms, such as house, tent, apartment, boat, or cardboard box.

"How should concepts be organized for instruction?" and "What teaching strategies should be used?" are difficult questions to answer. Most curricula are organized around topics, such as the "widening horizons" design that moves from family and home to school, community, state, nation, and world, while studying human activities at each level. Embedded in these topics are concepts from the social sciences. For example, when studying the topic of community (which is actually a concept) the concepts from geography might be population and landforms, such as mountains, rivers, and climate. Concepts from economics might be goods and services, market, and interdependence, while concepts from political science might include laws and government. The history concepts might be origin of the community and historical events; while sociology would contribute groups such as family, church, and social; and anthropology concepts might be culture, ethnic, and traditions. These same concepts should be encountered repeatedly when studying different communities or other topics.

Textbooks provide a structure and sequencing of topics. However, teachers may insert other topics or follow a curriculum guide. Concepts should be encountered over and over again throughout the grades always extending and broadening the meaning.

Different approaches to teaching concepts are advocated. One theory suggests that students learn a concept by memorizing a list of its attributes that is provided by the teacher or the textbook, by inferring a set of rules that explain the relationships among the attributes, and practicing classifying instances of examples and nonexamples (Gagne 1965; Tennyson & Park, cited in Yoho 1982). Other theorists (Parker 1988; Taba 1967) believe that students learn concepts best when they construct their own ideas of the concepts through a series of thinking activities labeled concept formation.

INTRODUCING AND EXTENDING CONCEPTS

If concepts are to formulate the curriculum framework for social studies instruction, then it is vital that students conceptualize—develop their own concepts or go beyond merely giving a name to a concept. As Beyer (1971) suggests,

> Concepts help organize data into patterns which may provide meaningful insights into that data. That is, they provide a set of interrelated categories into which evidence gleaned from data or from experience may be placed.
>
> Concepts also generate questions which can be asked of data in order to locate evidence for these categories. Knowing a specific concept enables us to use its elements as questions with which to probe data. (p. 15)

Thus, it is important for teachers to be knowledgeable of different teaching strategies that may be used to introduce and extend concepts.

Introduction of Concepts

Taba's Model

Taba's (1967) model for concept formation relies on teachers asking sequentially ordered questions.

Concepts are formed as students respond to questions which require them: (a) to enumerate items, (b) to find a basis for grouping items similar in some respect, (c) to identify the common characteristics of items in a group, (d) to label the groups, and (e) to subsume items that they have enumerated under those labels (Taba 1967). To further understand the concept, the students move on to interpret and apply the data.

Taba's Model of Cognitive Tasks illustrates the questions that might be asked, the overt activity, and the covert mental (not observable, occurs in the mind) activity.

CONCEPT FORMATION

Overt activity	Covert mental operations	Eliciting questions
1. Enumeration	Differentiation	What did you see? Hear? Note?
2. Grouping	Identifying common properties, abstracting	What belongs together? On what criterion?
3. Labeling, categorizing	Determining the hierarchial order of items. Super and subordination	How would you call these groups? What belongs under what?

INTERPRETATION OF DATA

1. Identifying points	Differentiating	What did you notice? See? Find?

162 • Teaching Concepts

2. Explaining items of identified information	Relating points to each other; determining cause and effect relationships	Why did so-and-so happen?
3. Making inferences	Going beyond what is given: finding implications, extrapolating	What does this mean? What picture does it create in your mind? What would you conclude?

APPLICATION OF DATA

1. Predicting consequences; explaining unfamiliar phenomena	Analyzing the nature of the problem or situation; retrieving relevant knowledge	What would happen if . . . ?
2. Hypothesizing; explaining and/or supporting the predictions and hypotheses	Determining the causal links leading to prediction or hypothesis	Why do you think this would happen?
3. Verifying the predictions	Using logical principles or factual knowledge to determine necessary and sufficient conditions	What would it take for so-and-so to be generally true or probably true?

An application of Taba's model to the concept of community might be introduced as follows:

CONCEPT FORMATION

Teacher question	*Possible response*	*Student overt activity*
What do you think of when you hear the word "community"?	Houses, stores, churches, ballgames, buses, taxis, trucks, cars, movies, schools, doctor, dentist, police, firepersons, mailman, lots of people, friendly, noisy	Enumeration and listing
If you look at the things listed and wanted to place those that are alike in a group, how would you group them?	Houses, stores, churches, schools Buses, taxis, trucks, cars Ballgames, movies Lots of people, friendly, noisy Doctor, dentist, police, firepersons, mailman	Grouping

What would you call each of these groups? How would you label them?	Buildings in community Ways to travel Places for fun How community feels People who work there	
	INTERPRETATION OF DATA	
How would you describe a community after thinking about the groups and their labels?	A community is a place where people live, work, and have fun. Some communities are large and noisy.	Identifying points
Why do people live in communities?	It is easier to find work and places to live. Possible to live near other people for protection and things to do	Explaining items of identified information
What are some disadvantages of living in a community?	May be too crowded, noisy, may not enjoy the recreation provided	Making inferences
	APPLICATION OF DATA	
What might happen if many people moved out of the community?	Some stores and other businesses would close, not as many doctors or dentists or places for people to work	Predicting, hypothesizing
Why might this happen?	Not enough people living in the community to support all the businesses	Supporting prediction
What would you conclude about communities?	Communities grow as people find places to live and work, but may become crowded causing people to leave	Verifying prediction

Parker Model

Parker (1988) uses a variation of concept formation by engaging students to think about three or more examples of the concept. He points out that the teacher should "be sure the concept is an important one—one that needs to be learned and learned thoroughly.... The teacher needs to verify the critical attributes of the concept" (p. 71). The teacher then selects examples of the concept that possess the critical attributes, but also show the diversity. A data-gathering chart should be formulated that presents the examples and asks questions that identify the critical attributes of each example. See the data-gathering chart for the concept of ethnocentrism (Figure 7.1).

The students should be given the data-gathering chart without the label for the concept. They may study it and complete it as individuals, in pairs, or small groups. They should note the differences and similarities among the examples. The students should summarize with individual students writing their statements to "begin with the words, 'These are all [statements] that _____.' The statements should reflect the critical attributes of the concept." The teacher then selects one of the statements containing all of the critical attributes and writes it on the board. Then the students should give the concept a label. If the students do not come up with the conventional label, then the teacher may state that this is what the concept is usually called.

FIGURE 7.1 Data-Gathering Chart on Ethnocentrism

	Is the speaker talking about his or her own culture?	Is the speaker making a negative judgment?	Which culture is judged to be superior? Inferior?	Does the speaker see individual differences among the members of the other culture?
1. A Japanese poet says, "Westerners are barbarians."				
2. Dr. Jane Smith, who has studied Asian cultures all her life, says, "Asians, especially the Japanese, are sneaky and untrustworthy."				
3. A Hindu farmer in India says, "Those Americans are immoral because they eat cows."				
4. An American teenager in California says, "If they're so hungry, why don't those Hindus get smart and eat their cattle?"				
5. Maria, a Hispanic, says, "Those Blacks just haven't been taught the value of an honest day's work."				

Students can then give examples and/or nonexamples of the concept. "Concept formation is a teaching/learning strategy that illustrates the idea: thinking to learn" (Parker 1988, p. 72).

Bruner (cited in Muir 1990) "describes a sequence of learning an unfamiliar concept in three stages of representation: enactive, iconic, and symbolic" (p. 215). First, *enactive* means encountering the concept in a concrete way such as actually observing a mountain or a close proximation by building one in a sand table. *Iconic* means looking at and observing a mountain in a picture or visual representation. *Symbolic* would mean representing the concept in an abstract form, such as a color key on a map that represents mountains. These learning experiences represent ways in which children can understand concepts and not merely give a definition.

Gagne Model

Gagne's (1965) model is an example of a deductive approach to the introduction of a concept. The steps in the model are listed as follows:

Conditions for a Concept-learning Task

1. Show the subject an instance of the concept and specify its name.
2. Show the subject another and different exemplar (or several) and again specify the concept name.
3. Show the subject a negative instance of the concept and specify that it is not the concept name.
4. Show the subject still another positive exemplar and, pointing appropriately to the positive and negative examples respectively, specify the concept name and specify that it is not the concept name.
5. As a test, give the subject a context and request that he or she illustrate or select the instance of the concept. (p. 191)

To apply Gagne's model to the teaching of the concept of "group," first present the students with the picture of a group (basketball team). You may want to list the attributes of a group, such as, These people play together to win a game; or These children play together to have fun. Then state, "This is a group." Show several pictures of a group (Girl Scouts, play group, band) each time stating, "This is a group." Then present a negative example (individual person) stating, "This is not a group." Then present another positive and negative example stating, "This is a group, but this is not a group." To determine if the students have learned the concept, give them a series of pictures which are examples and nonexamples and request that they place them in the appropriate stacks.

The concept of group is easily understood by children when reading Leo Lionni's *Swimmy,* a story about a small fish that organizes many little fish into a big group. "Why did Swimmy need all the other fish? What might have happened to Swimmy if he tried swimming alone? What are the advantages of a group? Disadvantages? Do you belong to any groups?" These questions will further clarify the understanding of the concept of group.

Martorella (1982) summarized the principles that lead to success in concept development. Those principles are as follows:

1. The instructor must begin with a clear and conventionally accepted definition of the concept.
2. At some point, instruction should include definition and/or its primary attributes.
3. Varied examples and nonexamples of the concept should be provided and some strategy should be included to help the learner determine which discussion pertains to examples and which to nonexamples.
4. Unless students know the critical attributes of a concept, they should be taught them prior to or currently with instruction.
5. Some opportunities to experiment with identifying examples and nonexamples should be incorporated, along with feedback on the correctness or incorrectness of the responses.
6. Finally, where young children are involved, pictures or other visual stimuli, rather than strictly verbal stimuli, may facilitate concept learning. (pp. 7–8)

Extending Concepts

Brainstorming

After the students have had some introduction to a concept or in order to determine what their ideas are about a concept, the following instructional strategy can be used.

Give them an envelope and a sheet of paper. The concept to be extended is *culture*. Ask them to brainstorm five things they think about when they hear the word culture. Then have the students place their lists inside the envelopes and pass them around until no one can determine whose envelope they are holding. Before they open them, have them write on the outsides of the envelopes the one thing they are sure is on the list inside. When they open the envelopes, determine if they were correct.

Then ask students to call out the lists so that they may be written on the board. After the list is complete, ask students if there are any things that are similar and could be put together. After grouping has occurred, label the groups and then ask if anyone disagrees with any of the things listed to describe culture. Discuss those items that are in question. Then ask if someone will generalize about the meaning of culture. What is culture? What is not culture?

Series of Pictures

In an attempt to extend the concept of shelter, collect a series of pictures that represent different types of homes (single family dwelling, row houses, apartment highrise, trailer, boat, nomad's tent). These examples can also represent styles from different cultures.

Show children the first picture and ask the question, "What do you see?" If children do not enumerate the attributes of the home such as windows, doors, etc., then ask specific questions like, "What is this?" After the visible attributes have been listed, ask questions such as, "What does this provide for people?" What do we call it?" Then present each one with the questions, "How is this alike?" "How is this different?" After all of the pictures have been utilized, ask the children if they can generalize about shelters. An example of a response might be: "Shelters may look different and be made from different materials, but they all provide places for people to live." If it has not come up in previous discussion, ask the question, "What is the difference between a 'shelter' and a 'home'?" This question should stimulate further extension of the concept.

Storybooks

Younger children are delighted by the antics of their favorite friends in storybooks; additionally, those same antics provide excellent opportunities for concept development. Read Virginia Lee Burton's *The Little House* (1942), which is a story about a house that is in the country, but growth causes a city to build around it. Extend the concept of change with questions such as, What was happening to the house? Why didn't the house like all the hustle and bustle of the city? Why did people ignore the house? Has anything similar to what happened to the house happened to you? Are there other changes in your life? What can you do about them?

Another children's book that extends the concept of family is *The Little Brute Family* by Russell Hoban. It is the story of the Brute family (animals) who seldom had things go right for them until Baby Brute found a wandering good feeling that made the family act differently toward one another. Questions such as, How did the Brute family members act before they found the good feeling? What do you think made them act that way? How did saying "please" and "thank you" make the family members feel? Why did the Brute family change their name to Nice? What is the story telling you about families?

SUMMARY

As indicated earlier in the chapter, concepts may be concrete or abstract, broad or narrow, single words or phrases. The ease with which children can acquire concepts will be dependent upon their level of abstractness, broadness, or length and difficulty. As indicated by Taba (1967), "Because concepts are hierarchical, or of different levels of abstraction, complexity, and generality, concepts of a high order can be learned only gradually over a period of time and by repeated return engagements in new contexts" (p. 36). Therefore, teachers will find concepts embedded in the conceptual frameworks supplied by the social studies textbooks and other instructional materials, but will need to determine what additional experiences are needed by children for those concepts to be learned.

SELECTED REFERENCES

Beyer, B. K. (1971). *Inquiry in the social studies classroom: A strategy for teaching.* Columbus, OH: Charles E. Merrill.

Burton, V. L. (1942). *The little house.* New York: Houghton Mifflin.

Gagne, R. M. (1965). The learning of concepts. *School Review, 73,* 191.

Gilmore, A. C., & McKinney, C. W. (1986). The effects of student questions and teacher questions on concept acquisition. *Theory and Research in Social Education, 14*(3), 225–244.

Hoban, R. (1966). *The little Brute family.* New York: Macmillan.

Lionni, L. (1963). *Swimmy.* New York: Pantheon.

Martorella, P. H. (1982). Cognition research: Some implications for the design of social studies instructional materials. *Theory and Research in Social Education, 10*(3), 7, 8.

McKinney, C. W., and others. (1987). The effects of ordinary and coordinate concept examples on first grade students' acquisition of three coordinate concepts. *Theory and Research in Social Education, 15*(1), 45–49.

Moore, V. D. (1970, February). Guidelines for the new social studies. *Instructor, 79,* 112–113.

Muir, S. P. (1990). Time concepts for elementary children. *Social Education, 54*(4), 215–218, 247.

Parker, W. C. (1988). Thinking to learn concepts. *Social Studies, 79,* 70–73.

Stanley, W. B., & Matthews, R. C. (1985). Recent research on concept learning: Implications for social education. *Theory and Research in Social Education, 12*(4), 57–74.

Taba, H. (1967). *Teachers' handbook for elementary social studies.* Palo Alto, CA: Addison-Wesley.

Thomas, J. L. (1972). Concept formation in elementary school social studies. *Social Studies, 63*(3), 110–116.

Yoho, R. F. (1982). Effectiveness of four concept teaching strategies on social studies concept acquisition and retention. *Theory and Research in Social Education, 14*(3), 211–223.

LEARNING ACTIVITY

Think back to your elementary school days. Think about the learning of concepts. Do you remember any concept that was difficult for you to learn, such as "isthmus" or "democracy"? Can you remember why you had difficulty with it? How was it presented to you? Did you read about it in the textbook? Did the teacher give you a definition? Were there any concrete examples of it? As you think about it, what do you think might have helped you to learn the concept? Record your thoughts in your journal. Think about them when trying to teach concepts to your class.

CHAPTER 8

PROBLEM SOLVING THROUGH INQUIRY

DEVELOPING THINKING SKILLS

The method of teaching problem solving through inquiry often has been misunderstood and misused because of discrepancies in the definitions given for the terms "problem solving," "inquiry," "reflective thinking," "inductive reasoning," and "discovery." Frequently, these terms are used interchangeably without explanation of their different meanings.

Problem solving is the process whereby an individual identifies a problem situation, formulates tentative explanations or hypotheses, verifies these tentative hypotheses by gathering and evaluating data, and restates the hypotheses or arrives at generalizations. The individual may then apply these generalizations to new situations.

Many authors use reflective thinking and inductive reasoning to identify the problem-solving method. Early in the 1930s, Dewey (1933) referred to the identification of the problem as the prereflective period, to the search for an answer as the reflective period, and to the dispelling of doubt as the postreflective period.

Inductive reasoning or inductive teaching is described as the process of leading individuals toward solving a problem by providing them with sufficient stimulation and a direction based on hypotheses. Inquiry is the method of searching for the solution to the problem.

"Inquiry is not conducted as an indiscriminant search for facts; it is instead, an organized, directed search" (Schwab 1962, p. 14).

> Hypotheses direct its activities. . . . Hypotheses determine what facts will be selected as relevant to the problem. They influence what interpretations are formulated and accepted in the end. (Fair & Shaftel 1967, p. 89)

Discovery may occur as the individual is conducting his or her search—the person reassembles or reorganizes information based on previous and newly acquired learning and gains insight into the problem. Bruner (1962) states that discovery

> is in its essence a matter of rearranging or transforming evidence in such a way that one is enabled to go beyond the evidence so reassembled to new insights. It may well be that an additional fact or shred of evidence makes this larger transformation possible. But it is often not even dependent on new information. (pp. 82–83)

Therefore, inquiry and discovery can be defined as steps in the problem-solving process.

The problem-solving approach in teaching rests solidly on the ability of children to think effectively. Taba (1967) relates, "The task of instruction is to provide systematic training in thinking and to help students acquire cognitive skills which are necessary for thinking autonomously and productively" (p. 87). There is a sequential order, as Piaget shows, in the development of forms of thought from childhood to adulthood; each step is a prerequisite to the next. A student should manipulate concrete objects in order to develop an intuitive grasp of the abstract concepts before engaging in abstract reasoning. Teaching strategies require the following for a proper developmental sequence: "The teaching strategies which helped students advance to higher levels of thinking involved what questions were asked; what the teacher gave or sought and at which point in the proceedings; at which point he permitted, encouraged, or bypassed elaboration and extension of ideas; and whether or not there were summaries of ideas and information before inferences of higher order were sought" (Taba 1967, p. 88).

As Taba so aptly points out, teaching children thinking skills depends more on what we get out of the children than on what we put into them. "Critical thinking must be more than simply an abstract mental exercise. It must involve the child in a real felt problem" (Tanner, cited in Sears & Parsons 1991, p. 50). The basic philosophy of the problem-solving approach is one of developing thinking skills in children that enable them to formulate generalizations about a given situation. These generalizations should be ones that can be applied in new situations, specifically in the problems in the everyday lives of the children, as well as the problems of our global world. If teachers are to help children develop thinking skills, they must know how to ask the right questions at approximately the right time—when the child appears ready for the question.

Some theorists would argue, however, as Tanner (cited in Sears & Parsons 1991) does that "critical thinking has gone the canned and packaged way . . . critical thinking has been reduced to a strategy, a series of steps or planned exercises that can be executed by a trained practitioner, the teacher. In its reduction, it has been weakened" (p. 50). On the other hand, those who advocate the use of inquiry teaching to develop critical thought strongly support its use. "Inquiry teaching is a teaching methodology for the education of students as active learners and problem solvers rather than passive receptacles of information" (Maher 1987, p. 186).

Sears and Parsons (1991) caution that

> Inquiry is harder to teach. It takes more work and preparation. Not everyone likes it. Discussion and argument is louder than memorization, and administrators have good ears. Parents feel that content knowledge is safer and certainly more "objective" than unsanctified knowledge. Even students, who have been encouraged to memorize, feel safer when they do what they have always done. (p. 51)

If teachers, particularly new teachers, are to stick with inquiry (critical thinking) "it must become more than a strategy to them." Sears and Parsons indicate "they must hold it as an ethic (a philosophy or system of morals). Only teachers committed to critical thinking as an ethic will persevere in the face of all circumstances which make it difficult to implement a social studies program focused on critical thinking" (p. 51).

ADVANTAGES AND DISADVANTAGES OF PROBLEM SOLVING THROUGH INQUIRY

Advocates of the method of problem solving through inquiry stress the value of developing rational critical thought and of the act of discovery encountered during the search for solutions to a problem. Bruner (1962) hypothesizes that discovery in learning "helps the child to learn the varieties of problem solving, of transforming knowledge for better use, helps him to learn how to go about the very task of learning" (p. 95). Retrieval of the information learned through discovery is more easily accomplished (Bruner 1962). Research indicates that we can teach for critical thinking in social studies and that our students can learn to think critically (Cornbleth 1985).

Motivation for learning becomes internal for learners in the problem-solving situation because they are actively seeking knowledge to solve a given problem. The excitement of discovery encourages them to continue their search; they learn by doing. The problems presented to the learners are concrete and related directly to their own experiences. The children can suggest a variety of solutions, but the situations remain open-ended, which can lead to further study.

Those who question the emphasis on the act of discovery of the inquiry method suggest that it places too little attention on the crucial role played by facts and skills in a student's mastery of a body of knowledge. Ausubel (1963) relates that "abundant experimental research has confirmed the proposition that prior learnings are not transferable to new learnings unless they are first overlearned" (p. 456). However, Sears and Parsons (1990) point out that "objective facts are always subjective" (p. 55). There are many "examples of 'established facts' which have been challenged by new evidence" (Sears & Parsons 1990, p. 56).

Friedlander (1965) questions the value of a child's curiosity in operating as a motivator and incentive for academic learning. He claims that children's curiosity may be unsystematic, noncumulative, immediate, and easily satisfied. He suggests that a child's curiosity may be satisfied with incorrect or partial information and that it may be strongest with issues not necessarily the proper concern of the school.

Concern is voiced by some for the inquiry method's practice of accepting "any answer." This group stresses the fact that the children might not have the opportunity to test all of their answers and it questions how the children will know if their answers are right or wrong. "Real world problems seldom have neat and tidy solutions . . . reflection and action about real issues rarely produced one, permanent resolution to the problem" (Sears & Parsons 1991, p. 59). However, it is not a question of whether an answer is right or wrong but rather when new or additional information is acquired, are the children willing to change their responses.

Questioning Skills

Reports of classroom instruction indicate that teachers rely heavily upon textbooks and ask questions that require the recall of information (Goodlad 1984).

Several models of questioning have been advanced to increase the teacher's ability to ask questions at higher levels of thought. One example is Taba's (1967) model based on three cognitive levels: concept formation, interpretation of data, and application of principles. At the first level, *concept formation,* as was described in Chapter 6, the child is asked to list, group, and categorize through such questions as, What did you see, hear, note? What belongs together? On what criterion? What would you call these groups? What belongs under what?

Next, the child is requested to *interpret the data* collected, draw inferences, and generalize through questions such as, What did you notice? See? Find? Why did so-and-so happen? What does this mean? What picture does it create in your mind? What would you conclude?

The last level, *application of principles,* requires that the child hypothesize about what he or she thinks will happen in the new situation and to support this prediction. These questions might include: What would happen if? Why do you think this would happen? What would it take for so-and-so to be generally true or probably true? A representation of Taba's model appears in Chapter 6.

FIGURE 8.1

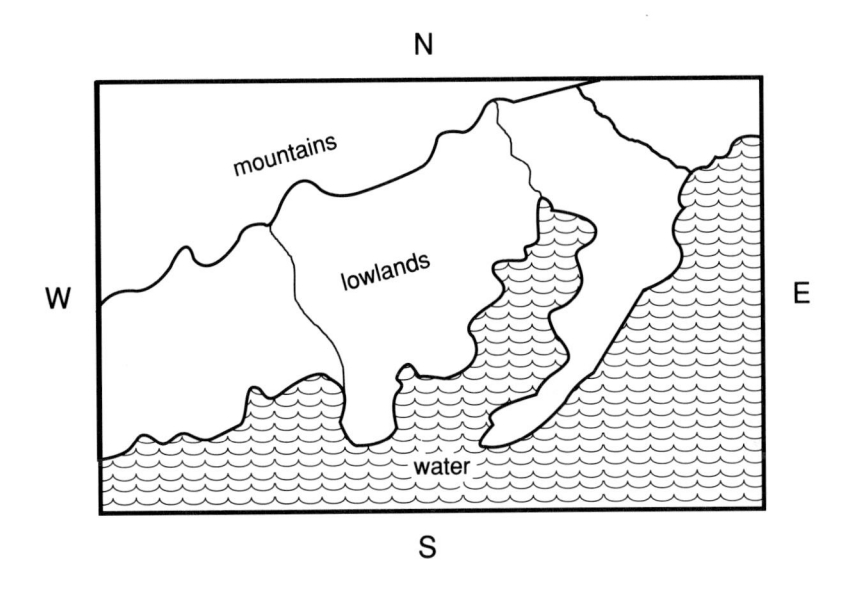

[Map drawing showing a coastline with labeled features: mountains (north area), lowlands (central), and water (south/east). Compass directions N, S, E, W marked on sides.]

Look at the transparency of the map drawing that should be used to introduce the learning experience (see Figure 8.1). This lesson might be used to introduce a study of cities or problems of cities. Figure 8.2 illustrates how Taba's three levels of questioning would be applied. Remember that these questions are only the key ones and others would be asked dependent upon the responses from the children.

FIGURE 8.2

CONCEPT FORMATION

Teacher question	Possible response	Student activity
What do you see on the map?	blue, green, rivers, brown, harbor, coastline	Enumeration and listing
What belongs together in a group?	blue—rivers brown—harbor green—coastline	Grouping
What would you call these groups?	color key natural features	Labeling Categorizing

continued

FIGURE 8.2

INTERPRETATION OF DATA

What are some natural features to be considered in selecting the location for building a city?	Climate, physical features, space, water supply, harbor, protection from elements, natural resources	Identifying
Why would you want to build your city near a good harbor?	Cheaper transportation, ease of access	Explaining items identified
How do climate and physical features of an area influence the development of a city?	They determine type of building, heating, or cooling	Making inferences

APPLICATION OF DATA

If you were to build a city somewhere on this bay, where would you build it?	Beside that big harbor along the coast	Predicting, hypothesizing
Why would you build it there?	It would be protected, access to interior, etc. Harbor would be deep enough for large vessels, natural resources nearby	Supporting prediction
What would you conclude about the location of cities?	Cities are built where they are accessible and near resources	Verifying the prediction

Another application of the model for use with younger children would be with the next picture (see Figure 8.3). Several concepts and generalizations can be developed by redirecting the focus of the questions.

Generalization: There must be a demand for your product in order for it to sell.

Questions	Possible response	
What do you see in the picture?	wood stand lemonade sign price change full glasses full pitcher trees	boy looks sad grass dog hammer nails glass spilled
If you were to group the things that are similar, what would you put together?	wood stand lemonade sign hammer nails full glasses full pitcher	boy looks sad dog

FIGURE 8.3

	glass spilled price change	trees grass
What would you label these groups?	lemonade stand	disappointed boy
	product not sold	where stand is
	INTERPRETATION OF DATA	
What did you notice about the boy?	He looks unhappy.	
Why do you think he is unhappy? What is his problem?	No one is buying his lemonade.	
How do you know the lemonade isn't selling?	Pitcher and glasses are full. Price has been dropped. No one is around to buy.	
	APPLICATION OF DATA	
What should the boy do if he wants his lemonade to sell?	Move it to a busy corner. Move it to a playground or a baseball game.	
Why should he move it there?	So there are more people around to buy it.	
What would you say is needed to be sure you can sell your lemonade?	You need people who are thirsty.	

Another generalization that can be developed with the same picture, but changing the focus of the question in the interpretation and application level, would be the following:

Generalization: Many people feel the same way when they face problems.

INTERPRETATION OF DATA

Questions	Possible responses
What did you notice about the boy in the picture?	He looks unhappy. He looks sad. He looks worried.
How do you know he's sad, worried, or unhappy?	The look on his face I've felt like that.
When did you feel that way?	I had a lemonade stand and I didn't sell any. I tried to sell cookies. I lost my dog. My friend didn't want to play.

APPLICATION OF DATA

What can we do when we have problems like these?	Try to find a way to solve them.
What will that do?	Make us feel better.
What can we say about how people feel when they have problems?	They're sad. They try to solve them.

The questions need to be asked in sequence so that the children will move from the concrete to the abstract. With experience the children will begin to organize their thinking this way and to formulate their own questions.

Classroom Conditions

If children are to receive maximum benefit from the questioning strategies and develop critical thinking, the atmosphere of the classroom must foster a feeling of trust and security within the children. Students need to know that they can ask questions and offer acceptable answers without fear of being wrong. Children should know that their ideas will be valued as well as learn to value the ideas of others. The classroom environment should provide excitement and stimulation for learning. Materials should be available to supply the needs of searching minds. The teacher should create an atmosphere of mental freedom that enables each individual to think without concern for boundaries.

Some would argue that teachers' desire for classroom control as well as their desire to be the source of knowledge and the authority for students corrupts the possibility for critical thinking in the classroom (Common 1982). If a teacher is to be successful in developing the inquiry process and hence critical thinking, then he or she must be willing to allow children to participate in the process of setting the limits for behavior, allow children to question their ideas, as well as ask them to explain their answers.

The responses given by a teacher, verbally and nonverbally, will relay much to the children. To state flatly "you're wrong" or "what a ridiculous answer" to children in front of their peers will cause them to be much more cautious with their next responses, if they respond again. Accepting their answers, asking them to discuss how they arrived at that response, or indicating your understanding by "yes, I see your point" are effective ways to acknowledge a contribution to the discussion.

Role of the Teacher

As mentioned before, in an inquiry-oriented classroom, the concept of the teacher's role undergoes a change in emphasis. Previously, the teacher assumed the major roles of information giver and disciplinarian with only minor roles of motivator, referrer, counselor, and advisor (see Figure 8.4). However, in an inquiry-centered classroom, the teacher assumes the primary role of motivator, while remaining an information giver, disciplinarian, counselor, referrer, and advisor (see Figure 8.5).

As motivator, teachers stimulate and challenge the students to think. They initiate problem situations for them to identify. Their questioning provides the focus and direction for the children's search. They assume the role of information giver only when the students request it or when it becomes necessary to redirect activities that may have wandered from the original goal. As

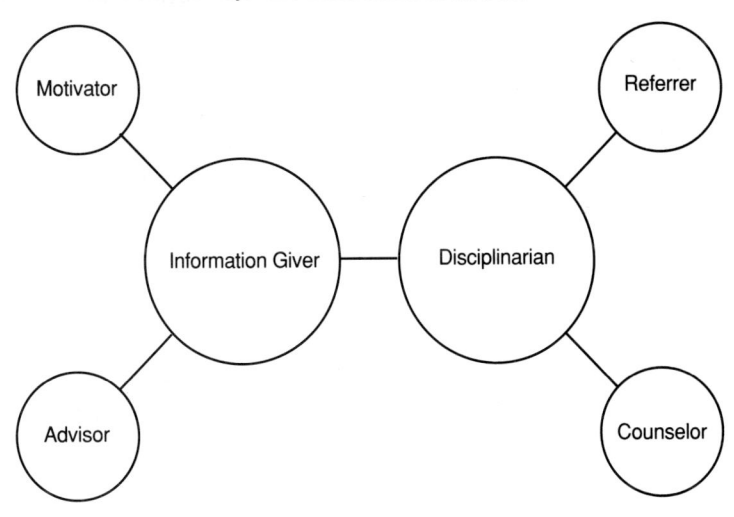

FIGURE 8.4 The Teacher's Major and Minor Roles in the Past

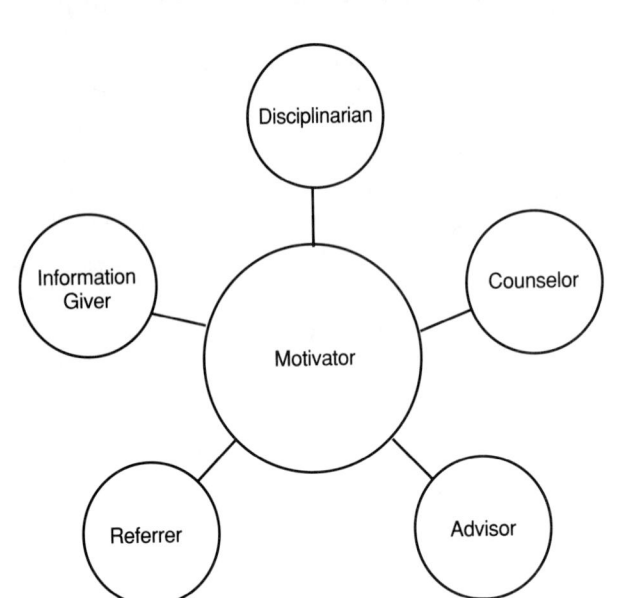

FIGURE 8.5 The Teacher's Major and Minor Roles in an Inquiry-Centered Classroom

(Diagram: central circle labeled "Motivator" connected to five surrounding circles labeled "Disciplinarian," "Counselor," "Advisor," "Referrer," and "Information Giver.")

referrer, they guide children to materials and sources of information. As advisor and counselor, they supply children with encouragement when it is needed and diagnose difficulties and give assistance. Discipline is necessary to avoid chaos; however, it is vital that children be guided toward self-discipline, which is important in the problem-solving approach.

To summarize the teacher's role, it is one that:

1. Helps children seek an answer rather than to serve as a fountain of knowledge.
2. Provides motivation and direction for the inquiry.
3. Establishes an effective classroom climate where children can question and seek answers without fear of being penalized for wrong answers.
4. Provides materials expressing different points of view.
5. Helps children to learn to accept the opinions of others.
6. Helps children develop an organized method of thinking about and dealing with information so that they will become independent thinkers.
7. Becomes an effective questioner—leading children from the concrete to the abstract level of thought.

Teachers should be aware that the use of the inquiry process in the classroom does require more planning time on their part. They must know how they will initiate the activity, what questions they will ask, and how to refocus the thinking of children. To accomplish these tasks it is necessary to have sufficient background knowledge of the problem from a variety of sources.

Responsibility of the Child in an Inquiry-Centered Classroom

The children become active inquirers into their own education. They make decisions about their learning experiences and interact more with teacher and peers. They are active thinkers—seeking information, probing, and processing data, and asking questions rather than always being questioned. The children often pose the problem to be solved, suggest the hypotheses to be tested, search for the necessary information, determine the discrepancies in the information, accept or reject the hypotheses, and draw generalizations. They participate in the self-discovery of certain basic concepts and principles as they move from observation, classification, interpretation, and application to generalization. The children acquire insight into their own behavior that will enable them to apply the generalizations to their own lives. They also learn to express themselves so that all may understand their views while learning to be open-minded and willing to accept the thoughts and opinions of others. Not all children enjoy inquiry experiences. Some do not like the uncertainness of the answers.

Goals/Outcomes

The goals/outcomes for the method of problem solving through inquiry are based on the processes or steps in which children are involved (identifying a problem stating and testing hypotheses, and generalizing).

These broad goals/outcomes are outlined as follows:

Develop the student's ability to:

1. Identify and define a problem situation.
2. Use a variety of materials to secure information relative to the problem.
3. Formulate hypotheses for tentative problem solutions utilizing the information presented and previously acquired knowledge.
4. Use rational thought processes by constructing hypotheses and testing, revising, and refining those hypotheses.
5. Discover the relationships between previously and newly acquired information to acquire new insight into the solution of a problem.
6. Compare and evaluate various theories, data, and generalizations in testing tentative hypotheses.
7. Select relevant facts necessary for testing hypotheses.
8. Express opinions on issues after an analysis of available information.
9. State generalizations from results and apply them to new situations.

Develop an attitude of:

10. Open-mindedness toward all sides of an issue before arriving at a decision.

11. Acceptance of the opinions of others and understanding of why opinions vary.
12. Concern and interest in the problems of society by active participation in problem-solving activities.

These goals/outcomes are general and based on the major values of the problem-solving methods as purported by its many advocates. More specific objectives should be developed within the content boundaries and needs of the individual classroom.

Problem Selection

How successful will the problem-solving-through-inquiry-process be? Will students who have not been exposed to this type of study be excited to pursue several possible answers to questions or will they continue to expect one right answer? Much of the success of the problem-solving method may lie in the selection of the problems for inquiry. One of the issues that has long been discussed is whether the teacher should select the problem to be studied or students should be allowed to choose. Some theorists believe that one of the reasons why the issue exists is the misinterpretation of Dewey's ideas about problem solving (Maxcy 1986). Dewey stated that the problem should be "vitally real to students," that such problems be connected with the student's present experience, be within their capacity, and arouse in the learner a search for new knowledge and ideas. Dewey did not say that the problem must be the student's own to prompt such arousal. Students could very well be moved to inquire by a teacher-selected problem (Maxcy 1986).

However, it is important that the teacher use certain criteria in the selection of the problems.

Dunfee and Sagl (1966) identified the following criteria:

1. Does the problem challenge the children intellectually, stimulate critical thinking, allow them to seek cause-and-effect relationships, and offer opportunity for formulating and testing generalizations?
2. Does the problem relate directly to the lives of the children, based on their past experiences, and have an impact upon them presently?
3. Is the problem concerned with a basic human activity and does it thus illumine man's efforts to meet his needs?
4. Are there sufficient community and classroom instructional resources available for developing the problem?
5. Does the problem offer opportunities for expansion of interests?

Fox, Lippit, and Lohman (1964) assume "that the way for children to inquire in a social science area is to begin with incidents that are microcosms of the larger scene—incidents that are representative of their own life experiences" (pp. 156–157). Here is an adaptation of their model of inquiry.

1. Identify problem. Set goals. Make design for study. Why do people behave in this way?
2. Observation data collection. Children look for clues to determine why things turn out the way they do.
3. Advance theories for causes of behavior.
4. What behavior might lead to better consequences? Make hypothesis. Test hypothesis.
5. Draw conclusions.
6. Research theories of others.
7. Generalize. How can I apply this to my own life?

An example of the method of problem solving through inquiry will be developed with adaptations from this model.

Initiation

The initiation (designated in the model as step 1) sets the stage for the problem-solving situation. It should stimulate inquiry and develop a continuing interest in the problem. Unless sufficient background is provided, problem identification will be difficult; however, too much information may stymie the quest. The initiation establishes the focus or direction of the search and serves as a springboard for action. The most effective initiations are those that actively involve the children either mentally or physically. Possibilities for this stimulation are contained in these illustrations of initiations.

Incident

This next example from a sixth grade classroom is designed to initiate inquiry.

Step 1. The teacher, without giving any reason for the action, uses chairs and desks to build a separating wall between two sections of children in the classroom. The teacher deliberately separates good friends and any brothers or sisters. The children soon ask questions: Why are you doing this? What have we done to deserve this? My best friend is on the other side—when will we get to sit together again? How long are you going to leave this here? As a result of this experience, the children begin to analyze the motives for and results of such actions. The remaining steps of the model are easily identified.

Step 2. Observe the behavior of the children as the incident takes place. Help the children look for clues to understand their own behavior.

Step 3. Advance theories about causes—what negative or positive feelings were produced?

Step 4. What behavior might lead to better consequences? Was there some way to avoid the building of the wall? Make and test a hypothesis by classroom action.

Step 5. Draw conclusions and summarize learnings.

Step 6. Discuss places in the world where cities or countries have been divided in such a manner—Berlin, Korea, Vietnam, and more recently Yugoslavia and Czechoslovakia. By introducing questions and materials, the teachers can provide direction or focus toward one of these areas of the world if they desire. The inquiry can now take on as much emphasis as necessary through research, reading, and discussion.

Step 7. Generalizations can be drawn from the study. Final applications are made to the children's own life—a possible question might be: "What behavior leads to hostile feelings toward me?"

How does problem solving/inquiry fit into the structure of a curriculum guide or the outline of a textbook? Quite easily. The previous initiation might be used to pursue the Vietnam War, the history of Eastern Europe, or any situation where divisiveness has occurred. The following problem-solving and inquiry activities are designed to be used to stimulate thought about topics in curriculum guides or textbooks, but also events that may be occurring within the child's world.

PROBLEM-SOLVING AND INQUIRY ACTIVITIES

Presentation of Facts

Another activity designed to initiate inquiry is this graduated presentation of a series of facts about a country to a fifth grade class (Hoffman 1992, pp. 643, 778, 779).

FIRST TRANSPARENCY

Information about a country
Country
Area: 761,604 sq. mi.
Population: 90,007,000
Birthrate: 29/1,000
Suicides: 1.6/100,000
Life expectancy:
  male 68
  female 76
Literacy: 88%

Information about a state
Texas
Area: 266,807 sq. mi.
Population: 17,348,206
Birthrate of U.S.: 15.7/1,000
Suicides in U.S.: 11.6/100,000
U.S. life expectancy:
  male 72
  female 78.8

Questions:
As you compare the area and population of this country with those of Texas, what conclusions can you draw?

What does the comparison of birthrates indicate?

What does the comparison of suicide rates suggest about the country?

From your limited knowledge of this country, identify any problems you think it might have.

Some problems the children might suggest would be overpopulation and lack of food.

SECOND TRANSPARENCY
Major crops

cotton	wheat
coffee	sugar cane
corn	vegetables
rice	

Questions:

What indication of the physical features of the country do these products give you?

What type of climate do these crops suggest?

What discrepancies in the climate might these crops suggest?

Do the crops indicate the country's location?

THIRD TRANSPARENCY
Minerals and Natural Gas

silver (world's leading producer)	copper	natural gas
	oil	
gold (7.5 million; U.S. 63.1 million)		
lead		

Questions:

Do the minerals indicate anything different about the physical features?

What can you hypothesize about the technology and industries of the country?

FOURTH TRANSPARENCY
Industrial Products

iron and steel	rubber	petroleum
chemicals		
electrical goods		
textiles		

Questions:

What can you conclude about the country from its industrial products?

Would you change any of your previous hypotheses as a result of this added information?

FIFTH TRANSPARENCY

Imports:	30 billion
Exports:	27 billion

Questions:
What does the imbalance between exports and imports suggest about the economy of this country?
Hypothesize concerning the problems you see this country facing.

SIXTH TRANSPARENCY
Tourism
Tourists: $4.9 billion   Texas: $17.6 billion

Questions:
Does the information about added income from tourism change any of your hypotheses?
What country do you think it is?

The country is Mexico. This is often a topic in the fifth grade curriculum. The class can now begin to seek information to test their hypotheses about the country. Small cooperative groups can be organized to test specific hypotheses or individual children can search out information for an assigned hypothesis. The information on the transparencies was selected to focus primarily on economics, but other facts can be selected to change the focus.

Wastebasket Technique

The teacher collects assorted articles from the wastebasket in one of the rooms of the house or one from another classroom in the school. For example, items from the kitchen might include a cereal box with the vitamins listed, a soft drink can (be sure to include the pull-ring), frozen orange juice can, other vegetable or fruit cans, a pair of scissors, a box or can that has a person's picture on it, a knife and fork, an ice cube tray, a penny, a plastic milk container, can opener, and glass bottles. Other materials may be added as the teacher plans to focus the search for information. Pose the problem thus: If you were an archaeologist in the year 2500 and during a dig had unearthed these articles from a lost culture, what could you hypothesize about that culture? Could you draw any generalizations about the culture without further information?

This type of activity should increase the child's skills of observing, classifying, and interpreting data and formulating hypotheses. Another approach to this same type of activity would be to substitute artifacts from other cultures. Using the articles from another class's wastebasket might be interesting to hypothesize what that class was doing.

Discrepant Data

The utilization of the discrepant data technique is intended to create cognitive dissonance within the individual, which should help break down stereotypes.

For example, to introduce the study of another culture, choose slides or pictures that would reinforce the stereotypes about that culture—such as wooden shoes, windmills, tulips, and chocolate from Holland. Present the slides or pictures to the children and ask them to formulate a generalization about the culture. An example of the generalization they might arrive at would be: Most people in Holland wear wooden shoes and grow tulips.

Then introduce the discrepant data in the form of slides or pictures featuring large cities and factories to show the modern aspect of Holland. Ask the children to restructure their generalization to accommodate the new information. The restructured generalization might be formulated thus: Some people in Holland still wear wooden shoes on special occasions and grow tulips, but many live in modern cities and work in factories.

Role Playing

Role playing is an activity that can be used for initiation in any grade. Following is an example of its use at the primary level. The teacher presents and discusses a particular situation with several selected children who, in turn, role play for the class. Their dialogue follows:

KEVIN: Did you hear what happened to Billy on the playground yesterday?
SARAH: No, I was absent.
KEVIN: He was sliding backwards down the slide and cracked his head.
JESS: He's in the hospital with a concussion.
SARAH: I'm sorry, but he knows we shouldn't slide backwards.
KEVIN: He always did like to show off.
JEFF: Other kids do it all the time and don't get hurt, so why shouldn't he?

Questions:
Why do you suppose Billy behaved this way?
The class discusses the situation and recognizes the problems and consequences of breaking safety rules. They try to understand why things turn out as they do. Why did Billy get hurt when others do the same thing without being hurt? What type of behavior would lead to better consequences? The class makes and tests hypotheses and draws conclusions. Teachers may then direct the search for information in any direction they prefer—for example, bike safety, home safety, or highway safety.

A variation of this initiation can be accomplished by role playing using an unfinished story for which the children seek solutions. An example might be:

Terry had borrowed a great snake book from Kim to finish his report for science. While he was working at the kitchen table (where his mother had told him not to do his homework) eating cookies and drinking a glass of milk, his baby brother knocked over the milk, drenching Kim's book. What should he do? His mother wouldn't allow him to go on the trip to the zoo Saturday if she knew he had disobeyed, but he couldn't return Kim's book the way it looked now.

Children can take turns playing the roles of mother, Terry, and Kim as they work out the solutions to the problem. Other similar role playing situations can be found in *Role Playing for Social Values* by Fannie R. Shaftel and George Shaftel (1967).

Tape Presentations

Another interesting technique to utilize is a taped presentation which provides the opportunity to include several voices and sound effects. Teachers can tape segments of historical diaries or fiction stories that introduce problem situations and can be quite effective. An example of one follows:

Rob Nelson added a flashlight to the collection of clothes and other articles he had placed in his gym bag. He thought he'd better go to the kitchen and get some cookies and a sandwich or two since he didn't know when he might find food again. Rob was running away from home. He was tired of all the rules, rules, rules. Go to bed by 9:00, you can't watch TV on school nights, and on and on.

Rob left the house and started for the main highway, where he hoped to get a ride. Rob walked for a long time, but no one seemed interested in giving him a ride. When he spied a police car coming down the road, he quickly dashed off into the woods. All of a sudden from the direction of his city came a blinding flash and loud booms. Rob dove for a covered ditch and that was all he remembered.

Hours later Rob came to; he ached all over. Gradually he crawled toward the opening, which was almost closed with debris. He looked out and was stunned at what he saw. The landscape was scarred and nothing could be seen. No sound, human or mechanical, could be heard. No birds sang.

For a while he just stood there. Then he . . .

The generalization to be reached by the children from a discussion of this episode is: Written laws are an attempt to clarify the rules by which society operates and to promote the impartial treatment of its members.

Dialogue between teacher and children might go like this:

T: What would be one of the first things you might do?
S: I'd run.
S: I'd look around and maybe just go back and see what happened.
S: I'd just run as fast as I could the opposite way.
T: Well, suppose you did look around; what might you look for?
S: Some way to survive.
S: For people.
T: Why would you look for people?
S: To see if any were alive.

S: You heard the big sound (on tape) and then you couldn't hear anything after that.
T: Is there any reason that you would look for people? Do you think that perhaps others escaped?
S: Yes.
S: Yes, you need to start working together and build to survive. Everything is barren.
S: It's natural to look for somebody else.
T: Why do you say that?
S: I don't think one person could lie in a destroyed city by himself.
S: Yeah, he's right there—you need someone to help you. You can't do everything yourself. You need help.
T: Good!
S: If the city was destroyed, I'd try to get out of there and go someplace else.
T: Suppose you do find a few more survivors; perhaps some had hidden in a cave, and soon you found five or six people. What would be one of the first things that you people might do?
S: Look for food and shelter.
S: Yes, you would be hungry after a day and you can't go without it.
S: You need shelter.
T: Remember, everything was destroyed. What would you use for food and shelter?
S: You would look for plants and stuff in the ditch.
S: I think you would look for food or anything left over you might be able to find.
T: What might be the safest thing for you to eat?
S: Something that was in your ditch because everything else could have been poisoned by the explosion.
T: What kind of food would you look for?
S: Mostly plant life—that would be about the only thing left.
T: Could you eat the top of the plant?
S: You could eat the root.
T: Why would the roots be the only thing left really?
S: Because the top of the plants would be destroyed and the roots would be left underground.
T: You're right; you remembered in the story that everything was scarred. Do you know anything about plants that might tell you about a water supply? What do you know about plants?
S: They need water, sunlight. . . .
S: The roots collect something like that so I guess you might get something out of the roots to eat.
T: Good! Now we've discovered people. We've discovered our next basic need is our food, water, shelter. . . .

S: Well, water, that might be our first. It depends. It may be way back in a cave and there would be blind fish, lobster, crab....

T: OK, after we get our food, water, and our little group of people, what are we going to have to do now? For example, when you go on a camping trip, what do you do to make things easier?

S: You work together.

S: Yeah, you work together in groups.

T: How do you work together?

S: Have somebody go get firewood, and some get water.

S: Some get water, and you know—everything that wasn't destroyed?

T: Yes, that's good. I'm glad you came up with the idea of organizing; this is what you have to do. Now suppose you have this group of people, how are we going to make sure everyone plays fair? For example, if we have a big, strong man over here and also someone was hurt in the blast and is not too strong, who do you think should get the most food?

S: He would.

T: Who would?

S: The injured guy.

T: Why?

S: Because he'd need the nourishment.

S: I don't agree with that because there may be so little food that they will have to fight over it and the stronger one is going to take it.

T: Do you think the strong should take it?

S: No, I think that it should be divided, but that's not the way it is. If I was in that position, I'd probably take the most if I could, or as much as I could.

T: But what do you think we could do to make this a little more fair? We may have some strong people and some weak people....

S: I think we should give the weak person more food and he might get better and then we would have another person helping. I don't know.

T: What can we do to make sure this doesn't happen, that one person gets all of it?

S: Split it up evenly or something like that.

S: Depends on how many people you had in on this. It might be easier, you know, if we had five or six people, or it might be harder to find that much food. But if there were three or four people it might be easier, I think.

S: Make rules.

S: Make the rules and everybody gets the same amount of everything.

S: Like in Monopoly you would get the same amount of money, even though you aren't equal at the end of the game.

T: That was the important thing; you said you need a set of rules, good!

S: And Rob was trying to get away from rules (referring to tape).

S: Ah-hh.

T: Yes, he was, wasn't he?
S: Uh-huh.
T: What do you think might happen if we didn't have any rules at all?
S: You couldn't do a thing. If you wanted to play a game, you couldn't play it.
T: Why not?
S: Because one guy could say, well, there's no rules and I can have as much money as I want.
T: And who do you think is going to?
S: The stronger person.
S: It's right there. If you don't have rules, the stronger person always gets it. You know it's that way!
T: Suppose someone breaks the rules?
S: Give him a penalty.
T: What kind of penalty?
S: Depends on what you're doing.
T: Suppose we catch one of the group stealing food.
S: Make his next ration less than he usually gets.
S: See how much he took. If he took an awful lot and if he had any extra, put it back and he can't eat for the rest of the day or something.
T: What else could you do? What do you think some people might want to do to him?
S: Physically hurt him.
S: That's a good idea—ha, ha!
T: How could we decide on a proper punishment to give a person? If we find someone taking more than his share—in other words, breaking a rule—how can we punish him?
S: Make him have a little less than his share.
T: OK, thinking over the little story you have just heard and the discussion we've had, what would you consider an important idea you developed? Everyone think carefully! What is one important idea you came up with from today's story and our talk?
S: Well, rules are very important because if somebody breaks them, the stronger person always gets his way, then it's just not fair to the weaker person.
T: Anyone else have an important idea?
S: Well, if a person is going to participate in something, everyone has to work together. . . .
S: And play fair and not break the rules.
S: Because there are too many people in the world to live without rules.
S: Laws you mean. (Sterling, "Dialogue.")

This lesson could be an introduction to the study of government. Why do we have laws? Who makes the laws?

Continuing Activities

After the problem has been initiated with the class, testing the hypotheses may take many forms, depending on the needs of the class. For example, the class could be divided into cooperative groups or small groups with each group selecting a hypothesis to test and then reporting back to the class on their findings. At that time, the class can decide, on the basis of the information given, whether to accept or reject the hypothesis or determine whether additional information is needed. Another approach would be for each child to test his or her own hypothesis.

Gathering data may take many forms—such as viewing videos or filmstrips, listening to tapes or records, interviewing people in the school or community, and utilizing resource books or textbooks. After the hypotheses have been tested utilizing the data collected, the children should draw generalizations based on their new knowledge. When possible, these generalizations should be applied to the child's own life.

Evaluation/Assessment of Problem Solving/Inquiry/ Critical Thinking

A typical paper and pencil test of factual information will not be useful in evaluating/assessing the problem-solving/inquiry process. It will not assess children's critical thinking ability. Why not? Too often students memorize information for such a test. Simon (cited in Cornbleth 1985) states that "rote memorization . . . produces the ability to repeat back the memorized material but not to use it in solving problems" (p. 87). The outcomes that are expected from the problem-solving process are not information based. This does not mean that information is not a part of the process nor that the children will not acquire additional information, however. What it does mean is that acquisition of information is not the primary goal. Rather what the children do with previous knowledge and new information, how they think about it, and the questions they ask in arriving at a solution to a problem, is the primary goal and what should be assessed. With this goal in mind, it should be noted that performance assessment is the type of evaluation that is advocated for problem solving/inquiry, not a traditional short answer or multiple-choice test. Performance assessment says that the student has to do something with the knowledge, whether it is hypothesizing a solution, forming a generalization, or speaking and/or writing about it. "An authentic assessment is one that would be much more a simulation or representation or replication of the kinds of challenges that face . . . citizens when they need to do something with their knowledge" (Nickell 1992). Therefore it follows that if authentic assessment of problem solving is to occur, it should be in the form that children will find useful in their everyday lives.

One of the difficulties in the assessment of problem solving is that each problem situation is set within a particular context. The critical thinking that occurs within that context (when critical thinking is conceived as questioning the ideas we encounter, the questions raised, and the means needed to pursue them) will depend to a large extent on the situation (Cornbleth 1985). If that is so, then presenting a new situation for assessment, where children identify the problem, ask questions about the situation, and hypothesize a solution, will not necessarily be an accurate assessment. Why? It's possible that the children may not have as much previous knowledge or experience with the new situation and therefore not be as able to think critically about it. Therefore, choosing a problem that is within the same context for assessment would be important.

An example of a performance assessment after the children have pursued the problem of the division of a city or country (let's assume they pursued the division of Berlin and Germany) might be the following:

You are a resident of East Berlin after the division of the city and your country, Germany. You have relatives in West Berlin. The Berlin Wall has been built and you cannot go to visit them. Write a letter to relatives in America describing the events that led up to the division and building of the wall, what you think were the causes and how you feel about it, describing your life under Communism and what if any possible solutions you can suggest for the problem of being separated from other members of your family.

To assess this example, the following criteria might be used:

1. ability to explain historical background
2. ability to describe events from different perspectives
3. ability to place self in another's situation
4. ability to use knowledge to suggest feasible solutions.

The History–Social Science Assessment Advisory Committee of California developed a large collection of performance-based tasks to be administered to fifth graders. These were intended for use in a statewide assessment instrument, but do provide a model. An example of one of those tasks follows (Palmquist 1992). This is a group activity.

"Declaration of Independence"

In your group, study and discuss the painting of a meeting of the Second Continental Congress (John Trumbull portrays five leaders of the new nation presenting documents to the leaders of the Second Continental Congress). Choose one of the following delegates who later signed the Declaration of Independence.

>   Benjamin Franklin   Thomas Jefferson
>   John Hancock   John Adams
>   Sam Adams

Pretend you are that delegate and write a letter to a friend describing your thoughts and feelings as you sign the Declaration of Independence. Discuss your ideas with your group before you write your letter. Include information about

- the importance of the Declaration of Independence
- the basic ideas contained in the document
- how you became a delegate to the Continental Congress
- what might happen to you after you sign the document
- the types of people who were present and why women, Native Americans, and African Americans were not included (p. 100).

Scoring is based on six points: for including a thesis statement giving direction to the essay, for giving meaning of historical data in own words, for demonstrating an understanding of significance in time and place and to present, for providing historical detail with multiple perspectives, for drawing conclusions or generalizations with supporting evidence, and for going beyond requirements to relate events past and present, show cause and effect, and demonstrate historical empathy.

Assessment for younger children can take the form of role playing, drawing pictures to show solutions to problems, or writing individual responses to problem solutions. Second graders are shown a picture of a lake with trash polluting the water and beach. The children are asked individually or as a group to identify the problem, and what might be some solutions to the problem. Children can choose their solution and either role play, draw, or write about it. The teacher can follow up with "Why did you choose that solution?" and "How do you know it will work?"

What is important to remember in assessing problem solving/inquiry/critical thinking is that it cannot be assessed in the same manner as the acquisition of information or by assessing individual skills (Cornbleth, 1985). It requires a holistic approach. Being able to accomplish one aspect of the process, such as identifying the problem, does not ensure that a completion of the process will occur.

SUMMARY

Problem solving through inquiry gives children the opportunity to question, to seek solutions to problems, to think critically about the problems, to formulate tentative hypotheses, and to come to some generalizations.

Children become active participants in the learning process. They do not merely accept answers that are given to them, but consider alternative possibilities. They use their own experiences and perspectives to arrive at the generalizations. They are then able to apply those generalizations to situations in their own lives. They can make connections between what they are learning in school and what's happening in their lives.

SELECTED REFERENCES

Ausubel, D. P. (1963). A teaching strategy for culturally deprived pupils: Cognitive and motivational considerations. *School Review, 71,* 456.

Beyer, B. K. (1971). *Inquiry in the social studies classroom.* Columbus, OH: Charles E. Merrill.

Brubaker, D. L. (1970, March). Indoctrination, inquiry, and the social studies. *The Social Studies, 41,* 120–124.

Bruner, J. (1962). *On knowing.* Cambridge, MA: Belknap Press of Harvard University Press.

Bruner, J. (1966). *Toward a theory of instruction.* Cambridge, MA: Harvard University Press.

Common, D. L. (1982). Small group instruction in social studies classrooms and the corruption of critical thought. *Theory and Research in Social Education, 10*(4), 49–67.

Common, D. L. (1985). Teacher authority in the social studies classroom: Erosion of a barren ground. *Theory and Research in Social Education, 12*(4), 25–37.

Cornbleth, C. (1985). Critical thinking and cognitive process. In W. B. Stanley (Ed.), *Review of research in social studies education: 1976–1984* (pp. 11–63). Washington, DC: National Council for the Social Studies. (Bulletin 75)

Dewey, J. (1933). *How we think.* Boston: D. C. Heath.

Dunfee, M., & Sagl, H. (1966). *Social studies through problem solving.* New York: Holt, Rinehart, & Winston.

Fair, J., & Shaftel, R. F. (1967). *Effective thinking in the social studies.* Washington, DC: National Council for the Social Studies.

Fox, R., Lippitt, R., & Lohman, J. (1964). *Teaching of social science material in the elementary school* (USOE Cooperative Research Project E-011). Ann Arbor: University of Michigan.

Friedlander, B. A. (1965). A psychologist's second thoughts on concepts, curiosity, and discovery in learning. *Harvard Educational Review, 35,* 25.

Glenn, A. D., & Ellis, A. K. (1982). Direct and indirect methods of teaching problem solving to elementary school children. *Social Education, 46*(2), 134–136.

Goodlad, J. (1984). *A place called school: Prospects for the future.* New York: McGraw-Hill.

Hoffman, M. S. (Ed). (1992). *The world almanac and book of facts: 1993.* New York: Pharos Books.

Maher, F. A. (1987). Inquiry teaching and feminist pedagogy. *Social Education, 51*(3), 86–88.

Massialas, B., Sprague, N. F., & Hurst, J. B. (1975). *Social issue through inquiry—Coping in an age of crises.* Englewood Cliffs, NJ: Prentice-Hall.

Maxcy, S. J. (1986). The conception of problem and the role of inquiry in social education. *Theory and Research in Social Studies, 14*(4), 295–306.

Nickell, P. (1992). Doing the stuff of social studies: A conversation with Grant Wiggins. *Social Education, 56*(2), 91–94.

Palmquist, K. (1992). Involving teachers in elementary history and social science test development: The California experience. *Social Education, 56*(2), 99–101.

Schwab, J. J. (1962). The teaching of science as inquiry. In J. Fair & F. Shaftel (Eds.), *Effective thinking in the social studies* (n.p.). Washington, DC: National Council for the Social Studies.

Schwab, J. J. (1963). *The teaching of science as inquiry.* Cambridge, MA: Harvard University Press.

Sears, A., & Parsons, J. (1991). Toward critical thinking as an ethic. *Theory and Research in Social Education, 14*(1), 45–68.

Shaftel, F. R., & Shaftel, G. (1967). *Role-playing for social values.* Englewood Cliffs, NJ: Prentice-Hall.

Skeel, D. J., & Decaroli, J. G. (1969, May). The role of the teacher in an inquiry-centered classroom. *Social Education, 33,* 547–550.

Sterling, R. E. Dialogue from classroom presentation by R. E. Sterling and a group of fifth and sixth graders.

Taba, H. (1967). *Teacher's handbook for elementary social studies.* Reading, MA: Addison-Wesley.

LEARNING ACTIVITY

Try an inquiry activity with your classmates. Collect a series of personal items that would indicate something about you as a person, such as theater tickets, music programs, running shoes, etc. Place these in a *plain* brown bag. Your classmates should do the same. Bring them to class and place on a table and have your instructor move them around so that no one knows who they belong to. Then select a bag and try to discover something about the person to whom it belongs. Draw some generalizations about that person. Then find the person and determine how well you analyzed the items.

Variations on the activity can be done by each person collecting things in their wastebaskets for one day. Or another variation might be to bring a collection of pictures you've taken on a visit to some other country and have your classmates hypothesize some things about the country.

Record your responses to the inquiry activity in your journal. How did you feel about trying to discover something about the person from the artifacts? Did you feel uncomfortable not knowing if your answers were "correct"? What thinking skills were you using in trying to hypothesize? To generalize? What was the difference in trying to figure out something about the person and being told that information?

How do you think you'll react as a teacher using inquiry in the classroom? Will you be worried that you won't have as much control over the children? Will you be excited as the children discover things on their own? Will you feel they are learning valuable skills?

CHAPTER 9

SKILLS OF VALUING/MORAL REASONING: A BASIS FOR MORAL EDUCATION

VALUE ISSUES confront children daily as they attempt to make decisions about their lives. Should I take the money in Sylvia's desk? Will I be a friend to Herby who is African-American? All the other kids are going to boycott Mr. Jim's market because he won't hire Puerto Ricans: Should I? My mother wants me to be a doctor and make lots of money; I want to drive a truck. What should I do? How do children make these decisions? Why don't people behave the way they say they should?

Possibly now, more than at any other time in our history, children observe tremendous conflicts in the values that people say they possess and what they actually exhibit by their behaviors. Equality of opportunity for all is a phrase often heard, but children witness discrimination against minority groups and women, particularly for jobs and schooling. Children find advertising claims on television suggesting the virtues of certain products to be untrue. Parents warn children against breaking laws, but serve as poor examples by exceeding speed limits when they are late. Everyone talks about how important it is to protect the environment, but litter is everywhere and the local strip-mining company attempts to leave without reforesting the area. Government is supposed to operate for all people, but some officials can be bribed to grant special favors.

Different subcultures and life-styles in our society possess varied value beliefs. Children from these backgrounds come to school with different value structures, as was witnessed by the description of the children in Chapter 1. Often, the teacher does not possess the same values as the children.

Obviously, the teacher's behavior will demonstrate value beliefs as will the policy statements of the school. For example, if the teacher tells the children that each individual is unique and important, but disregards individual differences in planning learning experiences and expectations, children will question whether the teacher values the worth of the individual. If school policy requires that children form lines to move about the school, but teachers and the principal tell students that they are to develop self-control, children will quickly observe the discrepancy.

Much discussion relative to values, moral reasoning, and moral education centers on the role that the school should assume. Does the school have any responsibility for the moral education of children? Should it? If so, how should this be approached? *Moral education* is defined by Purpel and Ryan (1975) as "direct and indirect intervention of the school which affects both moral behavior and the capacity to think about issues of right and wrong" (p. 659). Overvold and Konrad (1983) state: "Moral beliefs help us decide what to do. In general we decide what to do in any matter on the basis of the things we think are important (our values)" (p. 394). Another aspect of morality is justifying

> our conduct to others by providing reasons in support of our conduct. It is this process of reasoning rather than specific beliefs about what is right or wrong which we believe should be at the center of any program in moral education. The primary goal should be to show students how to think about moral questions, to teach them the canons of moral reasoning. (p. 395)

Several approaches to develop skills of valuing and moral reasoning will be discussed, including the cognitive developmental, character development, values clarification, and values analysis approaches.

COGNITIVE-DEVELOPMENTAL APPROACH

The cognitive-developmental approach is most frequently identified with Lawrence Kohlberg. Research findings by Kohlberg (1966) suggest that children achieve the ability to make value judgments dependent upon the stage of development in moral concepts they have reached. He indicates that there are six stages through which a child must go step-by-step. These are as follows:

Level I—Premoral
   Stage 1. Obedience and punishment orientation.
   Stage 2. Instrumentally satisfying the self's needs and occasionally others.
Level II—Conventional Role Conformity
   Stage 3. Good-boy orientation.
   Stage 4. Authority and social-order maintaining orientation.
Level III—Self-accepted Moral Principles
   Stage 5. Recognition of an arbitrary element or starting point in rules or expectations for the sake of argument.
   Stage 6. Orientation to conscience as a direct agent and to mutual respect and trust. (p. 7)

This developmental view strengthens the position of the school to stimulate the individual child's moral judgment and character rather than teaching fixed values. "The sign of the child's moral maturity is his ability to make moral judgments and formulate moral principles of his own, rather than his ability to conform to moral judgments of the adults around him" (p. 20). Therefore, it is the responsibility of the school to provide opportunities for the child to assess real and challenging conflict situations. These should be situations that do not have the obvious adult answer at hand to discourage the child's own moral thought.

If the developmental stages of Kohlberg are to be followed, it is suggested that the teacher first determine the stage that the children have reached before deciding on the types of instructional materials to use (Mackey 1973).

"The moral stages are *structures of moral judgment* or *moral reasoning*. Structures of moral judgment must be distinguished from the *content* of moral judgment" (Kohlberg 1975, p. 671). The *content* is the choice a person makes in a moral dilemma, while the *structure of moral judgment* is the reasoning the person gives for making that choice. To determine the stages that children have reached, teachers should pose a moral dilemma, have children choose how they would act, and then give their reasoning for their choice. Research indicates that posing value judgments that are one level above the children's present stage of development proves most effective. Kohlberg (1969) uses examples of moral dilemmas to determine the levels of development. These can be used as instructional materials in addition to those developed by the teacher. An example of one of them follows:

> In Europe a woman was near death from cancer. One drug might save her, a form of radium that a druggist in the same town had recently discovered. The druggist was charging $2,000, ten times what the drug cost him to make. The sick woman's husband, Heinz, went to everyone he knew to borrow the money, but he could only get together about half of what it cost. He told the druggist that his wife was dying and asked him to sell it cheaper or let him pay later. But the druggist said, "No." The husband got desperate and broke into the man's store to steal the drug for his wife. Should the husband have done that? Why? (pp. 347–480)

At Stage 1, the reasoning would be that it was his wife (life is valued in terms of the power or possessions of person involved); Stage 2, he would feel badly if something happened to his wife (life is valued in satisfying the needs of the individual and sometimes others); Stage 3, he would want others to recognize what he had done for his wife—reasoning might be what would people think if I let my wife die (life is valued in terms of the individual's relations with others and their valuation of him); Stage 4, I'll always feel guilty if I let my wife die—it is my duty to save her (life in terms of social or religious law); Stage 5, every life is worthwhile and stealing to save a life shouldn't be against the law (each life is inherently worthwhile); and Stage 6, every person has the right to live (regardless of other considerations, every life is inherently worthwhile) (Kohlberg 1975).

What effect does the classroom peer group have upon the child's value structure? Kohlberg (1966) found that children with extensive peer group participation advance more quickly through the stages of moral judgment than those who are isolated from participation. Active participation with value issues in the classroom with peers fosters the development of the valuing process.

Gailbraith and Jones (1975) suggest that alternative dilemmas to the original dilemma should be developed to promote disagreement within the class so that different positions will be taken. An example for the previous dilemma might be the following:

If the class agrees that the husband should steal the drug, one of the following dilemmas can be used to provoke disagreement.

A. Suppose someone overheard the druggist and the husband talking and would know it was the husband who broke into the store.

B. Suppose the man was not her husband, but a good friend.

If the class agrees that the husband should not steal the drug, one of the following alternatives might be used to provoke disagreement.

A. Suppose other people have stolen the drug to save their loved ones.

B. Suppose the husband learns that his wife's death is imminent without the drug.

The class can be divided into small groups that consist of students who agree about the appropriate action to take regarding the dilemma. They should decide on the reasons why they take that position. Rank these reasons according to their priorities. Each group should present their list of reasons. A general discussion on moral reasoning should follow.

Another strategy is to form groups of students who disagree on the appropriate action. Have them follow the same procedures. Since most classes will have children who are at different stages of development, they will have different reasons for their actions.

Critics of Kohlberg indicate that the developmentalist's view of changes in morality that take place as human beings pass from childhood, through adolescence, to adulthood is development in the sense of improvement. Beck (1989) believes "that the distinctive moral orientations of different child and adolescent age groups are a function of their life circumstances, including their political status, rather than their cognitive capacity" (p. 182). He further believes "that eight-year-old children in fact have enough mental capacity to achieve typical adult moral thought structures. What they do not have is the need to develop such structures given their life circumstances" (p. 182).

Peters (1975) criticizes Kohlberg's theory for ignoring other forms of morality and failing to recognize the "affective side of morality of moral emotions such as 'guilt,' 'concern for others,' 'remorse,' and so on" (p. 678). Senchuk (1981), unlike Kohlberg, stresses the role of responsive feelings or moral sensibility in moral development. He states it thus, "moral reasoning and moral sensibility are inseparably intervolved, and when our moral sensibility moves forward, reasoned moral judgment cannot be very far behind" (p. 273).

CHARACTER DEVELOPMENT

Character development or character education may well be another label for moral education in an attempt to avoid being identified with the "value neutral" approaches of values clarification and analysis (Dapice et al. 1988; Ryan 1986). Having been ignored by educators for many years, there appears to be a movement "to return values to the standard curriculum" (Viadero 1992) through character education programs. Different groups have been attempting to identify deeply held values upon which all Americans can agree as a basis for these programs. The Aspen Declaration on Character Education identifies six core values: "respect, responsibility, trustworthiness, caring, justice and fairness, and civic virtue and citizenship" (Viadero 1992, p. 13). In 1991, about 40 percent of the states had a policy statement on values education.

Lickona (1988) suggests, given the nature of elementary students, the reasonable goals for character development would include the following:

- to promote development away from egocentrism and excessive individualism and toward cooperative relationships and mutual respect,
- to foster the growth of moral agency—the capacity to think, feel, and act morally, and
- to develop in the classroom and in the school a moral community based on fairness, caring, and participation
- such a community being a moral end in itself, as well as a support system for the character development of each individual student. (p. 420)

Assuming that the aforementioned goals are implemented in the classroom, the program would seek to develop in each child these specific qualities:

> 1) self respect that derives feelings of worth not only from competence but also from positive behavior toward others; 2) social perspective-taking that asks how others think and feel; 3) moral reasoning about the right things to do; 4) such moral values as kindness, courtesy, trustworthiness, and responsibility; 5) the social skills and habits of cooperation; and 6) openness to the positive influence of adults. (Lickona 1988, p. 420)

For such a program to be successful, there should be four processes going on in the classroom (Lickona 1988). First, it is vital to build self-esteem and a sense of community. "Self-esteem is important to character development because morality begins with valuing one's own self" (p. 421). If children value themselves and know that others in the classroom care about them, it is easier for them to do the things they know they should.

Activities that help children develop a sense of community and foster self-worth depend upon teachers who begin on the first day of school and continue throughout the year, not setting aside a particular time, but taking advantage of any opportunity for children to get to know one another, recognize how they are alike and different, and begin to trust one another.

Another process that is necessary is learning to cooperate and to help others. Working together to complete some academic task such as solving a problem, building a model fort, drawing a mural, or collaborating on a unit of study fosters helping relationships. Class meetings or circle meetings that are designed to solve problems that have arisen in the classroom or school develop collective responsibility. Solving the problem of too much noise while working in groups or the failure of some students to put away materials that were used becomes a group responsibility.

The third process is moral reflection, which "refers to a wide range of intellectual activities including reading, thinking, debating moral questions, listening to explanations by the teacher (e.g., why it is wrong to make fun of a handicapped child), and conducting firsthand investigation to increase children's awareness of the complex social system to which they belong" (p. 422). Moral dilemmas that come from real life situations in the classroom, school, or community "are far more effective in engaging children's thinking and feelings than any 'canned' dilemmas from a book or kit" (ibid.). Should I cheat on a test? Should I steal that video game from Traci's desk? Why do people treat others unfairly?

Participatory decision making is the fourth process that causes children to move from making judgments to acting upon them. It requires "children to participate in making rules or solving classroom conflicts; they are then held accountable for these decisions, which eventually become operative group norms" (p. 423). Some teachers use a suggestion box, "a Conflict Corner where two students go to work out a problem," and class meetings, which help "children apply their moral reasoning to their own behavior and to the society around them" (ibid.).

With these four processes reinforcing one another, teachers are able "to develop the rational, affective, and behavioral aspects of children's character" (ibid.).

Critics of character education still raise questions about the values that are reinforced in these programs. Some critics said they objected to the word patriotism because they were afraid it might mean blind obedience to authority (Viadero 1992). Others question whether teachers are imposing their values on children and not those which the parents would support.

VALUES CLARIFICATION APPROACH

Another approach to the classroom process of valuing is advanced by Raths, Harmin, and Simon (1966), who suggest that teaching strategies should help children clarify their values. The process of valuing as posed by them is based on the following criteria:

1. Choosing from alternatives.
2. Choosing after careful consideration of the consequences of each alternative.
3. Choosing freely.
4. Prizing, being glad of one's choice.
5. Prizing, being willing to publicly affirm one's choice.
6. Acting upon one's choice, incorporating choices into behavior.
7. Acting upon one's choice repeatedly, over time. (p. 30)

This approach, labeled *values clarification,* "is based on the premise that none of us has the 'right' set of values to pass on to other people's children" (Simon 1971, p. 902).

As an example, headlines from the newspaper are given to children and they are asked to rank them in order of importance to them.

Democrats Conclude Deficit-cutting Plan
Homeless Contend Funds Not for Boat Dock
Nuclear Industry Must Face Problems
Liquor by Drink Wins in Close Vote

Afterwards, children are requested to write and then discuss the reasons behind their rankings. This gives children the opportunity to think about what things are important to them and why.

Newspaper articles also provide excellent situations for values clarification (see sample article and Figure 9.1). The news article may present only one side of the issue, and it will be necessary to search out factual information and possibly opinions from other sources. Children should not be forced to make their own value decisions until they are ready. It should be pointed out that with the addition of new information, new experiences, or hearing other opinions, their original decisions may change.

Another source for ranking values is the Values Survey developed by Rokeach (1971). There are two lists, each containing 18 items—instrumental (preferred modes of behavior) and terminal (end states of existence).

Following are the lists to be ranked; children should begin with the terminal values first.

TERMINAL	INSTRUMENTAL
___ a comfortable life	___ ambitious
___ an exciting life	___ broad-minded
___ a sense of accomplishment	___ capable
___ a world of peace	___ cheerful
___ a world of beauty	___ clean

___ equality	___ courageous
___ family security	___ forgiving
___ freedom	___ helpful
___ happiness	___ honest
___ inner harmony	___ imaginative
___ mature love	___ independent
___ national security	___ intellectual
___ pleasure	___ logical
___ salvation	___ loving
___ self-respect	___ obedient
___ social recognition	___ polite
___ true friendship	___ responsible
___ wisdom	___ self-controlled

The individual is requested to rank these values in order of importance to him- or herself in guiding his or her daily life. Fifth and sixth grade children should be able to rank these and discuss why they are so ranked. Of equal importance is the teacher's ranking. Such ranking may indicate wide discrepancy between the teachers' and the children's value beliefs (Skeel 1976).

FIGURE 9.1 Situation for Valuing

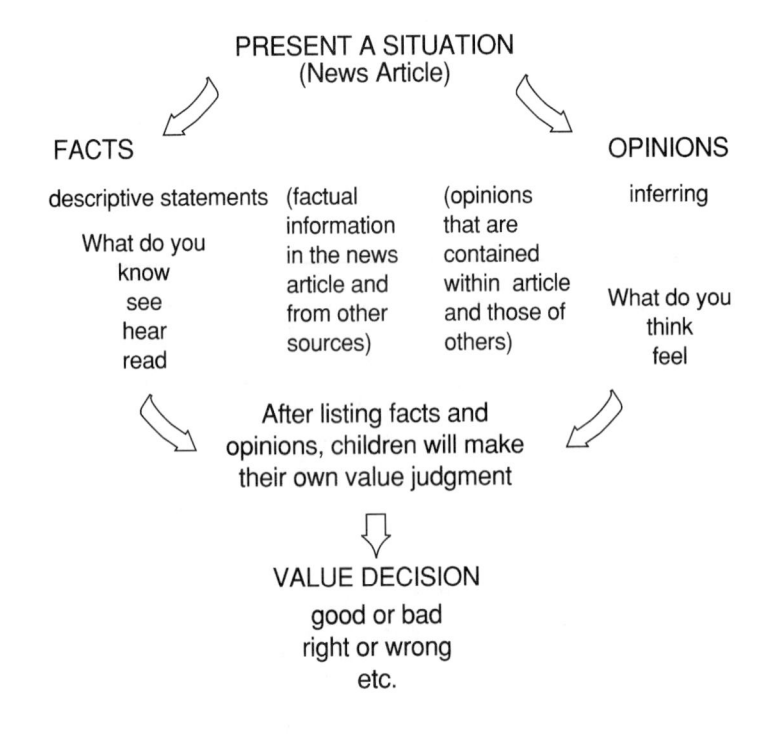

PRESENT A SITUATION
(News Article)

FACTS — OPINIONS

descriptive statements (factual information in the news article and from other sources) (opinions that are contained within article and those of others) inferring

What do you know see hear read

What do you think feel

After listing facts and opinions, children will make their own value judgment

VALUE DECISION
good or bad
right or wrong
etc.

FIGURE 9.1a

Town's only blacks leave to escape hate

VIDOR, Texas (AP) — Ugly catcalls have taken their toll on Bill Simpson and John DecQuir. After just six months, Vidor's only remaining black residents are packing their bags, frightened by too many instances of harassment.

"There are good people here, don't get me wrong," said Simpson, a 7-foot, 300-pound transplant from nearby Beaumont. "But it's overshadowed by the negativity, the hostility, the bigotry of this town."

A federal judge last year ordered the eastern Texas town, home to 11,000 whites, to desegregate its 70-unit public housing complex. A few blacks moved in last February, becoming Vidor's first black residents in at least 70 years. When they walked through town, they were hailed with racist slurs.

Simpson, 37, and DecQuir, 59, are the last of the arrivals to leave. They were preceded by two black women and their five children, who fled in July.

DecQuir moved out some of his belongings yesterday — he's heading back to his native Beaumont — and Simpson is planning to depart today to an undisclosed location.

While no one has physically attacked them, the men say the derisive yells, the threats and the oppressive fear have become all too much to bear.

"I've had people who drive by and tell me they're going home to get a rope and come back and hang me, physical gestures, derogatory words," Simpson said.

Simpson and DecQuir rarely leave their apartments, which are shielded behind the housing estate's chain-link perimeter fence.

"It's too much pressure," said DeQuir. "People just won't leave it alone."

The two moved to Vidor as the result of a 1980 class-action lawsuit filed against the U.S. Department of Housing and Urban Development by three blacks who were refused available public housing because of their race. ■

Sidney Simon (1971) suggests the following activity to help children find out what they really want. He suggests that the teacher provide Western Union telegram blanks or have children write on paper headed "Telegram." Ask the children to think of someone in their own lives to whom they would send a telegram that begins with the words *I urge you to*.

Children might send a telegram to their mother or father urging them to allow them to play football or urging them to stop smoking. These telegrams are used several times a year and are kept by the children so that they may refer back to them and write "I learned" statements from the messages carried by the telegrams.

The critics of values clarification indicate one of the major criticisms points to the superficiality. As Stewart (1975) claims,

> it deals primarily with the content of values and somewhat with the process of valuing, but ignores the most important aspect of the issue—namely, the structure of values and valuing, especially structural development. To oversimplify a very

complex subject, the content of values/moral judgments is the 'what' that is expressed by the person, the answer to a question or a dilemma; whereas the structure is the underlying cognitive logic on which the content is based, or the 'why' that generated the answer. (p. 684)

In other words, individuals may be expressing what they believe, but may not be requested to think about and explain the why of their beliefs. Also, individuals may not know how to use their beliefs to guide their decision making and behavior.

VALUES ANALYSIS APPROACH

Values analysis, whereby individuals discuss or list the alternative forms of action that are possible to resolve a value conflict, is another approach. The consequences of each of those actions are discussed or pursued in an attempt to realize how the action will affect all those concerned. The value issues that are raised by the conflict are listed and discussed. Individuals must decide which of the values issues are most important to them and why they are important. A choice of the action to be taken should be based on what is most important to the individual or what is valued most. Figure 9.2 outlines the process of value analysis.

This strategy can be implemented in a variety of ways. The problem can be presented to the children for discussion of the alternatives and consequences, or children can be requested to list their own alternatives and consequences to be discussed later with the class. Children should not be forced to express their solutions and value choices if they show any hesitation. The teacher should indicate that it is a free choice. The following is a sample problem presented to younger children and the classroom dialogue that it initiated.

What Should David Do?

David had the reputation for being the "character" of the class. He enjoyed his success as the "unpopular star" of the class. It was the only time he received any attention. If something happened, David was the first to be accused. One morning Susan discovered her week's lunch tickets were missing. David was the first person to be mentioned as the culprit. However, David did not take the lunch tickets and he knew Sammy had done it. Sammy had told him that morning that his mother did not have any money for his lunches that week. What should David do?

TEACHER: What are some ways in which David might solve the problem?
SARAH: He could pretend he doesn't know anything about it.
JIM: Tell the teacher what happened.
TEACHER: What about Sammy?

FIGURE 9.2 Value Analysis

```
                    PRESENT A DILEMMA
                     (Unfinished Story)

   What are the                        What are the
   possible alternative                consequences of
   solutions to the                    each of the
   problem?                            alternative
                                       solutions?

              What are the
              value issues
              raised by the
              problem?

         What is it you value most
         that helped you make
             your choice?

            Your decision or
         choice of alternatives
```

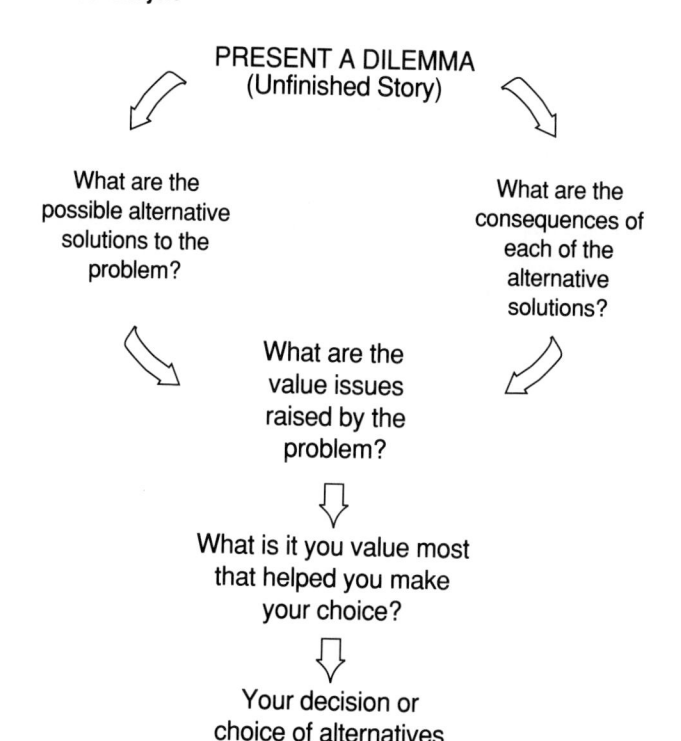

JIM: Let the teacher talk to Sammy.

KARA: Go to Sammy and ask him what he's going to do.

MARIA: Yes, and tell him that otherwise David will take the blame.

JUAN: That won't work. Sammy probably wouldn't care if David took the blame.

MARIA: No, I think Sammy would feel bad about that.

BOB: David should tell everyone that he isn't guilty, but that Sammy is.

SARAH: No, he should give Sammy a chance to confess.

JUAN: If David tells everyone, it will hurt Sammy. Maybe it is the first time he has taken anything. Maybe he was hungry.

BOB: You can't take things just because you are hungry.

SARAH: Have you ever been hungry and not had any money?

MARIA: It isn't that Sammy was right in what he did, but how do we work things out so that neither David or Sammy will be hurt any more than necessary?

TEACHER: Do you have any more ideas about what David might do? No? Then let's look at the consequences of each possible solution.

Alternative	Consequences
Ignore the situation.	David would be blamed for taking the tickets.
	The kids wouldn't trust David.
	Sammy would get away with it.
Tell the teacher.	David would not be blamed.
	Sammy would be punished.
	Sammy would be angry at David.
Talk to Sammy.	Sammy might not be willing to confess.
	Sammy might confess.
	David might lose Sammy as a friend.
Tell everyone that Sammy took the tickets.	Sammy would be hurt.
	David wouldn't be blamed.
	The kids might not believe David.

TEACHER: What are the value issues involved with the problem?
TRACEY: I don't understand what you mean.
TEACHER: What important things are a part of the problem? Is it a matter of money, trust, friendship?
TRACEY: Oh! I see! It's trust. The kids don't trust David.
SERENA: Also, friendship. David's friendship with Sammy.
JASON: How about the value of each person?
JUAN: Self-respect. When you are guilty and want to somehow make up for your mistake.
SKIP: Honesty.
BOB: If you tell everyone, then they will know you didn't do it.
TEACHER: Think about which of these values is most important to you. Ask yourself, "Why are they important?"
SKIP: Suppose honesty and friendship are equally important to you.
TEACHER: Then think about the effect on others as well as yourself.

The teacher then asked if any of the children were ready to role play their choice of solution. Role playing any of these value situations can be most effective. Children can be asked to reverse roles suddenly to get the feel of another view. Bob quickly volunteered and opted to tell everyone what had happened. Several of the children argued with him and role played their own solutions. This did not change Bob's mind and the teacher remained out of the discussion. The children completed this activity by recording in their logs or journals their choice and the reasons for it.

The previous example is included to emphasize the point that the teacher should not attempt to tell Bob his position is "wrong," because it is his choice and he feels strongly about it. If the teacher moralizes with Bob, he may not be as open in future discussions and the teacher's position is not likely to change

Bob's basic value beliefs. You may question whether the previous experience was worthwhile for him. The answer is "yes," because he is very much aware of what values are most important to him and why. It is possible that the other children's discussion with him may have quite an effect on similar future value decisions.

Frequently, specific problem-solving situations or units of study will contain value issues that should be confronted instead of avoided. When a fifth grade class studied the pollution problems of a local factory, the value issues of profit versus nonpolluted air were pursued. In playing the simulation game "Sunshine," the children identified the value issue of equality versus inequality. The unit of study that focused on India identified the religious value placed on the sacredness of animals, particularly the cow, versus the lack of food. An example of this type was given in the unit on Africa in Chapter 4. Young children, in their study of the community, encountered the value of community pride versus encouraging more industry to settle there.

One of the major concerns of this approach is that the value issues are most complicated and children have had limited experience with logical or moral reasoning. It is suggested that children will be too quick to make a decision without having all the knowledge or facts that are necessary to understand the issue. However, research has indicated that elementary children can use this model to make rational decisions (Dapice et al. 1988; Williams 1972).

SUMMARY

Discussions that give children the opportunity to express how they feel about important things in their lives are becoming increasingly more useful. Teachers have been learning that the things that they value are not always valued by others and that moralizing with a group of children has less effect on them than providing a forum where they can pursue these value issues with their peers. Valuing situations where children can talk (rather than be talked to) about what they believe, and why, should help them grow in their ability to understand what they value and be prepared to act upon those values.

The process of valuing and moral reasoning will develop skills and habits of thought rather than impart a specific set of moral beliefs.

> The skills and habits of thought to be developed include the following: the ability to give and ask for reasons about actions; the ability to identify moral principles implied by one's actions; the habit of striving for consistency, which means searching out counter-examples, both factual and moral, to one's moral judgments; the habit of getting clear about facts relevant to one's choices; being clear about the meaning of one's judgments; inferring and attending to the consequences of one's actions, including the effect they have on other people; and, finally, the ability to imagine how things might be experienced by someone else. (Overvold & Konrad 1983, p. 403)

SELECTED REFERENCES

Beck, C. (1989). Is there really development? An alternative interpretation. *Journal of Moral Education, 18*(3), 175–185.

Dapice, A. N., and others. (1988). Teaching and learning values. *Educational Horizons, 66*(3), 107–110.

Gailbraith, R. E., & Jones, T. M. (1975). Teaching strategies for moral dilemmas. *Social Education, 39*(1), 16–22.

Kohlberg, L. (1966, Spring). Moral education in the schools: A developmental view. *School Review,* pp. 1–30.

Kohlberg, L. (1969). Stage and sequence: The cognitive-developmental approach to socialization. In D. A. Goslin (Ed.), *Handbook of socialization theory and research* (pp. 347–480). Chicago: Rand McNally.

Kohlberg, L. (1975). The cognitive-developmental approach to moral education. *Phi Delta Kappan, 56*(10), 670–677.

Krough, S. L. (1985). Encouraging positive justice reasoning and perspective-taking skills: Two educational interventions. *Journal of moral education, 14*(2), 102–110.

Lickona, T. (1988). Four strategies for fostering character development in children. *Phi Delta Kappan, 69*(6), 419–423.

Mackey, J. A. (1973). Moral insight in the classroom. *Elementary School Journal, 73*(2), 35.

Metcalf, L. E. (Ed.). (1971). *Values education* (41st yearbook). Washington, DC: National Council for the Social Studies.

Overvold, M. C., & Konrad, A. R. (1983, Summer). Moral reasoning and the public schools. *Educational Forum, 47,* 393–409.

Peters, R. S. (1975). A reply to Kohlberg. *Phi Delta Kappan, 56*(10), 678.

Purpel, D., & Ryan, K. (1975). Moral education: Where sages fear to tread. *Phi Delta Kappan, 56*(10), 659.

Raths, L., Harmin, M., & Simon, S. (1966). *Values and teaching.* Columbus, OH: Charles E. Merrill.

Rokeach, M. (1971). The measurement of values and value systems. In G. Abcarian & J. W. Soule (Eds.), *Social psychology and political behavior* (n.p.). Columbus, OH: Charles E. Merrill.

Ryan, K. (1986). The new moral education. *Phi Delta Kappan, 69,* 228–233.

Schug, M. C. (1988). Economic reasoning and values education. *Social studies and the young learner, 1*(1), 6–9.

Senchuk, D. M. (1981). Contra-Kohlberg: A philosophical reinterpretation of moral development. *Educational Theory, 31*(3,4), 259–273.

Shaver, J. P. (1985). Commitment to values and the study of social problems in citizenship education. *Social Education, 49*(3), 194–197.

Simon, S. B. (1971). Values clarification vs. indoctrination. *Social Education, 35*(4), 902.

Skeel, D. J. (1976). How do children rank their values? *Viewpoints, 52*(1), 55–72. Bloomington: School of Education, Indiana University. (Bulletin)

Stewart, J. S. (1975). Clarifying values clarification: A critique. *Phi Delta Kappan, 56*(10), 684.

Viadero, D. (1992). Election talk aside, education in values gains momentum. *Education Week, 12*(7), 1, 12–13.

Williams, M. E. T. (1972). *A study of effectiveness of a systematic instructional model on the rational decision making behavior of sixth-grade students.* Unpublished doctoral dissertation, Indiana University.

LEARNING ACTIVITY

How do you rank values? Use Rokeach's Value Survey and rank both lists. Think about how you have ranked the values. Find a fifth or sixth grader; have that student rank the lists as well. Compare your rankings. Are they similar or quite different? Why might this be? How will this affect your work with children in the classroom? Will you find differences between the values the children think are important and your values? What will you do?

Consider how you'll approach values in your classroom. Record the thoughts in your journal.

CHAPTER 10

MAP AND GLOBE SKILLS

WHERE IS the Persian Gulf? Where is South Africa? Where are the Philippine Islands? Where do you live? What is the weather like in Japan? Where do most of the world's people live? How can I get to Europe from my home? Where do bananas come from and why? How can people live in deserts? How can I describe the community where I live? These are common questions asked by children. These questions may be stimulated by reports on television, communicating with people in other parts of the world, a trip to the local grocery store, or often from travel.

All of these questions can be answered through the study of geography. Geographers have established five themes that help us to organize geography in such a way that we can understand its meaning. Those themes are as follows with examples to clarify their meaning (Kemball et al. 1987).

1. *Location:* position on the earth's surface. Locations may be absolute, designated by specific addresses and degrees of latitude and longitude, or be relative, designated by such things as hemisphere, continent, or state.
2. *Place:* description by physical and human characteristics. Washington, DC, the capital of the United States, was built on a relatively small area situated on the banks of the Potomac River. Many of the streets radiate from a circle like the spokes of a wagon wheel. Many of the people who live there work in government offices.
3. *Relationships within places:* humans and environments. The volcanic eruptions in the Philippines not only affected the people who lived there, but volcanic ash circled the earth in the upper atmosphere affecting many areas of the world.

People in the Amazon Basin are changing the environment by the rapid cutting of the rain forest.
4. *Movement:* humans interacting on the earth. The building of the Panama Canal connected the Atlantic and Pacific Oceans. It was much easier for people to travel by water from the East Coast of the United States to the West Coast.

   Industrialization caused many people to move from the rural farms to the cities to find work.
5. *Regions:* how they form and change. The Persian Gulf region is an area where Iraq attempted to overrun Kuwait and annex the rich oil reserves to its own country.

   The school playground is an area where children can meet to exercise and play games. During most of the school hours it is empty.

These themes show the interaction of places with people and the environment. With learning experiences organized around these themes, children are better able to understand the world around them.

LEARNING EXPERIENCES FOR THE THEMES

Theme One: Location

"Where do you live?" "What is it near?" "How can I get there?" These are common questions asked by a person attempting to locate someone's house. Depending upon the location and the individual's ability in locational skills, he or she might answer by naming the place, expressing the distance from his or her present location to his or her home, expressing this distance in terms of the time required to go there; or, he or she might designate the location by readings of latitude and longitude to be more exact. With the increased speed of today's travel, the time involved in reaching one's destination has changed; however, many of the skills required to locate a place remain the same. The mass media, which include a great number of unfamiliar places in their reporting, and the increased mobility of people, enhance the study of locational skills. Map reading requires the learning of a new language, which enables the individual to interpret map symbols. Six basic skills have been recognized as comprehensive for map reading and interpretation:

1. Ability to orient the map and note directions.
2. Ability to recognize the scale of a map and compute distances.
3. Ability to locate places on maps and globes by means of grid systems.
4. Ability to express relative locations.
5. Ability to read map symbols.
6. Ability to compare maps and to make references. (Carpenter 1963, p. 157; National Council for the Social Studies [NCSS] 1984, p. 260)

On the basis of child development studies, Bacon (1970) contends that young children learn to think geographically much sooner than they learn to think historically (NCSS 1970). Rushdoony (1963) found that primary children were able to profit from instruction in map-reading skills recommended for fourth and fifth graders. He suggested that curricula be revised to introduce map skills to children at an earlier level. He also found a high positive correlation between map reading achievement and intelligence, reading achievement, and arithmetic achievement.

Blaut, McCleary, and Blaut (1970) state that map reading involves three transformations of perspective, distance, or scale, and semantic interpretation from abstract sign to signification. They found that young children (five, six, and seven year olds) could interpret an aerial photograph, hence performing scale reduction and projection; abstract from the photographic image to map signs; and solve a simulated route-planning problem. Thus, the children were participating in real, if primitive, map reading, map making, and map use.

Bluestein and Acredolo (1979) discovered that half of the three year olds, most four year olds, and all five year olds they tested were able to use symbolic map information to locate a hidden target, if map and space were physically aligned. Presson (1982) found that by rotating the maps 90° and 180,° kindergartners and second graders were not as successful, but concluded that children can extract information from maps to guide their search.

Landau (1986) "demonstrated that certain fundamental principles of map use can be accessed without any specific training" (p. 1). In experiments with a four-year-old congenitally blind child and four-year-old sighted children, she found they could use a two-symbol map to guide locomotion directionally in space and locate objects in front, behind, and to the left and right. The blind child had no training.

Uttal and Wellman (1989) found that "preschoolers' map-acquired representation of a space can support quite accurate identification of a configuration of hidden objects in that space on their very first trip through it. Because our results reveal impressive map-reading abilities in preschoolers, we believe that maps may be more useful to young children in their acquisition of spatial information than previously suspected . . . This suggests that young children can and do readily acquire a significant amount of information about a space from a map." (pp. 136–137).

The results of these studies suggest that map use can and probably should begin early. They also suggest that effective instruction in map and globe skills is accomplished through developmental tasks and that this instruction should be conducted in the context of the study of a topic. Thus, the six basic skills will be developed in the primary and intermediate grades in the context of a suggested topic. In the following discussion of methods for teaching map skills, the six basic skills (listed above) will be indicated by the number to which they correspond in the list. In mastering these map skills, children will need to build upon a progression of learning experiences. These suggested activities are representative and are not intended to be the only ones developed at each grade level.

Skills by Grade Levels

Kindergarten

As the children study the family and home, they develop a map of the community, using blocks placed on butcher paper to represent the school and their homes (5). A trip outside the school on a sunny day enables the children to note the location of the sun when they arrive at school and when they leave. With this knowledge the children are able to place the sun on their maps as a directional guide (1). The children place blocks on the map to locate other outstanding buildings, such as the fire station, library, and places of worship, relative to their homes (4). Beginning at the school, they count the number of blocks (in a city), kilometers, or miles (in a rural area) to their homes (2). The teacher draws the same map on a piece of paper, representing their homes and other buildings with drawings (5). The children compare their block map with the teacher's map to locate their homes (6). The simple slate or physical relief globe is then used to locate the placement of their homes in relation to the other areas of the world (3, 1, 5).

First Grade

Young children are fascinated by the study of a culture different from their own, especially one they think is quite far away. Japan is an example of a culture that might be used in first grade. The children first locate Japan on a simple globe and realize that it is a group of islands (1, 5). The teacher uses a tub of water and a cardboard representation of the islands to help develop this concept (6). The children note the direction of Japan from their homes (1). In an attempt to determine the distance of Japan from the children's homes, they compute the time in days it would take to reach the islands by plane or boat (2). By using a floor map of the world with land masses and water indicated, they place a toy plane and boat on the map, and move them at their approximate speed of travel—one day of school for the plane and five days of school for the boat (1, 2, 3, 4, 5). Using a globe that has an attachment showing the division of day and night, they interpret the time differences (6, 5).

Second Grade

Wall maps can be introduced at this level, but transition from the floor map to the wall map should be provided. During a study of community workers, children can make a large floor map using symbols to locate the buildings of the workers, such as the fire station and police station (1, 4, 5). The teacher should then draw to scale a smaller map of the area, hang it on the wall, and permit children to place buildings on the map (2, 3, 4, 5). Have the children locate their city or town on a simplified state map (1, 5, 6). Then refer them to a map of the United States to see where their state is located (1, 2, 3, 4, 5, 6).

Third Grade

During a study of contrasting communities, children learn that people wear different clothes in different parts of the world. The relationship of this understanding to map interpretation is then presented. Pictures of people in typical dress for a particular time of year are placed on a map of the world that has a three-color key—water, lowlands, and mountains (1, 5). People are placed, for example, on the equator, on lowlands and mountains, on a desert area, near the North Pole, and in the children's own community. Climatic conditions are estimated from the type of clothes worn and the effect of location on the climate (2, 3, 5, 6). The effect of altitude on climate and the resulting type of clothing also are interpreted. A representative relief map of clay or flour and salt is made to relate water, lowlands, and mountains to the three-color key (1, 5, 6).

Fourth Grade

Beginning a study of their state, the children use a large sand table to prepare a model representing the physical features of their state, such as mountains, valleys, lakes, rivers, and lowlands (1, 2, 3, 5, 6). As the study progresses, the children can locate major cities on the map, their own city or town, recreational areas, and major products of the state (1, 2, 3, 4, 5, 6). The products and characteristics of an area located in the same latitude with approximately the same land formation should be compared (1, 3, 5, 6).

Fifth Grade

Fifth graders should use degrees of latitude and longitude for locating places as they study the United States, Canada, and Mexico. As children report daily news events from around the world, they should indicate the location of the events in degrees of latitude and longitude and discuss their relative location to them. The children can use individual desk maps to locate the places (1, 3, 4, 5). A world map with time zones designated is used to determine the time difference between the children's location and that of the event (1, 2, 3, 4, 5). The children interpret the map key representing physical features and relation of latitude to determine the land formation and climate of the news events' locations (5, 6). The map key can also be used to interpret water formations or ocean currents that might be applicable to events (5, 6).

Sixth Grade

During a study of the United Nations, committees of children can select areas of the world where United Nations' organizations are operating, such as peace-keeping troops, and the economic advisory committee. Reproduce maps of these areas with the opaque projector to ensure accuracy (1, 2, 3, 6).

Reproduce physical features, using a five- or seven-color key (5, 6). These maps can be done on transparencies using overlays to represent political divisions, cities, physical features, products, and population (1, 2, 3, 4, 5, 6).

Theme Two: Place

Children learn about place by understanding the physical and human characteristics that are unique to places. Some places are flat while others are hilly. Some places have trees while others have none. Some places have houses, stores, and streets while others are barren. Some places have snow while others are always hot. As children learn about different places, they begin to differentiate them by these characteristics. Some of the learning experiences that will help them to distinguish the similarities and differences of places will be described by grade level.

Kindergarten

With the study of home and school, children can describe the surroundings. By taking a walking tour around the school, children describe both physical and human characteristics. What does the area look like? Is it flat? Do we have a river or stream? Are there many trees or none? Do we have people or miles of open space? Are the people all the same or are different groups of people living there? By developing a sand box model of the area, children can depict the terrain, but also add models of buildings and people.

First Grade

In their study of another country such as Japan, children identify the land and water masses between them and the country. They identify the fact that Japan is a series of islands, but also, through pictures, that it has many mountains. They compare this with the land area around their own homes. Using pictures they compare the buildings and people in Japan with their homes, and discuss the ways they are similar and different. Children develop symbols to represent the different buildings in their area and Japan.

Second Grade

As the children study their neighborhood, they can distinguish between those things that are natural such as the terrain (hills, river, etc.) and those things that were built by people—or how people changed the terrain. Examples might be man-made lakes, tunnels through mountains, or the buildings that have changed the landscape. By securing pictures of the way their neighborhood looked many years ago and today, they can decide whether nature or people have caused the changes.

Third Grade

In studying communities, particularly their own, children use their relief map of the community to discuss the landforms and how they are represented on a map. They then determine the landforms of the other communities they are studying. Children identify the services that are provided in their community by using papers or phonebooks. In securing these from other communities, they identify the similarities and differences. Children discuss the difference between a neighborhood and a community.

Fourth Grade

During a study of their state, children can expand their understanding of physical characteristics by developing a physical map using symbols to indicate the landforms. As they study other regions of the world, they can compare these landforms with the other regions. Children also need to recognize that changes in the environment made by people in their state may be different from those made in other regions.

Fifth Grade

As children study the United States, they identify the physical characteristics of the land that influenced where people settled. What effect did the rivers and mountains have on settlement? Did the richness of the soil or the climate affect where people settled? How did the type of transportation available affect the settlement of areas?

Sixth Grade

In a study of world civilizations, children discover why the early civilizations developed around rivers. Children should compare how the climate, resources, and physical features affected the growth and development of areas. Why are the major industrial regions located where they are? How have the political ideologies of people affected the ways in which countries have developed?

Theme Three: Relationships Within Places

As children begin to understand that places have unique characteristics, they also need to recognize how much people depend on the environment in these places. People not only adapt to environments, but they may make changes in the environment. People use technology that may have an impact on the environment, but it may not always be positive. For example, people pollute the environment by allowing waste to escape into the air, land, or water.

Kindergarten

Children who live in rural areas will not have a difficult time understanding how people depend on the environment. They can observe how the land produces food for them or for animals. Lumber from the forest is used to build homes. These children may have opportunities to use water for fun by boating or fishing on the streams, rivers, and lakes. Children who live in the suburban and urban areas may have more difficulty realizing how they depend on the environment but can recognize how the rain makes grass, flowers, and bushes grow or learn how milk gets to the grocery store. The children can readily see how people have changed the environment by observing all the buildings and freeways that have been built. Pollution of the air and water may also be easily observable during a walk around the school playground or neighborhood.

First Grade

As children study how they meet their basic needs of food, clothing, and shelter, they recognize how food is grown on the land, how the environment is adapted so they have shelter, and how cotton is grown for clothing or sheep feed off the land to produce wool. They should also recognize how children in other cultures have the same needs and how the environment supplies them. Children should observe that in different parts of the world people may wear different clothes due to the type of climate they live in, eat foods that are grown there, and live in homes that are adapted to the type of weather they have. Children can identify through pictures the way that environment is misused.

Second Grade

When children are studying their neighborhood, they can take pictures or draw the ways in which people depend on the environment. If there is an empty lot in the neighborhood, children can decide how it should be used. Should it be developed into a park or playground, should it remain as it is, or should a store or business be built there? Children can find early pictures of their neighborhood and compare them with the present to determine how it has changed. What tools or technology caused it to be changed?

Third Grade

In the study of different communities, children can identify how the environment affects the work that people do. A community that has a fishing industry uses the water for their work while a community that has a lumber or paper industry uses the forests for their work. Children should also recognize that some communities do not have natural resources and are dependent upon other communities. As children study transportation in the community, they identify not only how the environment affects travel, but also how technology has changed the way people travel and how it affects the environment. More traffic results in more air and noise pollution.

Fourth Grade

As children study their state and other places in the world, they should examine how people have made different uses of similar environments. Why some people grow coffee on the mountains and others use it for vacationing with ski resorts or mountain climbing should be discussed. Make a plan to solve an environmental problem in their state as well as other areas of the world, such as waste disposal.

Fifth Grade

The study of the United States presents an opportunity to identify the major industrial areas of the country and also the areas where natural resources are found. Are they similar or different? Why? Children can research the environmental reasons for Pittsburgh becoming a steel manufacturing area. Children can debate the advantages and disadvantages that technology has had in improving/harming the environment.

Sixth Grade

As they study world populations, children can identify why dense populations are distributed as they are and what environmental factors have affected them. Develop a map of the world indicating places where people have made dramatic changes in the environment, such as dams, canals, etc. Discuss why they occurred where they did. How has technology impacted on these environments?

Theme Four: Movement

Why do humans move about the earth's surface and attempt to move into space? How does interdependence cause more movement of people and products around the world? Children should recognize why their families move or why their ancestors chose to move to another area of the world.

Kindergarten

Children discuss the different places where their families go to shop, visit for vacations, or visit their relatives. Why is this necessary? What types of transportation are used for traveling to these different places? They discuss how they travel from home to school. Visit an airport and find out all the places where people travel.

First Grade

Children, as they learn about their school, determine the places where the children, teachers, and other workers come from. They identify the types of transportation people use to come to school. By taking a field trip to a place outside their neighborhood, children identify how they travel and draw a map of their route. Discuss ways that people travel to different sports events.

Second Grade

Children can develop a map of the places where their family members go to work. They can also develop a chart of the means of transportation they use. Which means is used most often and why? Identify foods or other products in the neighborhood stores that came from other places. How were they transported there? Discuss the advantages and disadvantages of using different means of transportation in the neighborhood.

Third Grade

Discuss how much the local community depends on other communities for places to work, shop, and participate in recreational activities. What would happen if there were no transportation or communication with other communities? How would this affect their lives? Develop a map that shows how the community depends on other communities to market their products and the communities from which products come into their own communities.

Fourth Grade

As regions of the world are investigated, place on a map the location from which people in the class or their relatives have migrated. Make a graph of the number of different places that class members have lived. Trace patterns of movement that illustrate how different areas of the state were settled. Extend that pattern to show how people have migrated to cities in different parts of the world. Select a product made in the United States and map the different places in the world where the product can be found.

Fifth Grade

In studying about the United States, develop a map that shows the major routes of travel around the country. Determine the different means of travel and the length of time it takes to move from place to place. Develop a map that shows the routes and means of transportation that were used to settle the country—from the early explorers to westward settlements. Show how technology changed the means of travel when the most western states were settled.

Sixth Grade

As children investigate other areas of the world, including South America, Eurasia, and Africa, they will identify the amount and type of products that are imported from and exported to the United States from these countries as well as the exports and imports among the countries. A discussion of how Western ideas are transported to these countries will help children understand why certain entertainers are popular, why jeans are worn in many countries, and why certain foods from other countries are popular in the United States. On maps trace the routes of migration of people to and from South America, Eurasia, and Africa.

Theme Five: Regions

A region is an area identified by its common characteristics. A playground has swings, monkey bars, slides, and seesaws. Deserts are places where there is little or no water, limited plant life, and few animals. Regions may change, for example, so that when a desert is irrigated it can then have plants growing, while a playground may have a basketball hoop and a baseball diamond added.

Kindergarten

Children can draw a map of their classroom and describe different regions, such as the housekeeping corner, the games area, and the reading corner. Discuss what is in a region that makes it different from another area. Talk about how these places change when a rug and rocking chair are added to the reading corner or how their classroom may be different when they are in first grade. Discuss how the local shopping area changed when new stores moved in.

First Grade

Develop a map that shows where all the children in the class live. Discuss the regions where they live. Do they find the same characteristics in all regions or do some children live in single-family dwellings, apartment houses, near stores or parks? Discuss the characteristics of cities, small towns, and farms. How are they similar and how are they different?

Second Grade

Children make a map of their neighborhood. What characteristics make it a neighborhood? How is their neighborhood like other neighborhoods in their community and how is it different? Interview older members of the neighborhood to find out how it has changed. Draw a picture of how they would like their neighborhood to look in the future.

Third Grade

Children should discuss those characteristics that identify a community. Draw a map that shows the political boundaries of their community. What makes it unique? How is their community different from those in the surrounding area? What is the derivation of their community's name? How has their community changed? Develop a quilt with fabric squares that are collected from communities in regions around the world. Each square has a design characteristic of that region (Kepner 1990).

Fourth Grade

As children study regions of the world, use different thematic maps to compare the regions for climate, vegetation, physical features, population, and industries. Are the boundaries the same or different? Describe ways that regions can be identified.

Fifth Grade

Develop a list of common characteristics to identify regions of the United States. Eliminate some of the characteristics and determine how it changes the boundaries of the regions; for example, use physical features and then population. Apply knowledge of a region in North America to a similar region on another continent.

Sixth Grade

Develop criteria to determine different regions of your city. Apply these same criteria to a city in another country. Use physical and human characteristics to categorize regions of South America, Eurasia, and Africa. Determine criteria that would identify regions that are developed and those still developing. Apply these criteria to North and South America, Eurasia, and Africa (Kemball et al. 1987).

As children participate in these learning experiences organized around the five major themes of geography, they should develop a better understanding of the environment in which they live and how they and others interact with that environment.

PROBLEMS TO DETERMINE THE EXTENT OF CHILDREN'S SKILLS

As children begin to acquire skills in map reading and interpretation, they should be presented with problem situations that require them to use the skills they have learned. The following problem example might be presented to kindergarten or first grade children after they have learned directions and know where the sun rises and sets. The picture (Figure 10.1) following is placed on a transparency.

Question:
"If the sun is just rising, which way is the wind blowing?"

This problem requires the children to think about the direction from which the sun rises and the resulting shadows. The bending of the tree indicates the direction of the wind.

As children learn to identify the types of products grown in different climatic

FIGURE 10.1

and geographic regions, they should be able to describe conditions necessary for their growth. The teacher might present pictures of different types of vegetation and ask the children to name the type of climate and geographic conditions necessary for their growth.

The fact that the location rather than the physical appearance or natural resources of an area sometimes determines its importance offers an interesting problem for fourth through sixth grade children to analyze. Some examples follow:

Place "A"

This is a chain of islands that covers, in all, an area of about 6,400 square miles. Some small shrubs and mosses grow here, but there are no trees. The climate is very cold and foggy. The population survives largely through fishing. . . .

Place "B"

This is a rocky peninsula, which is largely a limestone "mountain" rising 1,400 feet above the water. It covers an area of about 2 square miles. . . .

Place "C"

This is an island of volcanic origin. It is about 65 miles long and 2 to 18 miles wide. It has an area of about 463 square miles. Its climate is hot and humid, and it is subject to a large number of wind storms each. . . . (Brock 1965).

After a discussion of possible reasons for the importance of these places, the teacher can reveal their names—The Aleutian Islands, Gibraltar, and Okinawa.

Many schools provide camping experiences for their students to enhance the in-class activities. These outdoor experiences provide excellent opportunities for students to try their mapping skills. They can be given an area of the campsite to map, including locating streams, hills, and trails. Students can learn to use a compass and their map skills for orienteering, which is "a competitive exercise in which participants find their way along a predetermined course using a map, compass, and perhaps a series of teacher-supplied clues. The objective is to find the shortest route around a series of control points" (Jacobson & Palonsky 1976). Also, the opportunity to find the "buried treasure" adds excitement to a map activity. Teachers can design the treasure map to utilize the map skills they want children to practice; for example, "Walk 10 paces east to the oak tree, then turn north, walking until you reach the river."

When older children have a good grasp of the color key on a map and knowledge of the various theories about building a city, the following problem (see Figure 10.2) as was suggested in Chapter 8 can be presented:

Questions:
"If you were to pick the site for a city in this area, where would you build it? Why?"

This map should be presented on a transparency, using a color key to distinguish the different physical features. The problem can be tackled individually or by the whole class. The teacher may wish to add additional information about the natural resources, the winds, or other physical features. It should be noted that this also can be used as an excellent inquiry activity to initiate a study of cities.

FIGURE 10.2

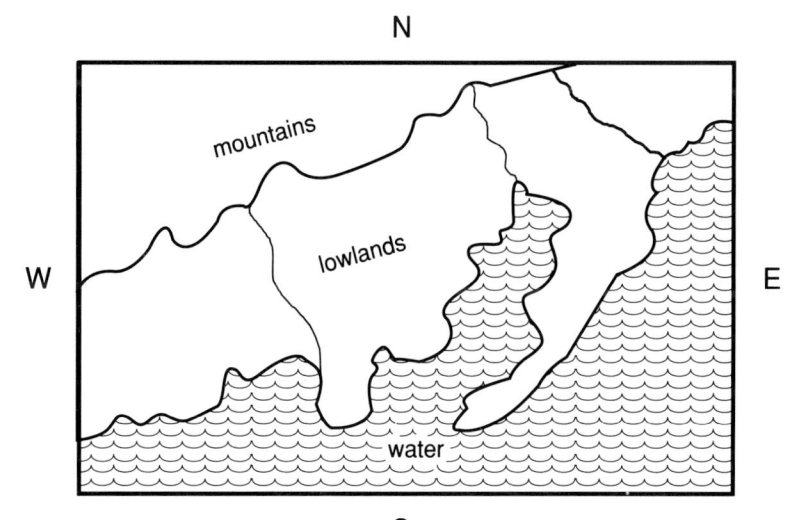

USING INTEREST CENTERS TO INCREASE SKILL

There are numerous activities related to maps and globes that children can complete on their own without the aid of the teacher. By developing an interest center for them in one corner of the room, the children can participate in the activities during free time or while the teacher is working with other groups. There should be a globe and a variety of maps available in the area. The following are some examples of the type of activities to plan:

1. Clip out downtown street maps of two city areas such as Savannah, Georgia, and Chattanooga, Tennessee. These two cities have quite different land-use patterns. Pose questions for the children to answer: What information can you find out about these cities? How are they alike? How are they different?
2. Clip from a map skill book the page which lists the geographic terms and the physical model that has examples of each type of land formation for them to match.
3. Find an enlarged physical features map of an area of the world such as Alaska and pose the question: How much information can you find about this area?
4. Supply a globe, a piece of string, and an air-age map (map used to plot airline routes) with questions about the "great circle routes."
5. Provide a map with the degrees of latitude and longitude plainly marked. Have children locate certain places in the world by their degrees of latitude and longitude.
6. Find a clipping of a news event that has occurred in some other area of the world. Ask questions relative to the geographic factors of the area. Example: Are there any bodies of water nearby? What types of landforms are found there? On what continent is it located?

Urban Map Skills

Since there are large numbers of people living in urban areas and a corresponding number of urban problems, it is important that children acquire an understanding of the urban concept. What is a city? How can it be described? The following presents an accurate conception:

1. A substantial number of people (number);
2. Living in close proximity (density);
3. Over an extended period of time (stability); and
4. Engaging in a variety of economic activities (occupational diversity).
   (Manson & Price 1969)

Activities introduced to acquire this concept include categorizing communities according to size, classifying occupations by community size, and working with aerial maps of cities.

Children can construct land-use maps of one part of the city (probably their own areas) or select a few functions, such as industrial and residential, for mapping the entire city. Listed below is a land-use category system that may be used by the children for city land uses:

1. Single-family residences;
2. Multiple-family dwellings or apartments;
3. Commercial or business—retail, wholesale, and service;
4. Industrial, manufacturing, and railroads;
5. Public schools, government functions, parks, and places of worship;
6. Streets;
7. Vacant and unused lands. (Lampe & Schaefer 1969)

Problems that confront cities, from the building of a new highway to urban renewal, are presented in a simulation such as *Urban Planning* and the MATCH kit, The City. The materials give children the opportunity to play out the solutions to these problems.

Maps and Globes

Every elementary classroom should contain a globe. In kindergarten and first grade, a simple globe of slate or one that shows only the outline of the continents should be used. The slate globe can be drawn with tempera or chalk and then washed or erased. Children should be permitted to manipulate the globe and locate places, such as their home and the United States. Reference to the globe by the teacher whenever feasible is important, for the children should form the habit of seeking it when the need arises.

Older children can use a more detailed globe—for example, the three- or five-color key of physical features can be used for the middle grades and a seven-color key for the intermediate grades. Use of a globe showing political boundaries with each country a different color has sometimes led children to believe that a country actually is the color shown on the globe. A globe that uses green for lowlands, brown for mountains, and blue for water might better orient children to globe usage.

Care should be exercised in the transition from globes to maps. The comparative size of Greenland is a good indicator of how shapes and sizes change from globe to map. Some map projections increase its size considerably, while others decrease the size. The teacher might have the children split a tennis ball or the peel of an orange and attempt to flatten it completely to help them to see what happens in the transition from a globe to a flat map.

Wall maps are generally not used by the children before the end of second or third grade, depending upon the ability and background of the children. As indicated earlier, the first maps used should be homemade. Commercial maps should not contain too much detail to avoid confusing the children. They should be large enough to be read easily across the classroom. Every upper-grade classroom should have a physical-political map of the world, and, if money allows, physical-political maps of North America and other continents. Little use is made of separate physical and political maps, and the combination saves money.

A chart of geographical terms is a useful instructional tool for older children. This chart pictorially shows most of the geographic terms such as "isthmus," "harbor," "bay," and "plateau." These terms, however, should be taught as the need arises. They should not all be taught from the chart at one time.

The wall map of the world should be pulled down each day for ready reference. Games utilizing locational skills can be introduced during free play time—for example, a box with slips of paper containing places to be located might be kept by the map rack. Depending upon the grade level, various clues to the areas' locations can be added. Intermediate-grade children may use only the degrees of latitude and longitude for their reference.

To increase the children's understanding of the grid system, a simple demonstration can be completed. Place an "X" anywhere on the blackboard and have children tell exactly where it is located. Place several other "X's" on the board and give the same direction. Children soon realize that some additional reference points are needed. Draw horizontal lines several inches apart and number them. Problems still arise in determining the exact location until numbered vertical lines have been added. Children should readily associate this method with that used on maps and globes to increase accuracy in locating places.

National Geographic Magazine supplies maps with each publication, but they usually contain too much detail for younger children. State chambers of commerce and embassies of foreign countries will provide maps of their areas. News magazines contain maps of areas where the news is happening. Weekly news maps with pictures of the events can be secured from *Time* magazine for a minimum charge.

SUMMARY

Maps and globes help children relate to where they are in the world in relation to where others are located. They begin to recognize why it is important to be able to locate places on a map and to learn about the environment in these places. They also recognize how the environment affects people and people affect the environment.

SELECTED REFERENCES

Bacon, P. (Ed.). (1970). *Focus on geography* (40th yearbook). Washington, DC: National Council for the Social Studies.

Blaut, J. M., McCleary, G. S., Jr., & Blaut, A. S. (1970). Environmental mapping in young children. *Environment and Behavior, 2,* 335–349.

Bluestein, N., & Acredolo, L. (1979). Developmental changes in map reading skills. *Child Development, 50,* 691–697.
Brock, J. (1965). *Geography: Its scope and spirit.* Columbus, OH: Charles E. Merrill.
Carpenter, H. M. (Ed.). (1963). *Skill development in social studies* (33rd yearbook). Washington, DC: National Council for the Social Studies.
Jacobson, M., & Palonsky, S. (1976). School camping and elementary social studies. *Social Education, 40*(1), 44–46.
Johnson, P. C., & Condesen, M. E. (1991). Teaching latitude and longitude in the upper elementary grades. *Journal of Geography, 90*(2), 73–77.
Kemball, W. G., and others. (1987). *K–6 geography: Themes, key ideas, and learning opportunities.* Washington, DC: American Geographic Society, Association of American Geographers, National Council for Geographic Education, National Geographic Society.
Kepner, T. (1990). Quilt-making as a window on the world. *Journal of Geography, 89*(4), 161–164.
Lampe, A., & Schaefer, O. C., Jr. (1969, May). Land-use patterns in the city. *Journal of Geography,* p. 302.
Landau, B. (1986). Early map use as an unlearned ability. *Cognition, 22,* 201–223.
Manson, G., & Price, C. J. (1969, May). Introducing cities to elementary school children. *Journal of Geography,* p. 296.
Muir, S. P., & Cheek, H. N. (1991). Assessing spatial development: Implications for map skill instruction. *Social Education, 55*(5), 316–319.
Muir, S. P., & Frazee, B. (1986). A developmental perspective. *Social Education, 50*(3), 199–203.
National Council for the Social Studies. (1984). In search of a scope and sequence for social studies. *Social Education, 48*(4), 249–262.
Presson, C. C. (1982). The development of map-reading skills. *Child Development, 53,* 196–199.
Rushdoony, H. A. (1963, November). Achievement in map-reading: An experimental study. *Elementary School Journal, 64,* 70–75.
Uttal, D. H., & Wellman, H. M. (1989). Young children's representation of spatial information acquired from maps. *Developmental Psychology, 25*(1), 128–138.

LEARNING ACTIVITY

With your classmates, develop an imaginary community, and decide upon its location and region. Is it at a fork of a river? Is it in the mountains or on a plateau? Plan your community to fit its location. Is it a port city or a ski resort? Describe the place and the relationships within the place. Each person should decide what role to assume in the community and discuss how the environment affects that role. Discuss any movement of people that might occur as a result of your place, such as tourists coming to ski.

Draw a map of your community placing each person's home and/or business on the map. Be sure all the physical features are included and their specific locations. Some may not live in the immediate community. Carefully construct a key for your map. Record in your journal your reaction to the map activity. Is it more exciting than map activities you remember? What aspects of the five themes would children learn?

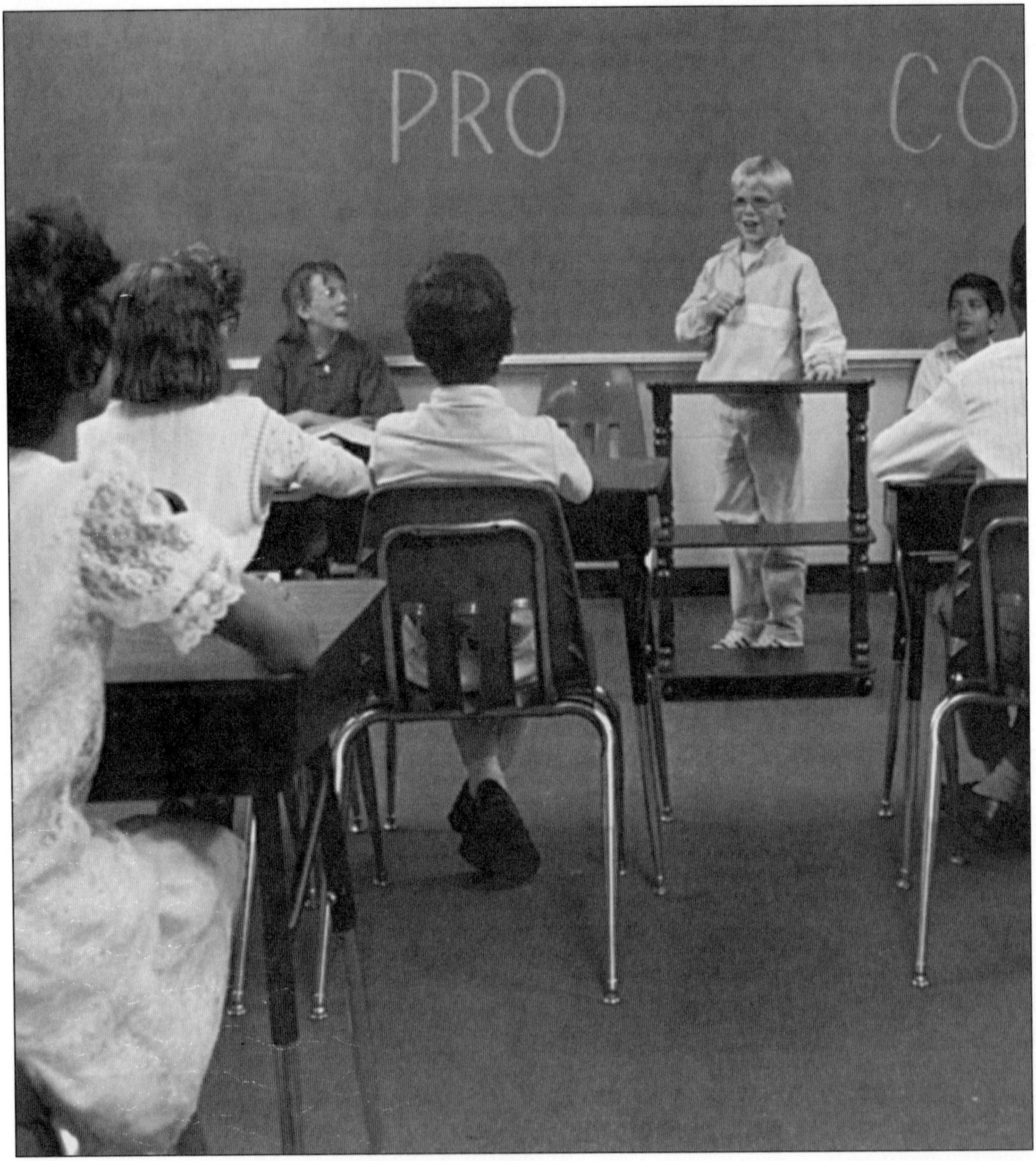
PRO
CO

PART IV
USING THE TEXTBOOK AND OTHER MATERIALS

EVEN THOUGH the textbook is the most frequently used instructional material, there are criticisms of its use. Often textbooks are seen as bland, boring, and lacking in substantive knowledge. There are teaching strategies that can adapt textbooks to better meet student and teacher needs. These strategies are discussed in Part IV. Another way to make better use of the textbook, or to use it less, can be accomplished by supplementing it with the vast array of rich and inviting materials now available.

Videotapes and filmstrips can be found to supplement almost any study; children's trade books add a spark of interest; the combined media present opportunities to interact with materials and artifacts of many countries; simulations, with and without computers, promote active learning; and cartoons, pictures, graphs, and charts can add to the understanding of topics.

CHAPTER 11

USING THE TEXTBOOK AND OTHER MATERIALS

INTRODUCTION

Research tells us that the textbook continues to be the most frequently used instruction tool in social studies classes (Armento 1986; McCabe 1993; Morrisett 1982). There are numerous reasons for this practice, but probably the most logical reason is the fact that a textbook provides both structure and content for social studies instruction. Its relative ease of use, requiring limited planning and preparation, appeals to the elementary teacher who is plagued with teaching all or most of the subjects and is often more concerned with how to teach reading, language arts, and mathematics. Too often social studies instruction comes at the end of the day, if there is time. Therefore using a textbook that can be picked up, read with the children, that provides questions to be asked in the teacher's guide, is a reasonable practice. However, is this practice effective social studies instruction? Are the intended objectives/outcomes achieved?

Critics of textbooks (Anyon 1978; Larkins, Hawkins, & Gilmore 1987; McCabe 1993; White 1988) would argue that they are often bland, boring, lacking in substantive knowledge and considerateness ("considerateness refers to the clarity with which verbal and nonverbal information is presented" [McCabe 1993, p. 129]). If in fact these criticisms are true, then totally relying on textbooks would be unfortunate. Even if they aren't true, good social studies instruction shouldn't be based exclusively on the textbook. Some critics would suggest that if a choice had to be made between abandoning social studies in the primary grades or being forced to use current texts, they would abandon social studies (Larkins et al. 1987). Earlier Anyon (1978) had argued that textbooks, particularly in the elementary school, are a part of the socialization process. "A definitive characteristic that emerges from the texts is that the information which 'counts' as elementary textbook knowledge tends to be that knowledge which sanctions and justifies prevailing institutional arrangements" (p. 50). She points out, however, that by sanctioning what is, certain groups in power are favored, students are not encouraged to seek change, and disagreement is channeled into "safe" political behaviors such as voting.

Another criticism of textbooks is their treatment of cultural and racial groups. Cortes and Fleming (1986) claim that textbooks have improved, but cultural biases and ethnocentrism remain, even though they are not as blatant as in the past. "However, the very subtlety of the continuing biases—such as the omission of critical themes or clarifying perspectives—may make these biases even more powerful influences than the flagrantly distorting adjectives and assertions of the past" (p. 376).

Treatment of Native Americans and African Americans in textbooks has received much attention. Stereotyped images of Native Americans "still group all Indians together, believe they live in tepees, wear feathers in their hair, and throw tomahawks" (Musser & Freeman 1989, p. 5). In addition, "Textbooks tend to treat Afro-American history and culture with a general unevenness, with little attention to Afro-American thoughts and activities" (Dhand 1988, pp. 25–26). Frequently, textbooks are criticized for presenting information from a Eurocentric perspective.

Often, in an attempt to be comprehensive, elementary textbooks lack in-depth information on various regions of the world. Areas such as Africa, Latin America, the Middle East, and Asia have limited space devoted to them (Bullard 1986; Crofts 1986; Greenfield 1986; Griswold 1986).

Woodward, Elliott, and Nagel (1986) state that "social studies textbooks are of poor instructional quality because of a number of factors: preoccupation with superficial yet broad content coverage, lack of care in content choice and presentation, absence of 'point of view' and the use of readability formulas that result in 'inconsiderate' content presentation involving short sentences, simple vocabulary and the exclusion of connectors and referents that help make text easier for youngsters to comprehend" (p. 52).

If these criticisms are true, what then can be done to achieve a more effective use of textbooks? Probably two of the best ways are: one, to develop strategies that adapt the textbooks to meet student and teacher needs; and two, to supplement the textbook with other materials. The remainder of the chapter will be devoted to these two activities.

TEACHING STRATEGIES WITH THE TEXTBOOK

One of the most frequent criticisms leveled at social studies materials is that children cannot read the material that is necessary for background information, whether it's in a textbook or a library resource book. Most recent studies, analyzing textbooks for readability, disclose that in a fifth grade text the reading level may range from fourth to tenth grade (McCabe 1993). Often, the difficulty is increased by the number and method of introducing new concepts. Concepts may be presented too frequently without giving sufficient exposure for development. Also, concepts may be presented without explicit enumeration of their critical attributes. Therefore, the reader does not understand the concepts and cannot comprehend the material read. In Chapter 7, which discussed concepts, teaching suggestions were outlined for teachers to introduce and extend concept development. It is important that these concepts be introduced before the children begin to read the materials.

CONCEPT DEVELOPMENT AND THE TEXTBOOK

The following lesson plan uses the Taba (1967) model to introduce the concept of independence before the students begin to read the section in the textbook about the American colonies seeking their independence from Great Britain.

CONCEPT DEVELOPMENT

Concept: Independence
Teaching Strategy: Inquiry, questioning
Outcomes: Students will identify the attributes of the concept of independence.
   Students will develop higher-level thinking skills.
Materials: Blackboard, textbook
Procedure: Teacher conducts lesson through a series of questions using the Taba model.

CONCEPT FORMATION

Teacher's Questions	Possible Responses
What do you think of when you hear the word independence?	on your own freedom not relying on others breaking away doing what you want separating yourself
How would you group these words? What goes together?	breaking away separating yourself freedom on your own not relying on others doing what you want
What would you call these groups?	*how you get it* breaking away

separating yourself
how you feel
freedom
on your own
not relying on others
doing what you want

INTERPRETATION OF DATA

How would you define independence?	means being able to function on your own, believe the way you want to, do things the way you want to
Why would someone want to be independent?	If they didn't believe the same way as others. If they wanted to make decisions on their own. If they believed others weren't being fair to them.
Give an example of someone with independence.	Child beginning to walk doesn't want help. Kids try to be independent of their parents. Countries try to be independent of one another.

APPLICATION OF DATA

What might happen if someone did not want you to be independent or have independence?	They would try to stop you. They might fight you.
Why do you think that would happen?	Because they didn't think you should be independent or didn't believe you could be—maybe you're not strong enough. They may not believe the same as you.
What could we say about people who try to have independence?	They want to do things on their own without other people bothering them.

Evaluation: Students apply the concept of independence to the United States, explaining why and how the nation received independence, after reading the textbook.

In addition to introducing concepts prior to reading the text, another way to increase the understanding of the concepts is to use the same strategy (Taba questioning) after the text material has been read. An example follows:

CONCEPT DEVELOPMENT

Topic: Europeans Reach America, grade 5, pp. 126–129, *United States and Its Neighbors,* Macmillan/McGraw-Hill, 1990.

Teaching Strategy: Inquiry (Taba model)
Skills: Concept formation and critical thinking
Objectives: To arrive at an understanding of the concept of explorer
   To arrive at a generalization of why the Vikings came to North America
Materials: Textbook, blackboard
Procedure: After students have read pages 126–129 of *United States and Its Neighbors,* ask the following questions:

CONCEPT FORMATION

Questions
What words do you think of or remember from your reading that would describe an explorer?

Responses
brave
adventuresome
fearful
seeking new places
looking for adventure
telling tales
sailors

FIGURE 11.1ab

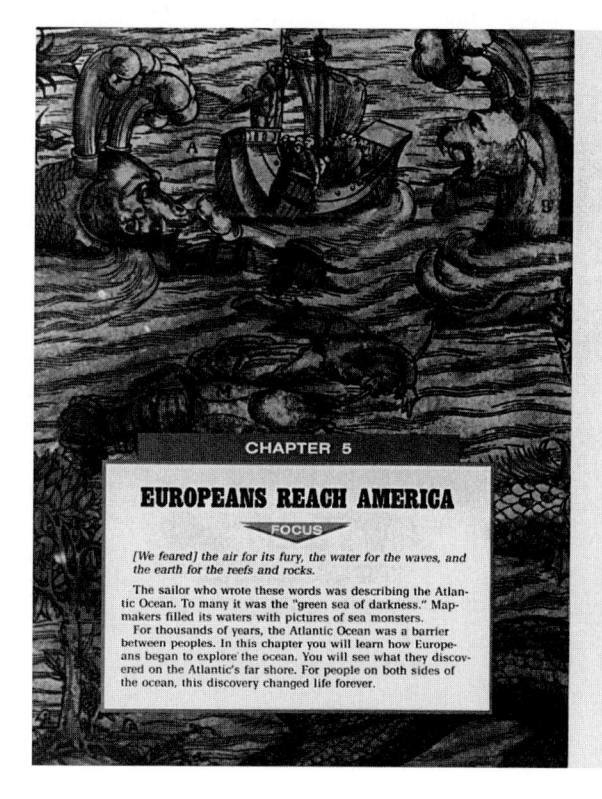

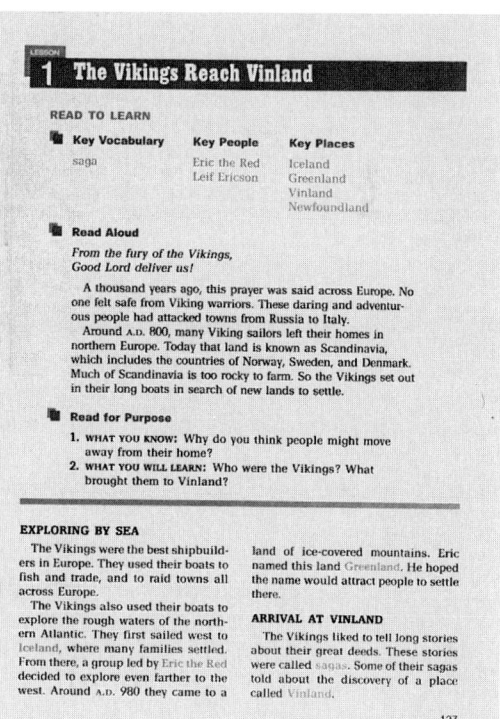

236 • USING THE TEXTBOOK AND OTHER MATERIALS

FIGURE 11.1cd

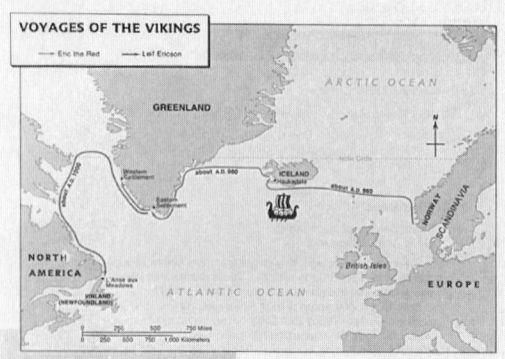

[Textbook page spread showing a map titled "VOYAGES OF THE VIKINGS" with routes of Eric the Red and Leif Ericson across the North Atlantic, and an illustration of Viking ships and helmets. Pages 128–129.]

Page 128 text:

MAP SKILL: Locate Scandinavia and North America on the map. Use the map to describe the stages of the Vikings' journey from Norway to Vinland.

According to the sagas, Vinland was first found in a fog by Bjarni Herjulfsson (byär′ nē här yōl′ sən), a young man who was sailing west from Iceland to Greenland when his boat got lost in thick fog. As the fog lifted, Bjarni saw a flat, wooded land. It was the Atlantic coast of North America.

"Is this Greenland?" the crew asked. "No," said Bjarni, "for there are said to be glaciers in Greenland." Bjarni had gone too far west. So he sailed back to Greenland and told the others about the new land he had seen.

Bjarni's story fired the imagination of Eric the Red's son, Leif Ericson. Around the year 1000, Leif and his crew sailed west from Greenland. They spent the winter exploring the new land that Bjarni had talked about.

One day a German sailor in Leif's crew came to Leif, rolling his eyes in excitement. "I have news!" he said. "I have found vines and grapes." "Can this be possible?" asked Leif, who had never seen grapes. "Certainly," answered the sailor, "for I was born where grapes grow." Leif named the new land Vinland, the land of wine and vines. Find Vinland on the map.

VIKINGS SETTLE IN VINLAND

Leif returned to Greenland filled with tales about Vinland. About five years later, a Viking named Thorfinn Karlsefni (tù′ fin cārl sev′ na), and his wife Freydis, convinced many Greenlanders to move to Vinland.

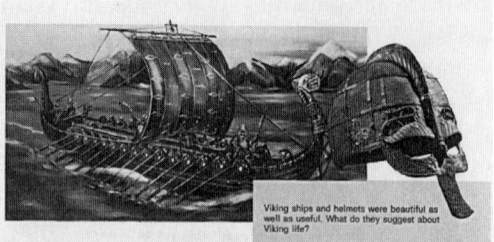

Page 129 text:

Viking ships and helmets were beautiful as well as useful. What do they suggest about Viking life?

After the Greenlanders had settled in Vinland, they were approached by black-haired men in skin boats. The strangers were probably Indians in birch-bark canoes. The frightened Greenlanders attacked, killing several of the Indians.

According to the sagas, the Indians later came out of the forests to fight back. They shot razor-sharp arrows at the Vikings, who fled in terror. Freydis could not believe her eyes. "Why are you running?" she shouted. She picked up the sword of a dead Viking. As the Indians rushed toward her, she spun around to face them, sword across her chest. Her surprising action stopped the attackers in their tracks. They turned and ran away.

VINLAND IS FORGOTTEN

Soon after the Indian attack, the Viking settlers returned to Greenland. The sagas say that Vinland was "an excellent land." Yet the Greenlanders feared they "could never live there in safety and freedom from fear."

Sagas of Vinland were told around the fire during long winter nights in Greenland. But as the years went by, the new land became a dim memory. Nearly 500 years would pass before Europeans would again come to North America.

Today we know that the Greenlanders probably settled in Newfoundland (nū′ fənd lənd), a large island off the coast of Canada. In 1960 archaeologists uncovered the remains of Viking houses there. These artifacts suggest that the sagas about Vinland are based on real events.

Check Your Reading

1. Who were the Vikings? What did they find in Vinland?
2. How do we know that the Greenlanders probably settled in Newfoundland?
3. GEOGRAPHY SKILL: How did the geography of Scandinavia encourage the Vikings to become skilled sailors?
4. THINKING SKILL: Beginning with the Vikings' leaving Scandanavia, write all the events mentioned in this lesson in the order in which they occurred.

If you were to group these words or thoughts that belong together, what would they be?	Vikings brave fearful adventuresome seeking new places looking for adventure telling tales sailors Vikings
If you gave those groups labels, what would you call them?	*traits* brave fearful adventuresome *what they did* seeking new places looking for adventure

	telling tales
	people who were
	sailors
	Vikings
Who were some of the explorers?	sailors
	Vikings

INTERPRETATION OF DATA

How would you define explorer?	a person who was brave and was seeking new lands
Why did they explore?	looking for new places to live or hunt
	looking for good land
	looking for adventure
What picture do you have of the Viking explorers?	they were brave and adventuresome
	they were seeking new places to live

APPLICATION OF DATA

What do you think might have happened if the Vikings had not sailed to North America?	They might have sailed somewhere else
	North America may not have been explored and settled as soon
Why do you say that?	They were brave to sail the oceans, others might not have tried if they hadn't
What generalization could you draw about the Viking explorers?	They wanted new land and they weren't afraid to explore to find it.

Other techniques to aid students with reading of text are outlined:

1. Tape-record important sections of the textbook so children can listen as they follow along in the texts. More able readers can help with the recording.
2. Have children work in pairs on reading assignments, matching a less able with a more able reader.
3. Have children prepare summaries or outlines of textbook sections. Use language experience techniques for younger children. These can be used year after year.
4. Use picture analysis questioning skills to focus on the important concepts such as "What do you see in the picture? What is happening? Why do you think that is happening?"
5. Have the class prepare a "cartoon" narrative of part of the text, depicting the major concepts.
6. Cut illustrative material and pictures from old texts and magazines. Make unit scrapbooks and bulletin boards to illustrate main concepts of the text.

7. Develop "textbook learning centers" where groups of children are each responsible for developing learning experiences for the other children for a small section of the text (Turner 1976).

GROUP READING

Children with different reading abilities may need to be grouped at times when reading the textbook. A sample lesson plan follows:

Topic: Mexico
Objective: To understand the culture of Mexico by acquiring knowledge of its historical development.
Materials: Textbook study guide and visual aids
Procedure: Group I, Underachievers—Use a textbook that contains a physical-political map of Mexico, a historical map of early Spanish explorations, and a story of Cortez's capture of the Aztecs. Use realia of Mexico, including a record of Spanish and Mexican Indian language, dolls dressed in native Mexican dress, pottery, and musical instruments.

1. Using the maps in the textbook, discuss the location of Mexico in relation to the United States and its geographical areas. Using the historical map, trace the routes of the Spanish explorers to Mexico.
2. Read the story of Cortez's explorations and conquest of the Aztecs to the children. Observe the realia of the country and discuss how the Spanish conquest influenced its culture.

Group II, Average Achievers—Have the children read silently the chapter on Spanish exploration and conquest in Mexico. Establish a purpose for the reading with the following study guide questions.

1. Try to determine the reasons why Spanish explorers were interested in the New World, particularly Mexico.
2. Trace the route of Cortez in Mexico and discuss the type of problems the physical features and climate gave his men.
3. Why was Cortez able to defeat the Aztecs?

Group III, Above-Average Achievers—Use the same study guide as above with these additional activities and questions.

1. Read another account of the Spanish conquest from a different resource and compare the two descriptions.
2. Are there any discrepancies in the accounts?
3. If so, why would this difference occur?
4. Discuss what you think Mexico would be like if the French or English had conquered the Aztecs.

In this sample lesson plan, all groups utilize the same text, but each with a different level of abstraction.

The textbook can be used by small or cooperative groups for exploratory reading or research information. The suggested references included in the textbook provide excellent resources for extending research activities.

One of the most common practices in utilizing the social studies textbook is for the children to "take turns" reading a paragraph or two. After the reading is completed, the teacher will conduct a discussion, generally asking information questions. If the purpose of the reading is to acquire information, then poor readers won't help others achieve this goal or retain it themselves. Children usually fidget, look out windows, or create some disturbances while poor readers are stumbling along. This type of experience does nothing to improve the skill or the self-esteem of the poor reader. What are some alternatives if the teacher wants to use the textbook as a group experience?

1. The teacher reads while the children *do* or *do not* follow along.
2. Children who are good readers from higher grade levels read the selection. This provides experience for the older children as well.
3. The children read the selection silently; then, in response to teacher questions, read a sentence or two that contains the answer. In addition, teachers ask questions that go beyond facts to include interpretation and application.
4. Use Readers Theatre techniques to read the text. The text is scripted by the students or teachers and students are assigned to read their parts. They can practice or not, and use props to illustrate the text (Gallagher 1991).

VOCABULARY DEVELOPMENT

Since social studies materials frequently introduce a multitude of new vocabulary words, teachers will need to use similar techniques with social studies vocabulary as they do with reading or other content areas.

Vocabulary words can be introduced to the children prior to the reading in the following manner. Teachers should find pictures that illustrate the vocabulary words. Write the words on the board, leaving sufficient space. Using tape or magnets, have children match the pictures with the words and explain them. Leave them on the board during the reading so that children can refer back to them if they have any difficulty.

Flashcards

Make flashcards of the concepts or vocabulary words for a chapter in the social studies textbook. Place pictures of them on the backs of the cards. Have children work in pairs, learning the new words before beginning the reading. Games can also be played with them.

Illustrated Concepts or Vocabulary Dictionary

Have children cut out pictures from magazines or draw pictures to illustrate the concepts or vocabulary words in the social studies. Develop an illustrated dictionary of them. Children can refer to the dictionary as they are reading.

Language Experience Chart

After children have read a selection from their textbook, ask them to tell you about it in their own words. Prepare an experience chart with their responses. Have children illustrate the chart where appropriate. Use the chart as review the following day before beginning the next section.

Journal Writing

Children can keep a journal whereby they write their thoughts about the reading selection. They may indicate the vocabulary words that were new to them or exciting.

USING THE TEXTBOOK WITH VALUING STRATEGIES

Most content in social studies textbooks is value laden, not as a result of the author's perspective or bias, but more due to the fact there are values imbedded in the issues and situations that are reported since they involve people. It is important to recognize the values that were inherent in the decisions that people made in the past. What did the colonists value that caused them to come to the New World? What values were important to the framers of the Constitution? What values led Lincoln to free the slaves? What did the Native Americans believe about land ownership? By using valuing strategies that were introduced in Chapter 9 with textbook content, some of these value issues can be clarified. In the lesson that follows, value analysis is used to clarify values held by the framers of the Constitution.

Concepts: Justice, Freedom, Equality
Outcomes: Students will recognize the value issues facing the framers of the Constitution.
   Students will use their valuing skills to help them make a decision.
Teaching Strategy: Valuing
Materials: Textbook, blackboard
Procedure: After students have read pages 322–326 in *United States and Its Neighbors,* MacMillan/McGraw-Hill, 1990, begin the valuing lesson with the following questions.

FIGURE 11.2a–d

LESSON 2: The Constitutional Convention

READ TO LEARN

Key Vocabulary
- delegate
- constitution
- legislative branch
- executive branch
- President
- judicial branch
- Supreme Court
- republic
- House of Representatives
- Senate

Key People
- James Madison

Read Aloud

In May 1787 representatives from 12 states came to the city of Philadelphia. Congress had called a convention to revise, or change, the Articles of Confederation. Not everyone liked this idea. Rhode Island did not send anyone. And Patrick Henry refused to go, saying he "smelt a rat."

Read for Purpose

1. WHAT YOU KNOW: Why were people unhappy with the Articles of Confederation?
2. WHAT YOU WILL LEARN: What did the delegates achieve at the Constitutional Convention?

THE DELEGATES

The 55 delegates who met in the Philadelphia State House were men of property—bankers, lawyers, planters, and merchants. A delegate is a person chosen by people to represent them. Many of the delegates had fought in the American Revolution. Most had served in their state assemblies. At the age of 81, Benjamin Franklin was the oldest delegate.

George Washington was probably the most reluctant delegate. After the war he had returned to Mount Vernon, hoping never to leave again. But his friends said that the convention would fail without him. It was his duty to go. And Washington was not a man to turn his back on duty.

The best-prepared delegate was a planter named James Madison. He was a short man, "no bigger," someone said, "than half a piece of soap." But he came to Philadelphia filled with big ideas for his country.

Madison wanted the delegates to get rid of the Articles of Confederation. The nation needed a strong government to survive, he said. And James Madison had written a plan for just such a government.

THE CONVENTION BEGINS

The convention began on May 25. The delegates' first act was to elect George Washington president of the convention. They also decided to keep their meetings secret. That way they could speak freely without fear of what other people might think.

Fortunately, Madison took notes about everything that happened. "This was a task," he said, that "nearly killed me." From his notes we know what went on each day of the convention.

For several days the delegates looked at the plan Madison had written. They liked it enough to vote against revising the Articles of Confederation. Instead, they would write a new constitution, or plan of government, based on Madison's ideas. From that point on, the meeting in Philadelphia was a Constitutional Convention. And James Madison became known as the "Father of the Constitution."

THE NEW PLAN OF GOVERNMENT

The delegates began planning a government with three branches, or parts. One was a legislative branch, or lawmaking branch, called the Congress. The Congress would make laws and raise money for the government. The second was an executive branch to carry out the laws and run the government. The executive branch would be headed by a President. The third was a judicial branch that would decide the meaning of laws. This branch would be headed by a Supreme Court.

The summer of 1787 was the hottest that people in Philadelphia could remember. Madison's notes tell us that the delegates' tempers rose with the heat. Most delegates agreed that the government should be a republic. A republic is a type of government in which the people elect representatives to run the country. Under the new plan of government, the people would elect the members of Congress. But the delegates could not agree on how each state should be represented in the new Congress.

Delegates from large states had their own plan. Edmund Randolph of Virginia said the number of representatives in Congress should be based on each state's population. That way, larger states would have more representatives in Congress than would smaller states.

The delegates from small states disagreed. They wanted each state to have the same number of representatives. Then smaller states and larger states would have equal power in Congress. The argument went on and on until one delegate said that the convention was held together by "no more than the strength of a hair."

James Madison, called "Jemmy" by his friends, kept the best record of what happened at the Constitutional Convention

---

After four months of hard work, delegates signed the Constitution on September 17, 1787.

An agreement called the Great Compromise saved the convention. In a compromise, each side to a dispute gives up something it wants in order to reach an agreement. In the Great Compromise, the large states and small states agreed that Congress should have two parts, or houses. In the House of Representatives, each state would be represented according to its population. In the other house, the Senate, each state would have two senators regardless of population.

There were other arguments over slavery, trade, and the powers of the government. But by September, the work was done. To George Washington, the new Constitution seemed "little short of a miracle."

A RISING YOUNG NATION

On September 17, the delegates met for the last time. They had worked hard to create a good plan of government for the republic. Tears ran down Ben Franklin's face as he signed the Constitution. Looking at Washington's chair in the State House, he had often wondered if the sun carved on its back was rising or setting. Now, Franklin was happy to say, it was a rising sun—a symbol of a rising young nation.

Check Your Reading

1. Why is James Madison known as the "Father of the Constitution"?
2. What kind of government did the delegates to the Constitutional Convention try to create?
3. What agreement was worked out by the Great Compromise?
4. THINKING SKILL: You read that we know what went on at the Constitutional Convention from James Madison's notes. Do you think his notes give us an accurate picture of the convention? Why or why not?

LESSON 3: The New Constitution

READ TO LEARN

Key Vocabulary
- Preamble
- federal system
- checks and balances
- veto

Read Aloud

Before the Constitution could go into effect, it had to be approved by 9 of the 13 states. In each state Americans studied the new plan to find out what kind of government it would create.

Read for Purpose

1. WHAT YOU KNOW: What three branches of government were created by the Constitution?
2. WHAT YOU WILL LEARN: How did the Constitution create a system of checks and balances?

THE PREAMBLE

The first thing Americans saw in the Constitution was its Preamble, or introduction. It begins, "We the People of the United States. . . ." These words told Americans that the Constitution would create a republic. As you know, in a republic, power comes from the people, who elect their own leaders.

The Preamble, which appears on page 330, lists the goals of the nation's government. First, the government should unite the states into a "more perfect Union." It should "establish Justice" and keep peace within the country. It should also defend the country from attack and protect the freedoms of all Americans. These goals are as important to us today as they were to people in 1787.

A FEDERAL SYSTEM OF GOVERNMENT

The Constitution set up a federal system of government in which power is shared between the national government and the state governments.

Our Constitution gives some powers to the federal, or national, government alone. For example, only the federal government has the power to print money or declare war. Other powers, such as setting up public schools and running elections, are left to the states. Still other powers, such as the power to tax, are shared by both the federal and state governments.

FIGURE 11.2e

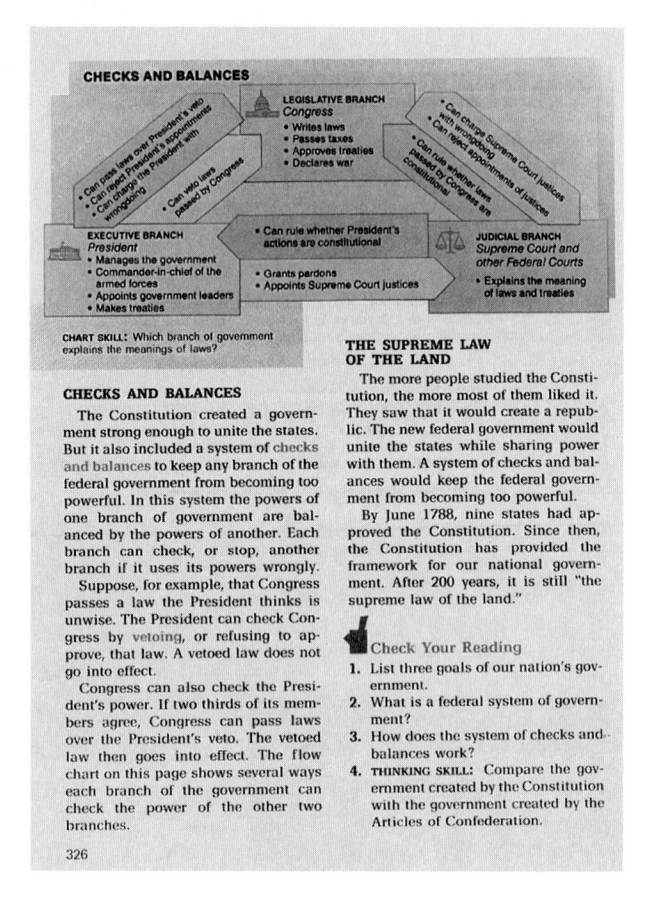

CHECKS AND BALANCES

LEGISLATIVE BRANCH
Congress
- Writes laws
- Passes taxes
- Approves treaties
- Declares war

- Can pass laws over President's veto
- Can reject President's appointments
- Can change the President with wrongdoing
- Can veto laws passed by Congress

- Can change Supreme Court justices with wrongdoing
- Can reject appointments of justices
- Can rule whether laws passed by Congress are constitutional

EXECUTIVE BRANCH
President
- Manages the government
- Commander-in-chief of the armed forces
- Appoints government leaders
- Makes treaties

- Can rule whether President's actions are constitutional
- Grants pardons
- Appoints Supreme Court justices

JUDICIAL BRANCH
Supreme Court and other Federal Courts
- Explains the meaning of laws and treaties

CHART SKILL: Which branch of government explains the meanings of laws?

CHECKS AND BALANCES

The Constitution created a government strong enough to unite the states. But it also included a system of checks and balances to keep any branch of the federal government from becoming too powerful. In this system the powers of one branch of government are balanced by the powers of another. Each branch can check, or stop, another branch if it uses its powers wrongly.

Suppose, for example, that Congress passes a law the President thinks is unwise. The President can check Congress by vetoing, or refusing to approve, that law. A vetoed law does not go into effect.

Congress can also check the President's power. If two thirds of its members agree, Congress can pass laws over the President's veto. The vetoed law then goes into effect. The flow chart on this page shows several ways each branch of the government can check the power of the other two branches.

THE SUPREME LAW OF THE LAND

The more people studied the Constitution, the more most of them liked it. They saw that it would create a republic. The new federal government would unite the states while sharing power with them. A system of checks and balances would keep the federal government from becoming too powerful.

By June 1788, nine states had approved the Constitution. Since then, the Constitution has provided the framework for our national government. After 200 years, it is still "the supreme law of the land."

Check Your Reading

1. List three goals of our nation's government.
2. What is a federal system of government?
3. How does the system of checks and balances work?
4. **THINKING SKILL:** Compare the government created by the Constitution with the government created by the Articles of Confederation.

326

When the framers began to write the Constitution, what were all the possible alternatives for government that were open to them?

| Possible responses: | They could have a king who would rule. They could be ruled by England again. There could be a national government. Each state could have its own government. They could have a national government and each state a government. |

What would be the consequences of each of these alternatives?

| A king would rule | ... who would be king, may not agree with king, people wouldn't get any chance to be heard |
| A national government | ... people could elect the members of the government, maybe the states wouldn't have enough say in the government |

Each state has a government	. . . states might fight with one another, who would speak for the country to other countries, bigger states would have more power
Be ruled by England again	. . . fighting the war would have been wasted, colonies had their freedom—couldn't go back to being ruled by England
State and national government	. . . share the powers, some for the state, others for national, all people would have representation
What were the values involved in setting up new government?	fairness justice freedom equality

What value issues were most important to the framers?

How would you make a choice about the type of government?

What values are most important to you? Make your decision (choice) based on those values.

Evaluation: Observation and assessment of students' ability to make decision. Have them write out their response (decision) and why they made that choice. Was their decision the same as the framers?

Teaching Strategy: Valuing
Materials: Textbook, blackboard
Procedure: After reading the textbook pages 216–218 from *Communities Near and Far,* Grade 3, Macmillan Publishing, New York, 1990, begin the valuing lesson with the following questions.

The people of Pittsburgh had so many steel factories that their city's air was polluted with dirt, dust, and ashes. What were the choices that the people could make about the pollution?

Possible responses:	They could let the city stay the way that it was. They could find ways to stop some of the pollution. They could close the factories. They could make the factories pay for cleaning up the cities.

What would be the consequences of each of these choices? What might happen?

Leave the city the way it was.	People might get sick. People wouldn't want to move to the city. The buildings in the city would look worse.
Find ways to stop the pollution.	It would cost the factories lots of money.

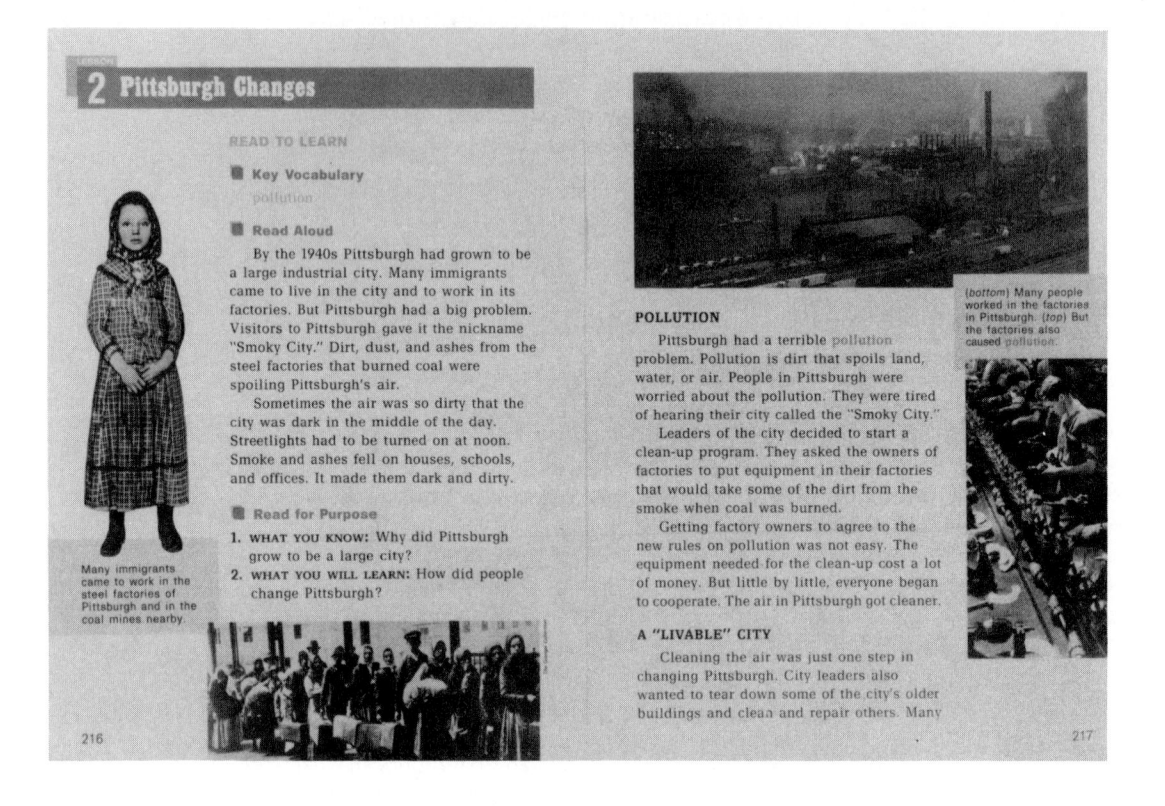

FIGURE 11.3a–b

2 Pittsburgh Changes

READ TO LEARN

■ Key Vocabulary
pollution

■ Read Aloud
By the 1940s Pittsburgh had grown to be a large industrial city. Many immigrants came to live in the city and to work in its factories. But Pittsburgh had a big problem. Visitors to Pittsburgh gave it the nickname "Smoky City." Dirt, dust, and ashes from the steel factories that burned coal were spoiling Pittsburgh's air.

Sometimes the air was so dirty that the city was dark in the middle of the day. Streetlights had to be turned on at noon. Smoke and ashes fell on houses, schools, and offices. It made them dark and dirty.

■ Read for Purpose
1. WHAT YOU KNOW: Why did Pittsburgh grow to be a large city?
2. WHAT YOU WILL LEARN: How did people change Pittsburgh?

Many immigrants came to work in the steel factories of Pittsburgh and in the coal mines nearby.

POLLUTION
Pittsburgh had a terrible pollution problem. Pollution is dirt that spoils land, water, or air. People in Pittsburgh were worried about the pollution. They were tired of hearing their city called the "Smoky City."

Leaders of the city decided to start a clean-up program. They asked the owners of factories to put equipment in their factories that would take some of the dirt from the smoke when coal was burned.

Getting factory owners to agree to the new rules on pollution was not easy. The equipment needed for the clean-up cost a lot of money. But little by little, everyone began to cooperate. The air in Pittsburgh got cleaner.

A "LIVABLE" CITY
Cleaning the air was just one step in changing Pittsburgh. City leaders also wanted to tear down some of the city's older buildings and clean and repair others. Many

(bottom) Many people worked in the factories in Pittsburgh. (top) But the factories also caused pollution.

216 / 217

Close the factories.	People might have to pay for the cleanup.
	The city would look better.
	People would enjoy being in the city.
	People wouldn't get sick.
	More people would move to the city.
Make factories pay for the cleanup.	Pollution from factories would stop and the city would look better.
	People would lose their jobs.
	There wouldn't be as much money to clean up the buildings and homes.
	Some factories might not be able to pay and would close.
	People would lose jobs.
	City would be cleaner and more people would come.
	Factories would charge more for their products.

FIGURE 11.3c

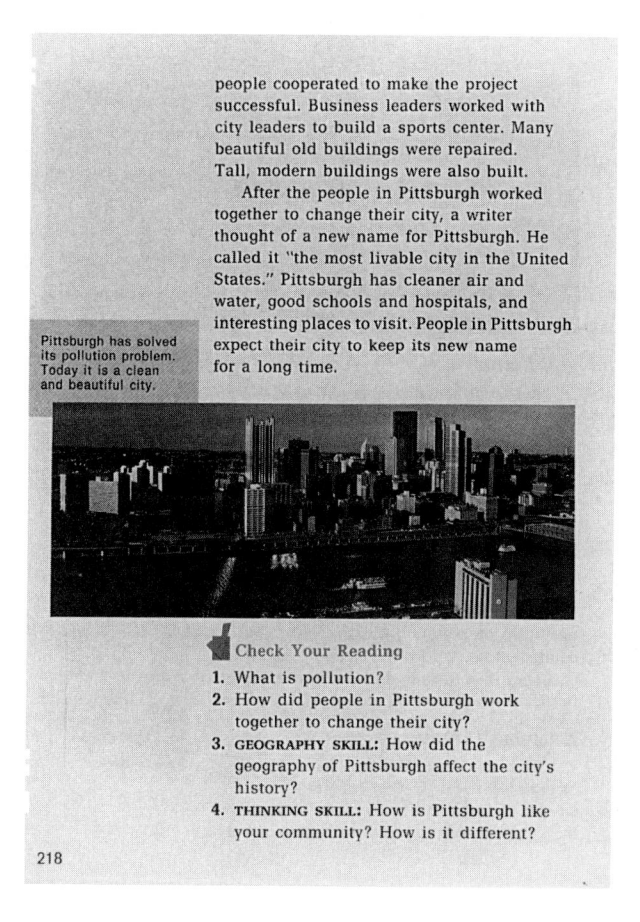

> people cooperated to make the project successful. Business leaders worked with city leaders to build a sports center. Many beautiful old buildings were repaired. Tall, modern buildings were also built.
>
> After the people in Pittsburgh worked together to change their city, a writer thought of a new name for Pittsburgh. He called it "the most livable city in the United States." Pittsburgh has cleaner air and water, good schools and hospitals, and interesting places to visit. People in Pittsburgh expect their city to keep its new name for a long time.
>
> *Pittsburgh has solved its pollution problem. Today it is a clean and beautiful city.*
>
> **Check Your Reading**
> 1. What is pollution?
> 2. How did people in Pittsburgh work together to change their city?
> 3. GEOGRAPHY SKILL: How did the geography of Pittsburgh affect the city's history?
> 4. THINKING SKILL: How is Pittsburgh like your community? How is it different?
>
> 218

What is important (values) in this situation?   clean city
health
jobs
costs

How would you make the choice of what to do?
What is most important to you?

Another valuing lesson is also historical, related to the controversy over land between the Europeans and the Indians.
Topic: Land Ownership, Grade 5, *United States and Its Neighbors,* MacMillan/McGraw-Hill, 1990, pp. 98–99.
Skill: Valuing
Objectives: To develop the ability to identify alternative solutions to a situation.

246 • USING THE TEXTBOOK AND OTHER MATERIALS

FIGURE 11.4a–b

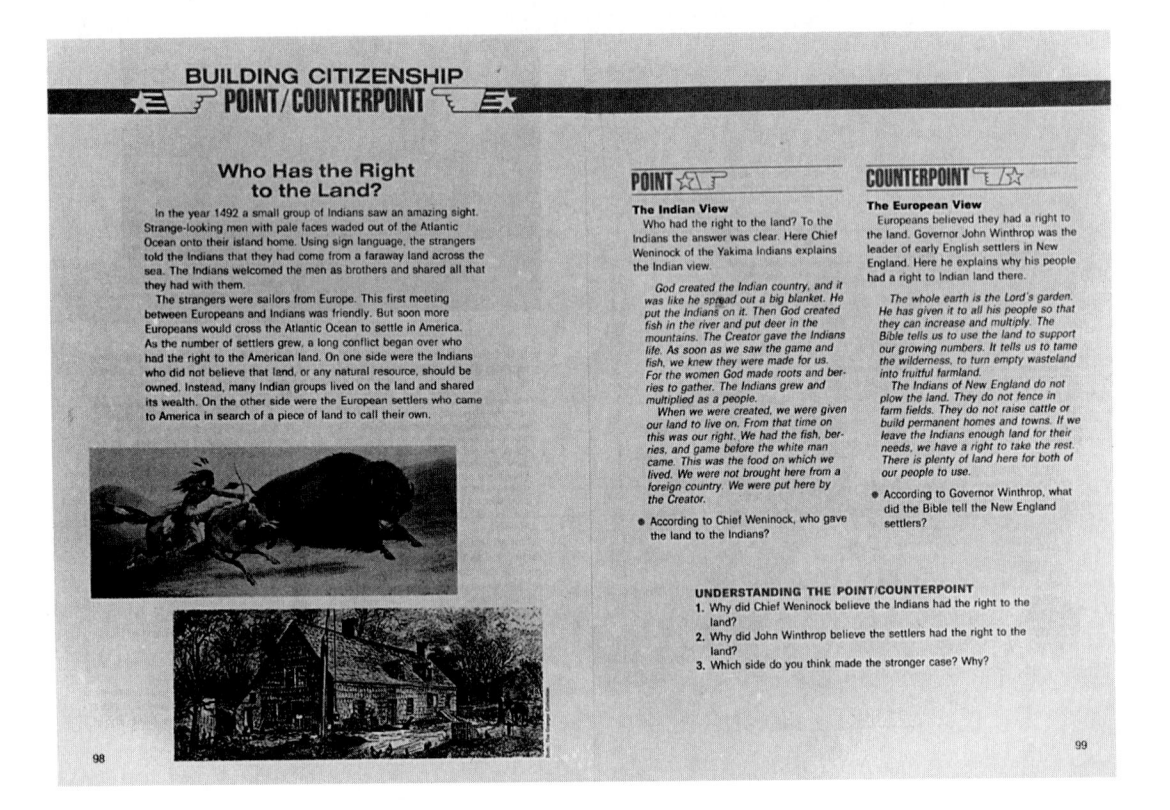

BUILDING CITIZENSHIP
POINT/COUNTERPOINT

Who Has the Right to the Land?

In the year 1492 a small group of Indians saw an amazing sight. Strange-looking men with pale faces waded out of the Atlantic Ocean onto their island home. Using sign language, the strangers told the Indians that they had come from a faraway land across the sea. The Indians welcomed the men as brothers and shared all that they had with them.

The strangers were sailors from Europe. This first meeting between Europeans and Indians was friendly. But soon more Europeans would cross the Atlantic Ocean to settle in America. As the number of settlers grew, a long conflict began over who had the right to the American land. On one side were the Indians who did not believe that land, or any natural resource, should be owned. Instead, many Indian groups lived on the land and shared its wealth. On the other side were the European settlers who came to America in search of a piece of land to call their own.

POINT
The Indian View

Who had the right to the land? To the Indians the answer was clear. Here Chief Weninock of the Yakima Indians explains the Indian view.

> God created the Indian country, and it was like he spread out a big blanket. He put the Indians on it. Then God created fish in the river and put deer in the mountains. The Creator gave the Indians life. As soon as we saw the game and fish, we knew they were made for us. For the women God made roots and berries to gather. The Indians grew and multiplied as a people.
>
> When we were created, we were given our land to live on. From that time on this was our right. We had the fish, berries, and game before the white man came. This was the food on which we lived. We were not brought here from a foreign country. We were put here by the Creator.

- According to Chief Weninock, who gave the land to the Indians?

COUNTERPOINT
The European View

Europeans believed they had a right to the land. Governor John Winthrop was the leader of early English settlers in New England. Here he explains why his people had a right to Indian land there.

> The whole earth is the Lord's garden. He has given it to all his people so that they can increase and multiply. The Bible tells us to use the land to support our growing numbers. It tells us to tame the wilderness, to turn empty wasteland into fruitful farmland.
>
> The Indians of New England do not plow the land. They do not fence in farm fields. They do not raise cattle or build permanent homes and towns. If we leave the Indians enough land for their needs, we have a right to take the rest. There is plenty of land here for both of our people to use.

- According to Governor Winthrop, what did the Bible tell the New England settlers?

UNDERSTANDING THE POINT/COUNTERPOINT
1. Why did Chief Weninock believe the Indians had the right to the land?
2. Why did John Winthrop believe the settlers had the right to the land?
3. Which side do you think made the stronger case? Why?

To identify the consequences of the various alternatives.
To identify the value issues related to the land ownership.
To use valuing skills to help them make a decision.

Materials: Textbook, blackboard

Procedures: Have students read pages 98–99 of *United States and Its Neighbors*.

As you read the situation about the Europeans reaching American lands that were inhabited by Indians, what possible alternatives are open to solve the problem of land ownership? What are the consequences of each alternative?

Alternative	Consequences
Indians keep the land	Indians would be happy
	Europeans would have no place to settle
	There would be no colonies
Europeans take the land they needed	Indians unhappy
	Europeans have land for settlement

	Conflict may occur between two groups
Share the land so that Indians and Europeans would meet their needs	Indians did not believe others should have their land
	Europeans would settle colonies
	Indians may be satisfied if they have enough land

What are the value issues involved in this situation? Religious beliefs, freedom. What do you value? What alternatives would you choose? Why? How do you make a choice of who should own or use the land?

Evaluation: Observation and assessment of student's ability to make a decision. Have students write out their response (decision) and why they made that choice. Role playing their decision is a good follow-up.

Additional information from other sources such as diaries of the settlers and Indian folktales may be needed for children to understand the situation. It is not expected that children will be able to feel as the settlers or Indians did, but rather to understand why there was a conflict.

Using effective teaching strategies to adapt and supplement the textbook makes it a more valuable resource. Other supplementary materials will be discussed in the rest of the chapter.

CHILDREN'S TRADE BOOKS

As related earlier in the chapter, textbooks often do not supply sufficient information on topics (Elliott, Nagel, & Woodward 1985). In addition, some children have difficulty comprehending the text material since it may include too many new concepts, may not be written with clarity, and may not include connectives (McCabe 1993). Children's trade books offer excellent supplementary material, as well as enliven the study of any topic. Children's literature books can open a whole new world to children. They can present events that occurred in the past in story form that are interesting for children to read as well as being historically accurate. Research suggests that children can better understand historical events that are written in narrative form (Levstik 1986). These books can also present clear pictures of current situations that children face every day.

Some of the older favorites that are informational books are Genevieve Foster's *George Washington's World*, *Abraham Lincoln's World*, and *Augustus Caesar's World*. These books provide a horizontal look at history to help children understand the events taking place in other parts of the world throughout the lifetime of each of these men. What a wonderful way to recognize how events in one place in the world may impact events in other places. *People and Places* by Margaret Mead discusses anthropological concepts of the similarities and differences among peoples of the world and offers suggestions that might solve humankind's problems so all may live together peacefully.

For the child who has an aversion to geography and history, fiction books like Holling C. Holling's *Paddle-to-the-Sea* or *Tree in the Trail* should prove fascinating as well as educational. *Tree in the Trail* presents the history of our westward movement through the experiences of a cottonwood tree on the Santa Fe Trail. *Paddle-to-the-Sea* is the story of a small, carved canoe containing the figure of an Indian. The canoe is set afloat from the Upper Great Lakes to make its way to the sea. These books contain accurate geographical and historical material presented in a way that should interest children and motivate them to learn more about the topics under consideration.

Depicting the forces of change, Virginia Lee Burton's *The Little House* finds itself in a country setting until the growth of the surrounding area overwhelms it and a city grows up around the house. Intended for young children, this book can be used in conjunction with a study of the local community. Pat Hutchin's *Changes Changes* will also help children understand the concept of change.

Children who read Eric Carle's *Have You Seen My Cat?* have a better understanding of multiethnicity. Lois Lenski is another author who has described the lives of children in various parts of our country. *Strawberry Girl* and *Cotton in My Sack* were written about farm workers in Florida and Arkansas. Her *Prairie School* discusses the hard life of the Plains states. Books about minority groups include *Striped Ice Cream* by Joan Lexan, *The Contender* by Walter Lipsyte, *A Ride on High* by Candida Palmer, *Lillie of Watts: A Birthday Discovery* by Mildred Pitts Walter, and *The Soul Brothers and Sister Lou* by Kristin Hunter. They are all stories about children who live in the ghetto. *Candita's Choice* by Mina Lewiton is a book about the adjustment problems of a Puerto Rican child in New York City. *That Bad Carlos* and *The Spider Plant* discuss respectively a boy who is acquiring a bad reputation and family life. Stories about poverty are depicted in *My Name Is Pablo, Maggie Rose, Her Birthday Christmas,* and *The Family Under the Bridge.*

Some more recent books can be found each year in "Notable Children's Trade Books in the Field of Social Studies" published in the April/May issue of *Social Education*. These books have been reviewed by a panel of experts and judged to be some of the best for children.

History becomes more realistic when told from journals or diaries. *I, Columbus: My Journal* edited by Peter and Connie Roop, retells the story of the explorer's first journey to the New World through excerpts from his journal. *Buttons for General Washington* by Peter and Connie Roop is taken from the true account of a Quaker family, telling how 14-year-old John Darragh takes coded messages sewn into his coat buttons from British-occupied Philadelphia to his brother at George Washington's camp. *Susanna of the Alamo: A True Story* by John Jakes is a vivid retelling of the battle at the Alamo and tells about a brave young woman, Susanna Dickinson, who survived the massacre to defy General Santa Anna and inspire Sam Houston to defeat the Mexicans.

Some books help to dispel stereotypes, such as *Happily May I Walk: American Indians and Alaska Natives Today* by Arlene Hirschfelder which describes the life, language, ceremonies, healing, roles of elders, arts, sports, education, and employment of Indian peoples and corrects popular misconceptions of their culture. *A Family in Brazil* by Olivia Bennett gives current and authentic information about a young girl and her family depicting daily life in Brazil. Other titles include *A Family in Chile* by Jetty St. John, *A Family in Ireland* by Tom Moran, *A Family in Morocco* by Judy Stewart, *A Family in Singapore* by Bridget Boom, and *A Zulu Family* by Darrell McKenna.

Often it is difficult to find information about current issues that young children can relate to and understand. Many children's trade books fill that void. *The Leaves in October* by Karen Acker May and *Monkey Island* by Paula Fox give firsthand descriptions of life in a homeless shelter and on the streets. *One Day in the Tropical Rainforest* by Jean Craighead George depicts a race to save a Venezuelan rain forest from developers. *Journal to Jo'burg: A South African Story* by Beverly Naidoo depicts the struggle of blacks to secure justice, freedom, and dignity in South Africa. *Poverty in America* by Milton Meltzer uses case studies, facts, and figures to dispel some of the myths about the poor.

Obviously, all the wonderful books that are available cannot be listed, but teachers should be reminded to seek out possible sources as they study different topics.

SIMULATIONS AND GAMES

A *simulation* was defined by Herman (1968) as a situation having human players and rules and outcomes that are sufficiently elaborate to require the use of calculators or computers. Games are more simplistic, more manual, and less amenable to computer analysis. Simulated games are situations in which the less sophisticated may "assume the roles of decision makers, in a simulated (imitated) environment according to specified procedures or rules" (p. 9). These materials give children the opportunity to participate actively in decision making in a variety of roles.

Without Computers

Computers and software are not always necessary to develop simulations in the classroom. Using information from the text, maps, and other resources, less complex simulations can be designed. Here is an example:

> You are about to lead an expedition from Independence, Missouri, to Santa Fe, New Mexico. You are responsible for determining what provisions will be needed for the 70 people and 18 wagons making the trip. Use your text and maps (other materials may also be provided) to decide what route you will take, locations where supplies may be obtained, and the natural obstacles that may impede the expedition's progress. Be prepared to justify your choices. Draw a map showing your route. . . . Such books as *Little House on the Prairie* (Wilder, 1935), *Oregon*

Trail (Feltskog, 1969), and *Tree Wagon* (Lampman, 1953) may be provided to supplement information in the text. (Miller et al. 1987, p. 486)

An example of a more sophisticated simulation that requires more teacher preparation to develop the roles and money cards is one that simulates the economic culture of Latin America (Reichenbach & Reichenbach 1991).

There are commercial simulations available such as *Rafa Rafa*, designed to give participants experience in observing and interacting with a different culture. *Gateway: A Simulation of Immigration Issues in Past and Present* is a four-part simulation on problems of immigrants and ethnic pride.

Simulations with Computers

Computer simulations are much more complex. Some of them require the use of a videodisc as well as a computer. Simulation software has been designed for use most frequently with Apple and IBM computers. However, research tells us that Apple computers are found most frequently in schools. Also, they are used most frequently with simulations (Northrup & Rooze 1990). There are some software packages that only work with one or the other. In making your selection, be sure it can be used with your computer.

The Market Place is a software package for grades 5–8 to be used with Apple II or Apple IIe computers. It contains three related programs: "Sell Apples," which introduces students to the concepts of price; "Sell Plants," which introduces students to advertising and its relationship to profit; and "Sell Lemonade," which seeks to reinforce concepts from the previous programs by having students develop marketing strategies for selling lemonade (Rose 1986).

Choices, Choices: Taking Responsibility, 1988, is a Tom Snyder Production, for grades K–5 for use with Apple or IBM. In this simulation, students must make a decision whether to tell the truth or not to tattle on a friend after witnessing a bad deed at school.

The Other Side, 1986, a Tom Snyder Production, for students in grades 5–12, can be used on Apple computers only. Two teams of students must cooperate to build a bridge to span the ocean between them. Students work in groups to resolve world disputes by communicating over a computer hotline.

Where in the World Is Carmen Sandiego, 1985, and *Where in America's Past Is Carmen Sandiego*, 1991, are Broderbund Software Productions for use in grades 4–8 with Apple and IBM computers. In each simulation, students become detectives trying to find Carmen Sandiego and thereby traveling all over the globe.

The New Oregon Trail, 1988, MECC for grades 5 and up is Apple II or IBM compatible. The children take the roles of trailblazers who must plan a trip across the United States to Oregon in 1848. They must decide on supplies to take as well as make decisions along the route.

There are numerous geography games including *Nigel's World*, 1991, produced by Lawrence Productions for grades 2–6 for IBM or Apple. This game introduces children to global geography by helping them recognize continents and countries as represented on maps and globes. Another is *Swamp Gas Visits the United States of America,* 1991, by Inline Design for grades K–12, designed for Apple II. In this simulation an extraterrestrial lands in the United States and must visit a number of states, cities, and landmarks. Children answer geography trivia questions as they move from place to place.

SimLife™ by Maxis, distributed by Broderbund, "challenges players to build and maintain a viable ecosystem in the face of declining species diversity, delicate food chains, and natural disasters" (White 1993, p. 114). The software is developed for Macintosh, but soon will have a DOS version released.

Research on the effects of simulations indicates that students who participate in simulations tend to remember what they learn longer than students who learn using other teaching strategies. Students' attitudes toward subject matter appear more positive in simulations as well (Van Sickle 1986).

CARTOONS

Cartoons are best used to stimulate discussions, present a particular point of view, and provide an opportunity to interpret the opinions of others. Most cartoons use symbols that require previous experience to be understood. If children lack this experience, teachers should assist in the interpretation.

Criteria for selecting cartoons for instruction include:

- Does the cartoon present an idea quickly and effectively?
- Does it present an idea that would be difficult to introduce using a different approach?
- Will it be understood by the majority of the students without too much assistance?

Cartoons that might embarrass children of a certain race, religion, or national origin should be avoided unless the discussion to be initiated concerns prejudice or a controversial issue. Frequently a cartoon expresses a view of a controversial issue better than most methods.

To enable all of the children in a class to see a cartoon at the same time, the teacher should make a transparency for the overhead projector. Children should be encouraged to collect cartoons that provoke thought. These cartoons can be used in school for committee presentations or individual reports. Children delight in developing their own cartoons. This activity aids them in understanding the subtle use of symbols.

The following cartoons are examples that should effectively provoke discussion. Discussion questions for the first cartoon can be: What idea is this cartoon attempting to portray? What does this cartoon suggest might happen if people continue to throw away so much garbage?

The next cartoon quickly presents an idea. The idea presented, however, is one that children might not readily perceive. What is the cartoon trying to say? How can the situation be solved?

FIGURE 11.5

TIME TO PRACTICE THIS... SO WE ALL DON'T END UP LIKE THIS...

RECYCLING

CIVILIZATION

FAIRFIELD CITIZEN-NEWS

GILL FOX
Courtesy Fairfield Citizen-News

The reluctant learner may be motivated about a topic by the use of cartoons where he or she would be otherwise uninterested.

GRAPHS AND CHARTS

Just as cartoons can present certain ideas more effectively, graphs and charts can often be used to illustrate an idea or present information more readily than other methods. Children who have difficulty with reading may interpret a graph or chart successfully and acquire the concept that others read.

It is necessary to assist children in learning to read and interpret graphs and charts. Young children should start with picture graphs that are related to something familiar to them. Figure 11.7, which uses stick figures to indicate the lunch count for the day, is an example.

Each child can readily perceive how he or she is represented on the graph. Children may wish to label the graph with their names to be sure that all are represented. Later, the teacher can explain that it is possible to represent several people with one figure, as shown in Figure 11.8. Bar graphs in the classroom can be used to represent the daily temperatures, as shown in

GRAPHS AND CHARTS • 253

FIGURE 11.6

BEFORE IT WAS TRENDY TO BE SENSITIVE TO OUR ENVIRONMENT THERE WAS ONE GROUP OF AMERICANS...

...WHO BELIEVED THE EARTH WAS A LIVING BEING DESERVING TO BE TREATED WITH CARE AND RESPECT.

WE CALLED THEM SAVAGES

WICKS
©THE SIGNAL 1990

Figure 11.9. After the children can interpret the bar graph, line graphs (illustrated by Figure 11.10) can be introduced using the same information as the bar graph for comparison and ease of understanding. Circle graphs, illustrated by Figure 11.11, are easily understood when they are used to show how a pie might be divided among the children.

Preparation of graphs using information related to classroom experiences during early primary grades will provide children with the understanding

FIGURE 11.7 Room 10 Lunch Count

Room 10 Lunch Count

Cafeteria   👥👥👥👥👥👥👥👥

Lunchboxes   👥👥👥👥👥👥

Home   👥👥👥👥👥👥👥👥👥

FIGURE 11.8 Room 10 Lunch Count

FIGURE 11.9 Daily Temperature (Bar Graph)

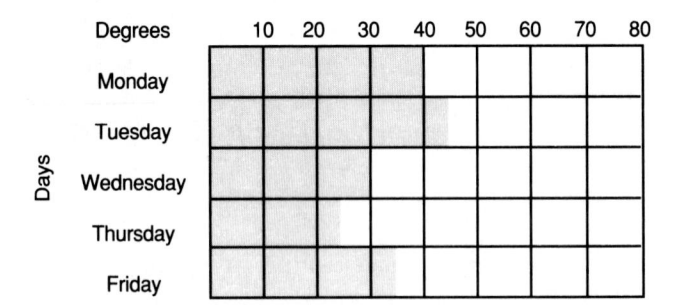

FIGURE 11.10 Daily Temperature (Line Graph)

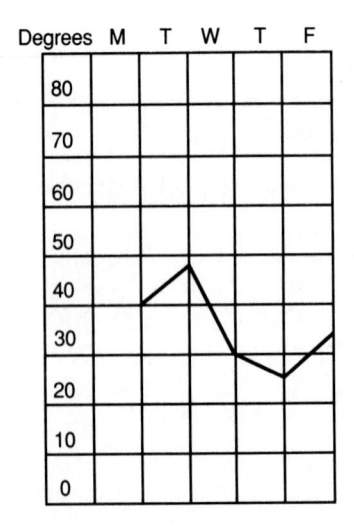

FIGURE 11.11 Apple Pie Shares

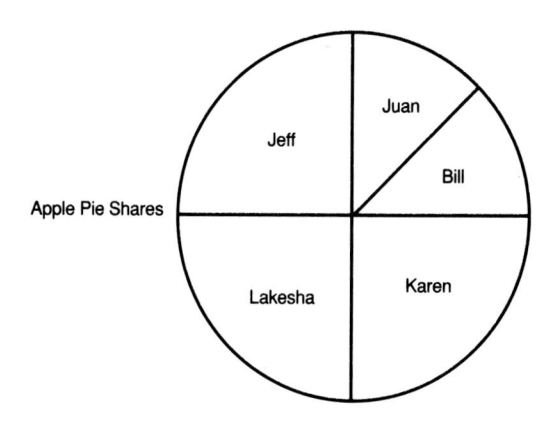

Apple Pie Shares

(Pie chart with sections: Jeff, Juan, Bill, Karen, Lakesha)

necessary to tackle the more abstract statistics presented in the middle and upper grades. Correct labeling of the graphs is vital, and emphasis should be placed on reading them accurately.

A variety of charts are found in every elementary classroom. Most children are introduced to school activities through the use of experience charts. Here, a mutual class experience is recorded, using the children's description for all to read (Figure 11.12). Charts also are developed to record the rules of a

FIGURE 11.12

Our Trip To The Zoo

Today we went to visit the zoo.
We saw many different animals.
The animals were not in cages.
They were in their natural habitat.
A polar bear was in an ice cave.
A giraffe was eating leaves.
We liked the koala best.
It looked like a teddy bear
The Koala comes from Australia.

game, the directions for committee work, and the helpers for the week (Figure 11.13).

A chart with pictures (for example, one depicting the process of making paper from the cutting of a tree through the finished product) is called a flow chart. These charts aid in understanding the steps involved in a process. In the primary grades, children can be introduced to them by using the book *Pelle's New Suit,* which describes how Pelle obtains a new suit—from the time he shears wool from the sheep until he picks up his suit at the tailor's shop. Young children can draw and interpret a flow chart of the process described in the book. More complicated processes, such as drilling and refining oil, can be understood by older children. Commercial flow charts are available on legislative processes such as "How a Bill Becomes a Law," or manufacturing processes such as "Milk from the Farm to You" (see Figure 11.14). Charts can be used for comparison—comparing the before and after, past and present, or another country's government with ours. A chart is described as a pictorial or line diagram of a topic.

PICTURES

Pictures are an extremely valuable resource in social studies. They can be used to develop numerous skills such as observing, classifying, grouping, comparing,

FIGURE 11.13

Responsibilities for the Week
September 10–14

Water Plants	Tara
Wash Blackboards	Roth
Pass Out Supplies	Joseph
Collect Papers	Reba
Class Leader	José
Collect Lunch Money	Samantha

FIGURE 11.14

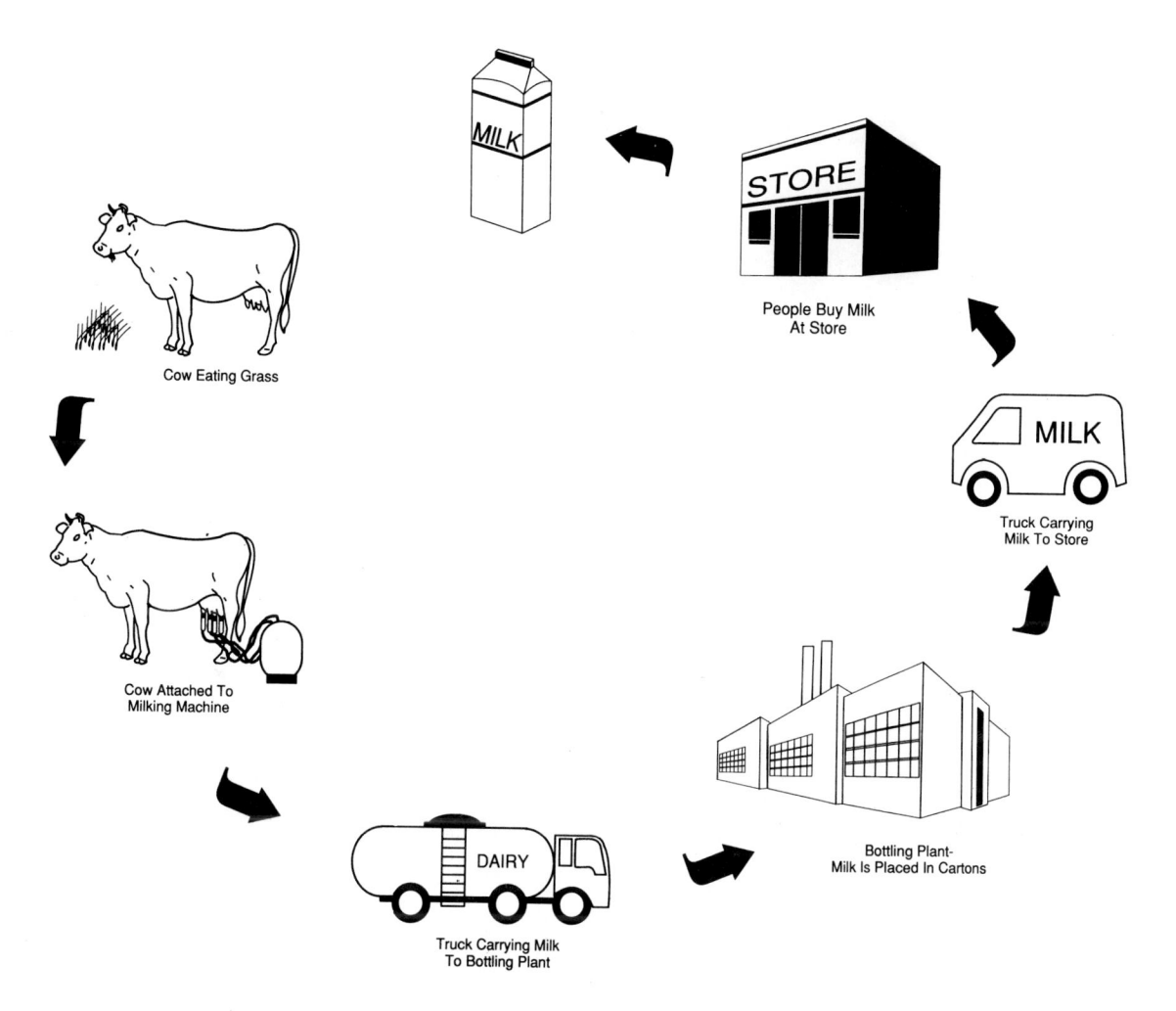

Cow Eating Grass

Cow Attached To Milking Machine

Truck Carrying Milk To Bottling Plant

Bottling Plant— Milk Is Placed In Cartons

Truck Carrying Milk To Store

People Buy Milk At Store

and contrasting and to introduce inquiry and problem-solving situations. Also, concepts that otherwise might be difficult to present may be done through pictures. Sources for pictures are extensive—including newspapers, magazines, posters, and slides and photographs that individuals have acquired through travels.

Commercial companies produce picture series that are valuable in that they often provide resources that are difficult for the individual teacher to acquire. Many sets of pictures have guidebooks with suggestions for presentations and a series of questions intended to provoke inquiry. *Historic Black Americans* from SVE is an example. *Interaction of Man and His Environment* from Rand McNally provides sets of pictures for contrast and comparison. Pictures to promote role playing situations are provided by *Words and Actions* from Holt Rinehart. *Cross*

Culture Study Prints by Inter Culture Associates is a set of 31 carefully selected photographs to uncover preconceptions and misconceptions about other lands and cultures.

MULTIMEDIA/MANY MEDIA KITS

Traditionally, *multimedia* has been defined as many media assembled for use in the classroom, such as films, filmstrips, records, and pictures; however, with the developing technologies, multimedia is beginning to be associated with an interactive video system, where text, audio, and visual data are offered within a single information video system.

The basic components of an interactive video system would include the following:

- One or more video monitors
- A computer that can communicate with the videodisc or videotape player
- Software that enables an instructor or students to provide directions to the computer and player
- An interface device or a cable that enables the computer and video players to communicate with each other
- Videodisc or videotape data
- A videodisc or videotape player. (Martorella 1991, p. 55)

Multimedia kits such as these are relatively small in number (Vote 88, Campaign for the White House), but teachers will be able to create their own software. The Library of Congress is recording on videodisc and CD-ROM (a large record type disk that is read by a laser) many of their special collections that provide primary data sources. ABC, which produced Vote 88, is developing other materials from its news archives.

Multimedia Kits

Media materials organized around a major topic have been assembled into kits for use in social studies instruction. These kits contain films, filmstrips, records, realia, written information, and a teacher's guide to instruction. The Learning Connection has assembled these kits for the study of other cultures. Many kits are available for countries such as Africa, China, Japan, Europe and for a multicultural learning center, for which it is often difficult to find sufficient information at the children's level.

Examples of the materials available are videos on aspects of the culture, records of the language and stories, flags and books with cassettes. Also included is a teacher's guide with background information and suggested teaching techniques for use of the materials.

As previously mentioned, MATCH kits provide multimedia materials organized around a specific topic. Currently available are these: *The City, A House of Ancient Greece,* and *Japanese Family. Free to Be You and Me* is a multimedia kit to explore gender stereotyping. *Children of the World* examines the similarities and differences that exist among the children around the world.

The advantage in using such kits is the accessibility of materials—many of the items included would be rather difficult for teachers to obtain elsewhere. Because some children will learn more from handling realia than from viewing a filmstrip about the items, use of the different media helps meet individual differences in the classroom.

These kits can be used with several teaching methods. Individual or committee research can be organized around the materials for unit teaching or problem solving. Because educationally disadvantaged children benefit from concrete materials, the kits can be used successfully with them. The kits also can be presented to the entire class as introductions to a new study or for enrichment.

VIDEOS AND FILMSTRIPS

Videos and filmstrips provide visual representations instead of the abstract representations provided by text descriptions. Both sources of information are important and must be carefully chosen. Criteria to be applied in the selection of every video or filmstrip include:

1. Is there continuity of content throughout the video or filmstrip?
2. Is the photography of good quality?
3. Is the sound of the video easily understood?
4. Will the presentation of the video or filmstrip contribute to the understanding of the topic under study?
5. Is the information presented accurate?
6. Can the information be understood by elementary school children?

Videos and filmstrips should be selected on the basis of their best use. Does the video introduce a new topic effectively? Does it provide background information? Does it motivate interest in a topic? Would it be effective as a culmination to a study? Guides are available to aid teachers in selecting videos and filmstrips. *Audiovisual Review* gives reviews of the recordings, filmstrips, and multimedia kits.

Videos

Some examples of videos include *Our Constitution,* produced by Focus Media for upper elementary, which explains the significance of the Constitution and its present-day meaning and importance. *Just the Two of Us* shows how elementary students can resolve common conflicts. It is produced by the Agency for Instructional Technology. *Going to Court,* produced by KIDS RIGHTS, has the

Muppets explaining courtroom procedures. *Sadako and the Thousand Paper Cranes* tells the story of a Japanese girl who died as a result of the atomic bomb. It helps children understand the realities of war and offers hope for peace. *The Right to Be Mohawk* presents the Mohawk view of land and how they believe it differs from that of the government. It is produced by New Day Films. *The Geography Tutor* is a series of six videos produced by Tell Me Why that gives definitions of physical features, weather, and climate, but in addition addresses global issues and problems.

Filmstrips

Most filmstrips include audio cassettes to enhance the learning derived from them. Children who have difficulty reading the textbook can benefit from filmstrips. Teachers' guides are included. Some examples are *Airports: A Community Need* for grades 2–6, produced by Enjoy Communicating; it gives an overview of all aspects of an airport from planes and runways to baggage handling. *Economics Primer: Making Choices* for grades 1–3, produced by SVE, develops some basic economic principles from a child's perspective. *A World of Food,* for grades 1–3 and also produced by SVE, introduces the growth and production of food. *Economics in Our World* is a series for grades 4–6, produced by SVE to provide students with a basic economic background as well as help them develop thinking skills in order to make reasoned judgments about economic questions. *Feeding the World* can be used when introducing the issue of feeding the world's population. It is for grades 4–8 and is produced by SVE. *Around the World with Lollipop Dragon* presents current factual information about North America, Latin America, Africa, and East Asia for children in grades K–3, produced by SVE. *A Child's Journey Through History* defines history as how people lived in the past. Timelines are used and colorful illustrations portray children in each age of history. It is intended for students in grades 3–5 and is produced by SVE. *Growing Up in Other Lands* for grades 2–5, produced by SVE, presents children in Peru, France, Thailand, and Israel, describing life in their homelands. *Let's Go Inside* uses rap music and multiethnic children to take viewers on a tour of a hospital, police station, and fire station. Produced by National Geographic, it is intended for preschool through Grade 2.

SUMMARY

Only a representative sample of the various materials available that will enrich the social studies curriculum can be presented here. This sample is intended to encourage teachers to use other resources in addition to the textbook.

SELECTED REFERENCES

Anyon, J. (1978). Elementary social studies textbooks and legitimating knowledge. *Theory and Research in Social Education, 6*(3), 40–45.

Armento, B. (1986). Research on teaching social studies. In M. Wittrock (Ed.), *Handbook of research on teaching* (3rd ed.). New York: Macmillan.

Brooks, C. (Ed.). (1991). *Best editorial cartoons of the year.* Gretna, LA: Pelican.

Bullard, B. (1986). Asia. *Social Education, 50*(5), 367–375.

Cortes, C. E., & Fleming, D. B. (1986). Changing global perspectives in textbooks. *Social Education, 50*(5), 376–384.

Crofts, M. (1986). Africa. *Social Education, 50*(5), 345–350.

Dhand, H. (1988). Bias in social studies textbooks: New research findings. *History and Social Science Teacher, 24*(1), 23, 25–27.

Elliott, D., Nagel, K. C., & Woodward, A. (1985). Do textbooks belong in elementary social studies? *Educational Leadership, 43*(7), 22–24.

Gallagher, A. F. (1991). *Acting together: Readers theatre.* Boulder, CO: Social Science Consortium.

Greenfield, G. M. (1986). Latin America. *Social Education, 50*(5), 351–356.

Griswold, W. J. (1986). Middle East. *Social Education, 50*(5), 357–366.

Larkins, A. G., Hawkins, M. L., & Gilmore, A. (1987). Trivial and noninformative content of elementary social studies: A review of primary texts in four series. *Theory and Research in Social Education, 15*(4), 299–311.

Levstik, L. (1986). The relationship between historical response and narrative in a sixth grade classroom. *Theory and Research in Social Education, 14,* 1–19.

Martorella, P. H. (1991). Harnessing new technologies to the social studies classroom. *Social Education, 55*(1), 55–57.

McCabe, P. P. (1993). Considerateness in fifth-grade social studies texts. *Theory and Research in Social Education, 21*(2), 128–142.

Miller, E. et al. (1987). One dozen ways to turn them on to reading. *Social Education, 57*(7), 486–487.

Morrisett, J. (Ed.). (1982). *Social studies in 1980s: A report of project span.* Alexandria, VA: Association for Supervision and Curriculum Development.

Musser, L. S., & Freeman, E. B. (1989). Teach young students about Native Americans. *The Social Studies, 80,* 5–9.

Northrup, T., & Rooze, G. E. (1990). Are social studies teachers using computers? A national survey. *Social Education, 54*(4), 212–214.

Reichenbach, B. R., & Reichenbach, S. H. (1991). Simulating Latin American economic culture. *Social Education, 55*(3), 188–190.

Robinson, M., & Schonborn, A. T. (1991). Three instructional approaches to Carmen Sandiego software series. *Social Education, 55*(6), 353–354.

Rose, S. A. (1986). Making market decisions in the classroom. *Social Education, 50*(1), 18–19.

Stetson, E. G., & Williams, R. P. (1992). Learning from social studies textbooks: Why some students succeed and others fail. *Journal of Reading, 36*(1), 22–30.

Taba, H. (1967). *Teachers' handbook for elementary social studies.* Palo Alto, CA: Addison-Wesley.

Turner, T. N. (1976). Making the social studies textbook a more effective tool for less able readers. *Social Education, 40*(1), 38–41.

Van Sickle, R. L. (1986). A quantitative review on instructional simulation gaming: A

twenty-year perspective. *Theory and Research in Social Education, 15*(3), 245–264.
White, C. S. (1993). Instructional technology news. *Social Education, 57*(3), 114–115.
White, J. J. (1988). Searching for substantial knowledge in social studies texts. *Theory and Research in Social Education, 16*(2), 115–139.
Woodward, A., Elliott, D. L., & Nagel, K. C. (1986). Beyond textbooks in elementary social studies. *Social Education, 50*(1), 50–53.

LEARNING ACTIVITY

Use the evaluation tools for textbooks and instructional materials that follow to assess their quality for use in your classroom. Select a textbook that has been written within the last five years. You may or may not want to compare it with an older one to determine how they have changed. Select different types of materials to assess.

Record in your journal your reactions to the textbooks. Will they be useful tools? How will you approach their use in the classroom? What exciting materials did you discover? How can you use them?

CRITERIA FOR EVALUATING TEXTBOOK MATERIALS

Subject _____
Grade Level of Materials _____

Student's Name _____

Textbooks evaluated were: (a) _____
(b) _____

Ratings on the form should be for the textbook you choose as the better of the two. Put an * by that book title. Comments should indicate why you made that choice. Evaluate this book in terms of the following scale:

SCALE: 0–2   No or little extent
3–4   To some extent
5–6   Great extent

I. SUBJECT MATTER CONTENT

1. To what extent do the materials focus on the major concepts and/or big ideas?   0 1 2 3 4 5 6
   Comments:

2. To what extent is the subject matter geared to a variety of interests, and the physical, mental, and social abilities of the students for which the materials are being considered?   0 1 2 3 4 5 6
   Comments:

3. To what extent does the content of the textbooks—both the pictorial and written content—reflect the pluralistic, multiethnic nature of our society, both past and present?   0 1 2 3 4 5 6
   Comments:

4. To what extent does the material depict both female and male members of various groups in society in situations which exhibit them unbiasedly in a wide variety of roles?   0 1 2 3 4 5 6
   Comments:

5. To what extent is the role of the various religious and socioeconomic groups, both past and present, accurately and fairly presented?   0 1 2 3 4 5 6
Comments:

6. To what extent does the book tend to encourage a positive self-image for children of all ethnic groups?   0 1 2 3 4 5 6
Comments:

7. To what extent does the author stress the importance of rational thought in discovering and testing the validity of values: e.g.,   0 1 2 3 4 5 6
   a. supporting opinions with facts?
   b. defining the nature of the value conflict?
Comments:

8. To what extent do the books support the use of higher level questions?   0 1 2 3 4 5 6
Comments:

9. Can the textbook function as a basis for decision making?   0 1 2 3 4 5 6
Comments:

10. Does the textbook consistently relate the knowledge presented to the immediate concerns of the learner?   0 1 2 3 4 5 6
Comments:

11. Does the textbook present a well-sequenced program of map and globe skills?   0 1 2 3 4 5 6
Comments:

II. ORGANIZATION

1. To what extent can the teacher depart from the sequence of materials prescribed by the author without impairing the effectiveness of the materials?
Comments:

0 1 2 3 4 5 6

2. To what extent are the materials arranged to clarify the scope and aims of individual lessons, units, and sections?
Comments:

0 1 2 3 4 5 6

III. VOCABULARY AND READABILITY

1. To what extent does the language of the materials accommodate the range of abilities and backgrounds of the students most likely to be using the materials?
Comments:

0 1 2 3 4 5 6

2. To what extent do the materials provide suggested strategies for the range of reading abilities of the students most likely to be using the materials?
Comments:

0 1 2 3 4 5 6

IV. TEACHER'S EDITIONS

1. To what extent does the Teacher's Edition combine reproductions of the pupil's page and lesson plans?
Comments:

0 1 2 3 4 5 6

2. To what extent does the Teacher's Edition provide optional as well as specific instructional procedures and interesting activities?
Comments:

0 1 2 3 4 5 6

3. To what extent is the Teacher's Edition clear in   0 1 2 3 4 5 6
format and an effective guide for the instructional
program?
Comments:

V. TEACHING AIDS
1. To what extent do the book and materials have   0 1 2 3 4 5 6
accompanying audio-visual aids, including records,
filmstrips, video tapes, laboratory kits, and skill cards?
Comments:

2. To what extent are testing materials available?   0 1 2 3 4 5 6

3. To what extent are the appendices and bibliography   0 1 2 3 4 5 6
adequate in terms of scope and content?

VI. PHYSICAL MAKE-UP
1. To what extent does the format of the materials   0 1 2 3 4 5 6
attract and hold a child's interest?

2. To what extent are the books substantial with   0 1 2 3 4 5 6
durable bindings?

3. To what extent are the printing, graphics, and   0 1 2 3 4 5 6
visuals suitable for the grade level being considered?
Comments:

EVALUATION OF TEACHING AIDS

Name of teaching aid being considered _____
Name of manufacturer _____
Address of manufacturer _____
Type of product (i.e., manipulative materials,
film, slides, game, etc.) _____
Discipline(s) in which the product might be used _____
Cost _____ Grade levels _____
Designed to foster concepts ____, skills ____, attitudes ____

I Instructions: List the rating you wish to make for each criterion: 3-excellent, 2-good, 1-fair, 0-not useful. Add all the ratings and determine the overall rating by using the following scale:

      33–42 excellent: highly recommended for purchase and use
      23–32 good: recommended for purchase and use
      13–22 fair: not recommended for purchase and use
      0–12 not useful: not considered useful

CRITERIA

____ 1. Approach suggested for use of the aid
____ 2. Concept, skill, and/or attitude development
____ 3. Extent of provisions for individual differences
____ 4. Can be used by children individually ____ or in small groups ____ (Check one.)
____ 5. Interest appeal to students (Do you think the product can be used in a way students will find interesting?)
____ 6. Can be used frequently during the year
____ 7. Can be used for more than one grade level
____ 8. Made of durable materials
____ 9. Easily stored
____ 10. Practicality
____ 11. Learning device vs. busywork
____ 12. Expectations of teacher for demonstration
____ 13. Commercial product vs. teacher-made product (If a similar aid were made by the teacher, would utility and attractiveness diminish?)
____ 14. Appropriate level of difficulty of content or format for intended age level

____ Total points ____ Rating of the aid

II Respond briefly to the following questions.
1. What concepts, skills, and/or attitudes are the product likely to foster?

2. Are the objectives cited in (1) above appropriate for the elementary school curriculum?

3. Does this material lend itself to the integration of at least two content areas? Explain.

4. What aspect of the product will make students interested?

5. Compare the quality of the product with the cost to determine the desirability of purchase.

Additional Comments:

SUBJECT INDEX

A

Activities
  culminating, 90
  current issues, 127–128
  dramatizations, 90
  economic, 150–154
  global, 138–141
  individual and group, 87
  initiation, 80, 83–84
  inquiry, 181–190
  integrating, 87–88
  law related, 144–147
  map and globe, 211–226
  multicultural, 105–106, 120
  problem solving, 182–190
  textbook, 231–247
  unit, 83–90
  valuing, 197–198, 201–207
Anthropology
  concepts, 37–38
  contribution, 38, 44–45
  definition, 37
  method of inquiry, 38, 44–45
  solution of problems, 44–45
Assessment
  children, 52–54
  inquiry, 190–192
  maps and globes, 221–223
  objectives, 91–97
Attitudes
  definition, 74–75
  measurement, 75, 80

B

Bandwagon technique, 129
Behavioral objectives, 72

C

Cartoons, 251–253
Charts
  experience, 255–256
  flow, 256–257
Checklist
  observation, 91–93
Children
  description, 3–5
  educationally disadvantaged, 110–120
  physically and mentally disabled, 108–109
Children's interest, 53
  inventory, 78–79
Children's trade books
  examples, 247–249
  uses, 139, 165, 167
Classroom atmosphere, 7–8, 113, 141–142,
  147–148, 176–177
Classrooms
  description, 7–8
Communication skills
  debate, 87
  oral and written reports, 80–83, 87–88, 90
  panel discussions, 87
  reading, 81, 235, 238–239
  role playing, 82, 87, 110, 120, 128, 146, 151,
  185–186, 206
Concept
  definition, 30–31, 159–160
  extending, 166–167
  introducing
    Bruner, 165
    Gagne', 165–166
    Parker, 163–165
    Taba, 161–163
  social sciences, 39, 46
Concept formation, 159–165
Conception
  of social studies, 5–7, 9–13, 16–21, 51–52
Conceptual framework, 16–21, 30–31, 39, 46
Content
  selection, 80–83, 114–116, 124–155
Controversial issues
  current, 124–125
  economic, 132–133
  environmental, 133–135
  learning experiences, 127–130
  political, 133

social, 131–132
Cooperative learning groups, 117, 190, 200
Current issues
    goals/anticipated outcomes, 125
    learning experiences, 127–130
    rationale, 124–125
    when to start, 126
Curriculum development
    assessment of children, 52–53
    community influences, 54
    decision-making, 51–52
    historical perspective, 54–58
    local school guidelines, 58–61
    multicultural, 106–107
    national agencies and projects, 64–69
    program planning, 71–98
    sample program, 59–61
    state requirements and guidelines, 62–64
    textbook, 61–62
Curriculum projects
    Bradley Commission on History in the Schools, 67
    Economics America, 153
    Joint Committee on Geographic Education, 67–68
    Juvenile Responsibility and the Law, 147
    Law in a Free Society, 68, 147
    MACOS, 65
    National Commission on Social Studies, 65–67
    We the People—The Citizen and the Constitution, 68, 147

D
Decision-making
    student, 11–12, 75, 207
    teacher, 51–52, 69
Discrepant data, 184–185

E
Economics
    concepts, 35–36, 150–154
    contribution, 36, 42–44
    definition, 35
    method of inquiry, 35–36, 42–44
    solution to problems, 42–44
Economic education
    goals/anticipated outcomes, 149–150
    learning experiences, 150–154
    rationale, 148–149
Environmental issues, 133–135
Ethnocentrism, 104, 164
Evaluation
    anecdotal records, 94
    checklists, 91–94
    groups discussions, 95–96
    individual conferences, 94–95
    materials, 267–268
    observation, 92–93
    problem solving, 190–192
    rating scales, 93–94
    self-evaluation, 96–97
    teacher-made tests, 97
    textbooks, 263–266
Experiential background, 52–53
Exploratory questioning, 83

F
Filmstrips, 260

G
Geography
    concepts, 32–33, 39, 211–216
    contribution, 33
    definition, 33
    method of inquiry, 33, 39
    solution to problems, 40–41
Global education
    atmosphere of the classroom, 141–142
    goals/anticipated outcomes, 136–137
    learning experiences, 137–141

H
History
    concepts, 32, 39
    contribution, 32, 38–40
    definition, 31
    method of inquiry, 32
    solution to problems, 38–40, 46

SUBJECT INDEX

I
Individual activities, 87
Inductive reasoning, 169
Initiation
   problem solving, 181
   unit, 83–86
Inquiry
   activities, 182–190
   advantages and disadvantages, 171–172
   classroom atmosphere, 176–177
   evaluation/assessment, 190–192
   goals/outcomes, 179–180
   questioning, 172–176
   problem selection, 180
   role of children, 179
   role of teacher, 177–178
   thinking skills, 169–171
Integrating activities, 87–90
Interest inventory, 78–79

K
Knowledge
   definition, 73–74
   evaluation, 97

L
Law related education
   classroom and school environment, 147
   goals/anticipated outcomes, 143
   learning experiences, 144–147
   materials, 147
   mock trials, 146–147

M
Map skills
   globes, 225–226
   grade level, 213
   interest centers, 224
   problems, 221–223
   themes
      location, 211–212
      movement, 218
      place, 215
      region, 220
      relationships within places, 216
      urban, 224–225
Materials
   cartoons, 251–253
   CD-Rom, 258
   children's trade books, 139, 165, 167, 247–249
   filmstrips, 259–260
   games, 249
   graphs and charts, 252–256
   multimedia, 258–259
   pictures, 256–258
   simulation, 140, 153, 249–251
   textbooks, 231–247
   video, 259–260
Methodology
   concept, 159–168
   current issues, 124–135
   economic, 148–154
   global, 136–142
   inquiry, 169–194
   law related, 143–148
   multicultural, 100–122
   unit, 76–98
   valuing/moral reasoning, 195–209
Multicultural education
   activities, 120
   content, 114–116
   cultural, racial, ethnic, and religious groups, 103–104
   curriculum development, 106–107
   definition, 100–102
   educationally disadvantaged, 110–120
   gender, 109–110
   goals, 102
   learning experiences, 105–106
   organizational patterns, 117
   physically and mentally disabled, 108–109
   poverty and homelessness, 110–112
   role of the child, 112–113
   role of the teacher, 113–114
   teaching strategies, 107–108, 117–119

N
Name calling, 129
Newspaper

class, 126–128
reading, 128–130
reporting, 127

O

Objectives
attitudes, 74–75
behavioral, 72
current issues, 125
developing, 72–76
economic education, 149–150
global education, 136–137
knowledge and understanding, 73–74
law related education, 143–144
problem solving, 179–180
skills, 75–76
unit, 79–80
values, 75
Outcomes, 73, 125, 136–137, 143–144, 149–150, 170–180

P

Pictures, 256–258
Plain-folks, 129
Political science
concepts, 34, 39
contribution, 35, 41–42
definition, 33
method of inquiry, 34
solution to problems, 41–42, 46
Pollution, 38–46
Problem solving
activities, 182–190
advantages and disadvantages, 171–172
assessment, 190–192
classroom conditions, 176–177
definition, 169–170
evaluation, 190–192
goals, 179–180
questioning skills, 172–176
problem selection, 180
role of teacher, 177–178
role of children, 179
thinking skills, 169–171
Program planning, 71–98
Progaganda techniques, 128–130

Q

Questioning
skills, 172–176
Taba, 172–176, 233–237

R

Reading
group, 238–240
questioning, 240–247
textbook, 232–240
Reflective thinking, 169
Role playing
current issues, 128
inquiry, 185–186
multicultural, 120
values, 206
unit, 82, 87

S

Schools
description, 8–9
guidelines, 58–61
Self-evaluation, 96–97
Simulations
with computers, 250–251
without computers, 249–250
Skills
definition, 75–76
map and globe, 210–226
valuing, 195–207
Small groups, 86–88, 190, 198
Social sciences
anthropology, 37–39, 44–46
economics, 35–36, 39, 41–44
geography, 32–33, 39–41
history, 31–32, 38–40
political science, 33–35, 39, 41–42
sociology, 36–37, 39, 44–46
Social studies
attitudes and values, 74–75
definition, 3–28
knowledge and understanding, 73–74
objectives, 13, 72–76
skills, 75–76
Sociology

concepts, 36–37
contribution, 37, 44–46
definition, 36
method of inquiry, 37
solution to problems, 44–46

T

Teacher-made tests, 94
Teacher-pupil planning, 77, 85
Teachers
   description, 5–7
   discussion, 9–11
Textbooks
   evaluation, 263–266
   group reading, 238–239
   research, 231–234
   teaching strategies
      concept, 233–237
      valuing, 240–247
      vocabulary development, 239–240

U

Unit planning
   bibliography, 90–91
   components, 77, 79
   content, 80–83
   culminating activities, 90
   evaluation, 91–97
   individual and group activities, 87
   initiation, 83–86
   integrating activities, 87–90
   learning experiences, 83–90
   lesson planning, 84–86
   objectives, 79–80
   sample unit, 79–91
   teacher pupil planning, 84–86

V

Valuing
   character development, 199–200
   cognitive developmental, 196–199
   value analysis, 204–207
   value clarification, 200–204
Videos, 259–260

W

Waste basket technique, 184

NAME INDEX

A
Aardema, V. 91
Acredolo, L. 212, 226
Akenson, J. E. 9, 14, 55, 69
Anderson, C. 148
Anderson, L. 136, 142
Anyon, J. 231, 232, 261
Arends, R. I. 148
Armento, B. J. 149, 154, 231, 261
Ausubel, D. P. 171, 193

B
Bacon, P. 212, 226
Bailey, W. 64
Bang-Jensen, V. 148
Banks, J. A. 14, 101, 102, 104, 106, 107, 121
Baptiste, H. R. 107, 121
Baptiste, M. 107, 121
Barr, R. D. 7, 14
Barth, J. L. 7, 14
Beal, G. 108, 121
Beck, C. 198, 208
Bereiter, C. 111, 121
Berry, R. 71, 98
Beyer, R. K. 30, 47, 159, 161, 168, 193
Blaut, A. S. 212, 226
Blaut, J. M. 212, 226
Bluestein, N. 212, 226
Bookchin, M. 41–43, 47
Bradley Commission on the Schools 67, 70
Broek, J. O. M. 33, 47, 227
Brubaker, D. L. 5–6, 14, 15, 16–21, 193
Bruner, J. 57, 65, 165, 170–171, 193
Bullard, B. 232, 261
Bullard, S. 102, 121
Burton, V. L. 139, 142, 167, 168
Butts, R. F. 14

C
California State Department 63, 70
Campbell, E. 91
Carpenter, H. M. 211, 227
Center for Civic Education 147, 148

Cheek, H. N. 227
Chiasson, J. 91
Cogan, J. J. 14
Comer, J. 113
Common, D. L. 193
Conard, B. D. 104, 121
Condesen, M. E. 227
Cornbleth, C. 171, 190–193
Cortes, C. E. 103, 121, 142, 232, 261
Crofts, M. 232, 261
Cushner, K. 101, 110, 121

D
Dapice, A. N. 199, 207, 208
Decaroli, J. G. 194
Dahand, H. 232, 261
Dee, R. 91
DeMasi, J. 145, 148
Dewey, J. 169, 180, 193
Dow, P. 65
Dreeban, H. 148
Dubois, R. 136
Dulaney, B. 145, 148
Dunfee, M. 180, 193

E
Eagan, K. 56, 70
Econ and Me 154
Edelman, M. W. 14
Elkins, D. 14
Elliott, D. 232, 247, 261
Ellis, A. K. 14, 193
Engle, S. H. 5, 7, 10–11, 14–15, 22–28, 135
Engelmann, S. 111, 121
Essery, M. 9, 14
Evans, R. W. 135

F
Fair, J. 170, 193
Fillmore, L. W. 102, 121
Fischer, B. 148
Fischer, L. 148
Fleming, D. B. 103, 121, 142, 232, 261

Fouts, J. T. 71, 98
Fox, R. 180, 193
Frazee, B. 227
Freeman, E. B. 108, 121, 232, 261
Freedman, P. I. 103–104, 121
Freidlander, B. A. 172, 193

G
Gagne, R. M. 73, 98, 160, 165, 168
Gailbraith, R. E. 198, 208
Gallagher, A. F. 146, 148, 239, 261
Garcia, J. 108, 121
Gibson, J. 64
Gilmore, A. C. 168, 231, 261
Give and Take 154
Glen, A. D. 193
Goldberg, M. 111, 121
Good, C. V. 77, 98
Goodlad, J. 172, 193
Goodman, J. 108, 121
Gordon, S. 91
Grant, C. A. 105, 121
Greenfield, G. M. 232, 261
Greig, M. E. 98
Griswold, W. J. 232, 261

H
Hadaway, N. L. 108, 121
Hahn, C. 65, 70, 124, 135, 142
Hanna, P. 55, 56
Harmin, M. 200, 208
Hawkins, M. L. 231, 261
Hoban, R. 167
Hodgkinson, H. 102, 121
Hoffman, M. S. 182, 193
Hunter, R. M. 148
Hurst, J. B. 193

I
Isadora, R. 91
Isham, M. M. 136

J
Jacobson, M. 223, 227
Jarolimek, J. 14
Jenkins, S. 147–148

Jenness, A. 139, 142
Jones, T. M. 198, 208
Johnson, G. 124, 136
Johnson, P. C. 227
Joint Council on Economic Education 154

K
Katzman, C. 154
Kemball, W. G. 210, 221, 227
Kepner, T. 221, 227
King, J. 154
Knapp, M. S. 53, 70, 111–112, 117, 119, 121
Kneip, W. M. 142
Kneller, G. F. 73, 98
Kohlberg, L. 196–198, 208
Konrad, A. R. 196, 207, 208
Krough, S. L. 208

L
Ladson-Billings 104
Lampe, A. 225, 227
Lampe, P. E. 100, 101, 121
Landau, B. 212, 227
Larkins, A. G. 231, 232, 261
Lendsey, J. 145, 148
Lenning, L. R. 152–154
Levstik, L. 247, 261
Lickona, T. 199, 208
Linehan, M. F. 110, 117, 121
Lionni, L. 165
Lippitt, R. 180, 193
Lohman, J. 180, 193

M
Mackey, J. A. 197, 208
MACOS, 65
Mager, R. F. 72, 98
Maher, F. A. 171, 193
Mallen, J. T. 14, 77, 98
Manson, G. 224, 227
Martin, D. S. 103–104, 121
Martin, R. S. 35, 47
Martorella, P. H. 14, 166, 258, 261
Massialas, B. 193
Matthews, R. C. 168
Maxey, S. J. 180, 193

McAulay, J. D. 55, 70
McCabe, P. P. 231, 233, 247, 261
McCleary, G. S. Jr. 212
McDill, E. L. 14, 53, 70, 110, 121
McDonald, G. J. F. 41, 47
McHale, J. 134, 136
McKinney, C. W. 168
Meadows, D. H. 136
Means, B. 53, 70, 111–112, 117, 119, 121
Melcher, K. 108, 121
Mehaffy, G. L. 136
Metcalf, L. E. 208
Michaelis, J. 14
Miller, E. 247, 261
Miller, R. G. 35, 47
Mollel, T. M. 91
Moncrief, L. W. 44, 47
Moore, V. D. 30, 47, 159, 168
Morris, A. 139, 142
Morrisett, J. 231, 261
Muir, S. P. 165, 168, 227
Musser, L. S. 108, 121, 232, 261

N
Nagel, K. C. 232, 247, 261
National Commission on Social Studies in the Schools 65, 67, 70
National Council for the Social Studies 210, 227
National Council on Economic Education 68, 153–154
National Education Association 55, 70
Natriello, G. 14, 53, 70, 110, 121
Naylor, D. T. 145, 148
Nelson, J. L. 142
Nelson, M. R. 14
Nickell, P. 190, 193
Nicol, A. 91
Northrup, T. 250, 261

O
Olson, L. 72–73, 98
Overvold, M. C. 196, 207–208

P
Pallas, A. M. 14, 53, 70, 110, 113–114, 121
Palmquist, K. 191–193

Palonsky, S. 223, 227
Parker, W. C. 30, 47, 159, 160, 163–165, 168
Parsons, J. 170–172, 193
Passe, J. 136
Passow, H. 111, 121
Pasternak, M. G. 105, 121
Pavan, B. N. 117, 121
Peters, R. 142, 198, 208
Pitkanen, M. A. 91
Pomerantz, C. 139, 142
Population Reference Bureau 138, 139, 142
Pratt, R. B. 70
Presson, C. C. 212, 227
Price, C. J. 224, 227
Project Social Studies 57, 64
Purpel, D. 196, 208

R
Ragan, W. B. 55, 70
Raths, L. 200, 208
Ravitch, D. 5, 14, 106, 121
Redding, N. 73, 98
Reichenbach, B. R. 250, 261
Reichenbach, S. H. 250, 261
Riekes, L. 147–148
Rice, M. 64
Riessmann, F. 121
Rivers, A. 139, 142
Robinson, M. 261
Rokeach, M. 74–75, 98, 201–202, 208
Rooney, R. C. 121
Rooze, G. E. 250
Rose, S. A. 250, 261
Rose, S. 43, 47
Rushdoony, H. A. 212, 227
Russell, A. 147–148
Ryan, K. 196, 199, 208

S
Sagl, H. 180, 193
Schaefer, O. C., Jr. 225, 227
Schermbrucker, R. 91
Schonborn, A. T. 261
Schug, M. C. 71, 98, 154, 208
Schwab, J. J. 169, 193
Sears, A. 170–172, 193

Seefeldt, C. 14
Senchuk, D. M. 198, 208
Shaftel, F. R. 120, 121, 170, 186, 193–194
Shaftel, G. 120, 121, 186, 194
Shaver, J. P. 208
Shermis, S. S. 7, 14
Simon, L. H. 5, 14
Simon, S. B. 200, 201, 203, 208
Skeel, D. J. 142, 151, 155, 194, 202, 208
Social Education 65
Social Studies and the Young Learner, 65
Sprague, N. F. 193
Stanley, D. 91
Stanley, W. B. 168
Stein, L. E. 145, 148
Steptoe, J. 91
Sterling, R. E. 189, 194
Stetson, E. G. 261
Stewart, J. S. 203–204, 208

T
Taba, H. 14, 160–163, 167–168, 170, 172, 194, 233, 235, 261
Tannenbaum, A. J. 111, 121
Tennessee Department of Education 64, 70
Thomas, J. L. 159
Thomas, P. 148, 168
Thornburg, K. 143
Todd, R. J. 71, 98
Totten, S. 136
Trifonovich, G. 101, 110, 121
Turner, T. N. 238, 261
Tye, K. A. 136, 143

U
Uttal, D. H. 212, 227

V
Van Sickle, R. L. 251, 261
Viadero, D. 106, 121, 199, 200, 208

W
Walsh, D. 104, 121
Ward, B. 136
Ward, P. 31, 41, 47
Webster, S. W. 14
Wellman, H. M. 212, 227
Welton, D. 14, 77, 98
Weir, B. 91
Weir, W. 91
West, E. 64
White, C. S. 251, 261
White, J. J. 231, 261
Williams, J. W. 5, 14
Williams, K. 91
Williams, M. E. T. 207, 208–209
Williams, R. P. 261
Willis, S. 104, 107, 121
Woodward, A. 232, 247, 261

Y
Yoho, R. F. 160, 168

Z
Zacharias, J. R. 57

CREDITS

28   (Brubaker article)© National Council for the Social Studies. Used with permission.

33   From Engle, S. H. (1989) "Whatever happened to the social studies?" *International Journal of Social Education* Vol. 4 (1), p. 42–51. Reprinted by permission of the International Journal of Social Education.

296 (social studies concepts chart) *Social Studies,* vol. 79, p. 72, March/April 1988. Parker, W. C. "Thinking to learn concepts." Reprinted with permission of the Helen Dwight Reid Educational Foundation. Published by Heldref Publications, 1319 Eighteenth St., N.W., Washington, D.C. 20036-1802. Copyright © 1988.

367, Fig. 9.1A   Reprinted by permission of Associated Press.

422, Fig. 11.1   Reprinted by permission of Macmillan/McGraw Hill School Publishers.

435, Fig. 11.2   Reprinted by permission of Macmillan/McGraw Hill School Publishers.

441, Fig. 11.3   Reprinted by permission of Macmillan/McGraw Hill School Publishers.

447, Fig. 11.4   Reprinted by permission of Macmillan/McGraw Hill School Publishers.

460, cartoon "Time to practice this . . ."   Reprinted by permission of Gill Fox and the *Fairfield Citizen.*

461, cartoon © Randy Wicks, The Signal (Valencia, CA)